Horse-racing: a book of words

Other Books of Words from Carcanet

Fly-fishing
C.B. McCully

FORTHCOMING:

Fashion
Helen Maclean

Cricket
David Palmer

Computing
David Timms

Drama
Martin Harrison

Music
Brian Morton

HORSE RACING

GERALD HAMMOND

CARCANET

First published in 1992 by
Carcanet Press Limited
208-212 Corn Exchange Buildings
Manchester
M4 3BQ

British Library Cataloguing in Publication Data
Horse-racing: a book of words.
1. Racehorses. Racing
I. Hammond, Gerald
798.4

ISBN 0 85635 930 0

The publisher acknowledges financial assistance
from the Arts Council of Great Britain

Set in 9pt Plantin by Bryan Williamson, Darwen
Printed and bound in England by SRP Ltd, Exeter

General Editors' Preface

The *Book of Words* series offers a new conception and analysis of the vocabularies used in our sports, pursuits, vocations and pastimes. While each book contains an essential lexicon of words and phrases – explored historically and in depth – each also contains generous quotation, practical reference, anecdote and conjecture. The result is more than a dictionary: specific, inclusive, thought-provoking, each *Book of Words* offers the past and present through a weave of words, in all their curiosity and delight.

Those intrigued by the language particular to their area of interest will find the relevant *Book of Words* a coherent and challenging treatment of the topic; those interested in the English language itself will find the series yielding significant material on semantic scope and change; and general readers who wish to understand the vocabularies of human endeavour will find the series tracing the necessary but implacable relationships between words and world.

Editors, chosen because of their intimate enthusiasm for their subjects, have been encouraged to be comprehensive in their coverage: vocabularies typically range from the demotic to the esoteric, from slang to the technical and specialised. Within that range, emphasis is also placed on *how* each lexicon developed, and *why* its terms acquired their peculiar descriptive power. These are books to read with pleasure as well as keep on the reference shelf.

Gerald Hammond
C.B. McCully

Acknowledgements

The author and publisher would like to thank the following for their kind permission to reprint copyright material:
Elizabeth Eliot and Longman for *Portrait of a Sport*; John Hislop Esq. for *From Start to Finish*; the Estate of Vincent Orchard for *Tattersalls*; Peter O'Sullevan Esq. and Random Century for *Calling the Horses*; the *Racing Post* and *Sporting Life*.

My chief debt, as it is for anyone who undertakes serious lexicographical work, is to the OED. We thank Oxford University Press for permission to include material from the Dictionary.

Every effort has been made to contact copyright holders, but the author and publisher apologise if any inadvertent omission has been made.

Introduction

A surprisingly large number of people make a living from horse-racing: jockeys, trainers, stable staff, valets, clerks of courses and their staff, racing journalists, bookmakers, settlers, tic tacs, betting-shop managers and counter clerks, compilers of form guides, and even a few professional punters. One man's career is another's hobby, and for many more people racing is a pleasurable pursuit. A list of these would include punters of the armchair and more active varieties, amateur jockeys, members of the Jockey Club, stewards, and, most of all, racehorse owners, very few of whom ever make any kind of profit from the game. Neither of these lists is remotely complete. Think of handicappers, commentators, starters and their assistants, among those whose careers are in racing, and among the hobbyists are book-makers like myself. The racing connections stretch on and on, each group having its own stock of words and phrases which make up the language of horse-racing.

Because horses were so important to our culture for so long, 'their' words have contributed much to the general language. *Career* and *hobby* are good examples. A career was, first, a race-course, then it described a gallop at full speed, and now it summarises a person's progress through life. A hobby was originally a small horse, then, as *hobby-horse*, it described the wickerwork figure of a horse used in morris dances, then a toy, until it emerged as a favourite occupation pursued merely for amusement or interest.

Some words or phrases in the general language seem to come from the world of horses or the racing of them, but turn out to have no such origin. A *last ditch* effort describes very well a chaser trying to keep up with the pace as the field jumps the last open-ditch, and *flying colours* exactly evokes the spectacle of the race seen from the rails, but both phrases really come from the battlefield. Others which one might not have suspected begin, like *career*, on the racecourse, or at least, like *hobby*, among horsemen. *Cavort* originally described a horse's capering. *Curry favour* derives from the curry-comb used in the rubbing down of a horse. *Daisy cutter* described a horse's action long before it was used about balls which keep low in cricket. *Gingering up* was a singularly unpleasant practice of horse dealers. To *back out* of something recollects the way a horse comes out of its stall; *in a lather* conveys the way it sweats,

9

and, corrupted, becomes *hell for leather*. Motor vehicles have *near*
and *off* sides, *pull up* at the lights, and *break down*. *Henchman*, from
Old English *hengest*, a gelding, was an early kind of stable lad. A
wild goose chase did not describe frantic efforts to catch a bird for
the pot, but an early form of horse race; as did *handicap*, whose
origins are as odd as the ways in which this word has broadened
into the general language.

Some common phrases are more obviously racing terms: winning
hands down, for instance, or *neck and neck*, *staying the course*, and
having a *run for one's money*. Others need a little thought: *easy going*,
geed up, and *flea-bitten* are examples. And in some cases the horse
connection has to be traced carefully. *Manage* and *interfere* have
certain limited racing usages now, which seem only to be by-
products of the words' applications to a large variety of pursuits
and practices in modern society, but both entered the language as
words which had solely horse senses.

Many of these words and phrases will be found here. With nearly
1100 entries, ranging from specialised terms like *furnished*, *scope*,
or *peck*, to common expressions like *get on*, *get out*, or *get up*, my
aim is to explore and explain the language of the racecourse. To
collect every word connected with horses would have resulted in
a multi-volumed work, so I have operated on two basic principles
of exclusion, leaving out words which one would be unlikely to
encounter now, or in earlier days, on a racecourse, and generally
omitting words whose meanings are so obvious that they have
nothing of interest to offer about the history of racing or the way
it is practised now. So, while the word *mount* is omitted, although
it is in common use on the racecourse, the word *leg* is included.
Every horse has four legs, apart from the ones I back, and everyone
knows what a leg is just as they know what a mount is; but there
are other kinds of legs in racing history, and to describe a horse
as having a leg means more than it seems.

A list of the many horse-related words missing from the book
would include examples as diverse as the verb *to bishop*, meaning
to file down a horse's teeth to make it appear younger, probably
so named after a gentleman given to doing this; *frog*, derivation
unknown, describing the thick, wedge-shaped piece of horn in the
middle of the sole of a horse's hoof; *gaskin*, from Gascony, originally
referring to a fashionable style of breeches in the sixteenth century,
and now describing the bunch of muscles at the lower and outer
part of a horse's thigh; *coffin*, to describe, for obvious reasons, the
unusually long head of some horses; the verb *to hog*, meaning to
cut the mane short so that it stands up like bristles on a hog;
dandy-brush, a stiff brush used in cleaning horses, named after the

fashionable gentlemen dandies of the eighteenth century; and numerous varieties of bit and bridle.

In every case my estimation is that such words and phrases are too peripheral to the activity on the racecourse. 'There where the course is' is the context for this book of words. That line begins the best thing ever written about racing, Yeats's poem 'At Galway Races'. The racecourse is the place, he says, where 'Delight makes all of the one mind.' All, following their career or hobby, have one mind and, accordingly, one language. But many who use this language do so carelessly, without properly realising what it means. One example is *the distance*. Everyone hears the course commentator say 'as they approach the distance', but few know exactly what the distance is – 240 yards from home – and fewer know why it is so called. Another example would be an apparently simple word like *nowhere*. 'Eclipse first, the rest nowhere' was the proverb which spread from racing to the general culture, and we echo it when, as is usually the case, we describe the horse we have backed as finishing nowhere. But the word's meaning was much more precise than our casual use of it implies. A famous 'plunger' of the eighteenth century won a fortune by predicting the exact placing of every horse in a race in which Eclipse ran. *Nowhere* meant that the horse had been beaten by such a distance that it was officially not placed, even if it finished second. That 'distance' by which it had to be beaten to be nowhere was 240 yards.

For those who like to chase words, then, as much as for those whose hobby it is to chase losses, the language of horse-racing offers many rewards. Horses have their own history, as does betting, the two coming together when men started to ride match races against each other in the sixteenth and seventeenth centuries. Actually, the racing of horses in Britain goes much further back: possibly to the Roman occupation, almost certainly to the Vikings. The name *Hesketh*, from *hestr*, horse, and *skeith*, track, in some sixteen locations in the North of England, points to a connection with horse-racing going back over a thousand years. One, Hesketh Wood, is virtually on the site of the still very active 'gaff' at Cartmel; another Hesketh is just two miles from the training centre of Gisburn; and Bunstock, originally Brunescayth, sits by Carlisle racecourse. A Viking moot began as a religious gathering and soon turned into a fair, with games, dancing and competitions:

> Horse racing and horse fighting seems to have been particularly usual . . . possibly they played a part in the selection of victims for sacrifice, possibly a victorious beast was looked upon as specially favoured by the gods.
>
> (Foote & Wilson, *The Viking Achievement*)

The bookmakers are missing, otherwise all the elements of Derby day were there; and it is no great step from *moot* to *meeting*, the word which describes present day gatherings for the purpose of racing horses.

Yeats's poem ends like this:

> ...somewhere at some new moon,
> We'll learn that sleeping is not death,
> Hearing the whole earth change its tune,
> Its flesh being wild, and it aloud
> Crying as the racecourse is,
> And we find hearteners among men
> That ride upon horses.

At Galway races, as at any racecourse, we see men, horses, and the landscape they ride over, the earth whose flesh is wild. From this wonderful combination comes a living language too, in which apparently simple words – such as *ask*, *waste*, *gone*, *home*, and *pull* – take on complex associations of delight, fear, effort, and humour.

The main principle of inclusion, then, is to collect words and phrases which take on a special sense when used on the racecourse. Their historical and linguistic perspectives are supplied by the Oxford English Dictionary (OED). Any otherwise unattributed definition is the OED's, as are the dates given for first appearances of a word, or one of its meanings – generally described as 'first attestation'. In both cases the reader needs to exercise common sense. A dictionary definition is a fairly arbitrary thing, a lexicographer's idea of how a word may be broken down into a variety of senses, and how each sense should be defined. In most of the entries here I have tried to fill out and qualify accepted definitions, often by offering examples of the word's use in accounts of racing over the last few hundred years and from contemporary sources. For the latter I have relied on the two major racing papers, *The Sporting Life* and *The Racing Post*, and for the former a number of representative books listed in the bibliography (p.243), with reference keys to the entries. As for first attestations, these can only be a rough guide. A word first attested in print in 1890 had probably been hanging around in the spoken language for at least half a century, and readers knowledgeable in racing history ought to be able to move back many of the dates given here by a few years at least.

One of the books I have used is Jon Bee's Dictionary of Slang, compiled in 1823. He described his work like this:

> A Dictionary of The Turf, The Ring, The Chase, The Pit, of Bon-Ton, and the Varieties of Life...For elucidating Words

and Phrases that are necessarily, or purposely, cramp, mutative, and unintelligible, outside their respective Spheres.

The phrase 'necessarily or purposely' gets it just right. Special usages are partly invented to hide things from outsiders and partly evolve to describe things for which there is, as yet, no word or phrase. To elucidate them is to reveal the beautiful complexity of the 'varieties of life', and to show how our language is most alive in one special place – there, where the course is.

Accept   At each *forfeit* stage owners *accept* when they pay for their horses to stay in the race. Such horses are known as *acceptances* or *acceptors*. 'Salsabil's half-brother Marju ... heads the list of acceptors for this year's third and final Cartier Million after Wednesday's second forfeit stage' (*Racing Post* 7 September 1990).

accumulator   A *multiple bet* in which four or more horses are backed in different races, all of the *returns* from one going on to the next, and so on, so that the winnings accumulate. The OED's first example of the word's use to mean a thing which accumulates itself (rather than a person who does the accumulating) is from 1833; its first betting example is from an 1889 Dictionary of Slang, but here the sense is of the better rather than the bet itself: 'a person who backs one horse, and then if it wins results (sometimes including original stakes) goes on to some other horse.' This sounds confused and it is possible that the dictionary compiler has not understood the bet, although Partridge also describes it as a 'better' rather than a bet and dates its use from *c*.1870. By the twentieth century its sole reference was to the bet itself.

acey-deucy   An American term for riding with one stirrup leather longer than the other: unnecessary on British courses which, with very few exceptions, are not all on the *turn²* like American tracks. Riding acey-deucy helps keep the jockey balanced when his mount is always required to lean in the same direction. Only one British course suits this style of riding: 'When Steve Cauthen came over here, before he got the knack of riding the other course, when he still rode acey-deucy, he was worth following at Chester' (*Racing Post* 9 May 1990). The expression looks as if it comes from card-playing, but I suspect that it is actually derived from A.C.-D.C. because of the strange appearance of such a style of riding.

act, action   Poets have often played on the inherent ambiguity of these words, meaning both 'to do' and 'to pretend to do' (like 'perform'). The racing sense fuses the two ideas most naturally, for while it is instinctive for a racehorse to gallop, it needs to be trained to do this in conditions which are not natural to it. A horse's *action* is, accordingly, the trained movement of its limbs, under the control of a rider, at all speeds, in the straight and coming round bends. Many a horse falls out of contention in the

15

Derby by 'losing its action' around Epsom's Tattenham Corner.
An important consideration in running a horse in a race is to
estimate how it will *act* on that particular track:

> On May 8 he ran for and won the Chester Vase, on the Roodeye
> at Chester – a race of a mile and a half – so in winning this he
> proved he could get the Derby distance, and also showed his
> complete adaptability for the sharp Epsom course. Chester
> racetrack is all on the turn and, like Epsom, a left-handed
> course. Papyrus, in that race, came round the turns there skim-
> ming along the rails, so I knew how well he could act at Epsom.
> (Donoghue, 214)

The *going*, too, affects a horse's action. Some horses only act on
the soft, some only on the firm, and these traits are frequently
passed on through the generations. A jockey's favourite excuse
for the poor performance of a fancied horse is to claim that it did
not act on the going or the track.

Act comes from the Latin *agere*, 'to drive, carry on, do'; and
its earliest English senses have more to do with movement than
with action – e.g. from 1603, 'thy senses five that acte thy life.'
The OED does not recognise this racing usage of act. It does identify the special sense of action, but its first attestation, from
Shakespeare's *Henry V*, 'imitate the action of the tyger', is a dubi-
ous example: its next example is from 1882, 'the action of the
competing horses'.

added 'Added money' in the terms of a race describes a sum
contributed to the prize money over and above the stake moneys
made up of owners' *entry* and *forfeit* fees, as in:

> Askham Bryan Novices' Handicap Hurdle. 2 miles. £2000
> added to stakes. Distributed in accordance with Rule 194 (iv)
> (b)...The Horserace Betting Levy Board Seventh Race
> Scheme provides for the inclusion of £2000 in the added money
> subscribed for this race.

age Whatever its foaling date, every racehorse's age is calculated
from 1 January of that year (since 1834: previously Mayday was
the starting point). South of the equator a horse's age is dated
from 1 August. Some races are restricted to horses of a particular
age: two-year-old races are for horses in their first season, and
the English *classics* are all limited to three-year-olds. The greatest
racing scandal occurred in 1844 when Running Rein won the
Derby and was then discovered to be a four-year-old, originally
named Maccabeus. Another horse in the same race, Leander, was
struck into and had to be put down: a veterinary inspection of
his mouth proved him to be another four-year-old. Both owners
were *warned off*.

The age of racehorses has gradually come down. In the early years of the eighteenth century it was rare for a horse under the age of six to be raced. Experimental runnings of four- and three-year-old races took place in the 1730s but did not catch on until a generation later, and the first two-year-old to appear on a racecourse ran at Newmarket in 1769. Today flat race meetings will generally have at least two of their six races confined to two-year-olds.

The OED records two specific senses with references to horses: to *age* a horse is to calculate its age by looking at its teeth (1887); and *aged* refers to a horse or mare of six years old and upward (1869). See *all-age*, *tooth*, *weight*.

aids Often taken to mean the things which help control and guide the horse – reins, whip, etc. – but really *aids* refers to the 'actions of a rider's hands and legs to show the horse what is required of him' (Hislop, 30). Another such natural aid is the rider's voice. The OED's first attestation is from 1751, when 'aids in the manage' are described as 'helps, or assistances, by which the horseman contributes towards the motion or action required of the horse.'

air The OED records, from 1641, the special horsemanship use of *air* to denote 'the artificial or practised motions of a managed horse' (see *manage*), an extension of the sense 'manner, appearance'. In practice, the word describes the horse's bearing and its rhythm while going through the managed paces, and in this respect may be extended to describe thoroughbreds: one can admire the air of a racehorse as it canters to the start.

airing Recorded early in the seventeenth century to describe the exercising of horses in the open air, its racing use is fairly cynical: a horse is said to be 'out for an airing' when it is not expected to win, either to lower its handicap *mark* or to help make it race fit. Partridge defines it as 'a race run with no intention of winning' (1870).

all in 'All in, run or not', commonly shortened to *all in*, was the rule in betting until the end of the nineteenth century. It meant that if a horse did not start the race, its backers still lost their money. Today the rule still applies in *ante-post* betting, but all bets on the day of the race, including *S.P.* bets, are subject to the 'non-runner, no bet' principle.

allow, allowance An *allowance* is a deduction from the weight a horse is required to carry in a race. Fillies and mares often get an allowance when racing against colts, and apprentice jockeys may claim a graduated allowance depending upon the number of winners they have ridden. In this example *maidens* are given an allowance of four pounds when running against horses which

have won, and fillies get a five pound allowance: 'Dee Stakes...
Weights: Colts and geldings 8st 12lbs; fillies 8st 7lbs. Penalties:
a winner of a weight-for-age race value £5000 4lbs. Maidens
allowed 4lbs.' Accordingly, a maiden filly, getting all the allowances, will carry 8st 3lbs in the race, twelve pounds less than a
penalised colt.

The word is first attested in this sense in 1823, but the practice
goes back much earlier. For example, Prior, in tracing the decline
in popularity of the Arabian horses in the eighteenth century,
shows how the race *conditions*[2] of the time were framed to favour
them: 'by 1782 those "by Arabians" were actually allowed 3lbs
in the Contraband Stakes at the First Spring Meeting at Newmarket.' By the middle of the nineteenth century, in the conditions
of the Goodwood Cup, '"horses got by Arabian, Turkish, or
Persian stallions" were allowed 18lbs, and if out of mares of the
same breeds, a further 18lbs.' To show how complex the system
of allowances had become, this same race had the further conditions that

> horses bred in America, or on the Continent, were allowed a
> stone, and those from Scotland or Ireland, 7lbs; horses that
> had run during the year at specific meetings in the North of
> England were allowed 3lbs; and those that had run at Liver-
> pool, or far-off Newcastle-on-Tyne, 2lbs in addition. (Prior,
> 123)

all right The *all right*, signalled by a blue flag over the number
board, shows that jockeys have *weighed in* correctly after a race.
Bets can then be settled.

all-weather Describes special surfaces on which horses can gallop
or race throughout the winter. *All-weather gallops* have been used
by trainers for some time; all-weather tracks were introduced in
the UK at Lingfield and Southwell in 1989, each offering a different surface. Lingfield has *equitrack*, Southwell *fibresand*. All-
weather soon turned out to be an over-ambitious designation: the
first meeting of the 1989-90 chasing season to be lost to the weather
was an all-weather meeting at Southwell in November, because
of fog. In February 1990 another was lost because of flooding.
'All-weather' functions as an adjective and a substantive: horses
race at 'all-weather tracks' or do well 'on the all-weather'.

also ran First attested in 1896, *also ran* describes a horse not
placed in a race: from the practice of listing in a newspaper after
the first three (or four) finishers all the other runners under the
heading 'also ran'. The phrase's general sense of a failure at anything comes from this racing usage.

amble From Latin *ambulare*, 'to walk', via French. The word's original sense, from the fourteenth century, was to describe a horse's irregular trot, when it raises both right limbs simultaneously and then both left. The word's extension to human movement is not recorded until the end of the sixteenth century; but this use is now the dominant one, so that if a horse is described as ambling down to the start the sense is probably only figurative, meaning 'making its way in a leisurely fashion'.

amiss Originally two words, *a*, the preposition of manner, and *miss*, 'failure, deficiency, shortcoming'. The word is frequently used slightly euphemistically in racing to describe an injury which occurs in a race: 'something badly amiss with him' might well mean that the horse in question has to be put down. A particular euphemistic usage comes when a mare is described as going amiss, meaning that she has come into *season*[2] at the time of her race.

answer A horse *answers* when it responds to the jockey's urging, normally towards the end of a race. This special racing sense is first recorded in 1894, identified as an abbreviated form of 'answer the question'. Today the verb alone is invariably used: 'If the horse answers sufficiently, keep on swinging your whip without hitting him. If he does not answer, give him a tap...' (Hislop, 128) See *ask*.

ante-post *Ante* is Latin, but *post* is not, otherwise this would mean before-after. The post here refers to the Betting Post, a distinctive feature of nineteenth-century racecourses:

> When regular fixtures were held at certain courses it became the custom to sink a stake into the ground, like a country sign-post, on some part of the course. All those who wanted a bet would ride or draw their carriage up to this stake...

which came to be known as the 'Betting Post'. (Sidney, 24) Betting at the Post was, therefore, equivalent to the modern betting in the *ring* before a race: ante-post betting was any betting transacted before this course betting-market opened. Today ante-post bets are those laid in the days, weeks, even months before the day of the race. The advantage of ante-post betting is that one may often obtain a better *price* about a horse than if one waits for the day of the race. The disadvantage is that if the horse does not run, the bet is lost. The OED's first attestation is from a 1902 *Encyclopedia Britannica* entry, where the 'post' is mistakenly identified as the **number-board**.

any price Said of a complete outsider, exaggeratedly: the horse has so little chance of winning that one may back it at 'any price' one cares to name.

> Turning into the straight Tophatter was any price to win. But Summons fell two out which left Green Bramble on his own,

and he blundered and unseated his rider at the last. (*Sporting Life* 23 May 1990)

any to come   A bet in which the *returns* from one successful selection are to be staked on later selections. Not the same as an *accumulator* because the stakes can be varied; e.g. '£10 to win Haversack. Any to Come £5 to win Certification, £5 each way Witch Doctor.' If Haversack wins at 2/1, then of the £30 returned (£20 win plus £10 stake) £15 will be staked on the other two horses. If they both lose, the better will get £15 back. Also known as *if cash*.

apprentice   'A learner of a craft'; from Old French *aprentis*, derived from *aprendre*, 'to learn'. An *apprentice*, learning his trade with a licensed trainer, is a young jockey who is normally given a weight *allowance* when riding against senior jockeys. There are special races confined to apprentices only. With the decline of trades and crafts the racing usage now provides one of this word's few literal applications. Apprentices are also known as *claimers*.

ask   To call upon a horse for a special effort, usually towards the end of a race: often expressed as 'asking the question'. The OED's first attestation is from 1894: 'Until the last ten strides, when I really asked King Lud the question.' If the horse quickens up, he *answers* it. In jumping the jockey *asks* the horse for a big jump when he gets him to *stand off*: 'Scudamore asked Tarquogan's Best for a big one at the last and got the response he wanted' (*Sporting Life* 7 September 1990). More loosely, 'ask' can be used to describe any pressure put on a horse to run faster or *keep up* to his work: 'According to Charlie Nelson . . . Lear Leader is "very idle and has to be asked for every last bit"' (*Racing Post* 31 July 1990).

at it   Slang for hard at work: 'Three furlongs out the rest of the field was at it while he was still going easily.'

auction   At the end of a *selling race* the winning horse is offered in auction. However, an *auction race* is one open to horses which have been bought at public auction. For typical auction race conditions, see the example given under *condition*.

autumn double   A popular *ante-post* bet which involves getting the winners of the two big autumn *handicaps*, the Cambridgeshire and the Cesarewich.

away[1]   Used to describe the start of a race. A horse which is fast *away* in a sprint has a distinct advantage over one which is slowly into its stride. In this sense the word is very close to its origin, in the phrase *on way*, i.e. on one's way. The contracted form *āwēg* is already found in Old English.

away[2] At the race's end a horse which wins *going away* is one which is increasing the distance between itself and the rest of the field.

away[3] On the racecourse, bookmakers who take bets on other meetings which are going on at the same time are said to bet at *away meetings*, or, simply, *bet away*.

Baa To go *baa baa*, or *baa baa black sheep*, is bookmakers' slang for barring the favourite; that is, offering it at so poor price that no one will back it (Partridge, 1932).

back The original equestrian sense of *back* was to break and mount a horse. When Hotspur says 'that roan shall be my throne. / Well, I will back him straight' (*1 Henry IV*, 2:3:74) he is not proposing to place a bet on it, but only to ride it away. Our modern sense of placing a wager on a horse may be related to the use of 'back' to mean 'support . . . with physical force', hence the connection with the strongest part of the body. Alternatively, it is possible that it derived from the original equestrian usage: if, in a *match*, each rider 'backed' his own horse. The OED gives this example from 1699: 'The lord Wharton's horse Careless has beaten another backt by the duke of Devon, etc, for £1900." When a horse is described as running *unbacked* this is not normally the literal case. It means that there has been relatively little money for it.

back-end Not a horse's posterior – although it can be used to describe this – but the last few weeks of the Flat season: 'He's taking a long time to get ready. I'm hoping to win a couple of races with him at the back-end.' The implication is that all of the valuable races have been run by then, so that the back-end races offer little in the way of competition. On the better course, however, back-end races give good, late-maturing animals a chance to win a race: 'River God shaped with a great deal of promise on his only start as a two-year-old, finishing 7½ lengths third to Rami in a typically competitive back-end maiden at Newmarket' (*The Independent* 20 June 1990). The OED records *back-end*, meaning 'the later part or "latter end" of a season' from 1820.

backer A *backer* is someone who bets on a horse. The first unambiguous example in the OED is from 1850: 'Take any odds against him that his backers may give.' From this example one can see that originally backers supported their horses by offering *odds* on it against the rest of the field. From this grew the practice of offering odds on several runners and, eventually, the whole field, the backer turning into the *bookmaker*. Today 'backer' is the most common general term for a member of the betting public, a little more professional in implication than *punter* and not so clinical as *bettor*.

backhander   John Hislop defines a *backhander* as a 'tap down the quarters without twirling the whip through your fingers – or pulling it through your hand to the ordinary hitting position' (Hislop, 130). Thus the racing sense is more gentle than either the common meaning of a blow delivered with the back of the hand or the other sporting senses, such as backhand shots in tennis and polo, with which the OED misleadingly includes it.

bad   More commonly than 'poor', *bad* is used in racing to describe a long distance between a horse and the horse of horses in front of it: 'To put it tersely, I just galloped past Brownrigg, sailed over the last two fences, and won by ten lengths. Stephen came in a bad third' (Sassoon, *Memoirs of a Fox-Hunting Man*).

bait   A horse is *at bait* when it stands in a stable for part of the day and is provided with food. 'Bait' meant, from the sixteenth century, 'feed for horses' and 'a halt for refreshment in the course of a journey'; derived ultimately from the Old Norse *beit*, 'pasture', and *beita*, 'food'.

ball   Even a light covering of snow will be enough to cause racing to be abandoned because of the phenomenon of *balling*, when the snow forms into hard lumps inside the horse's shoes, rendering it likely to lose its footing. The OED gives a general sense for the intransitive use of *ball* as 'to become clogged with balls of snow': it does not recognise this as specific to horses, but its three examples are all horse-related, including this one from Anne Brontë's *Tenant of Wildfell Hall*: 'The snow... clogged the wheels and balled the horses' feet.'

balloon   In chasing, a horse *balloons* a fence when it jumps it very *big[1]*, losing nearly all momentum: 'Midnight Strike easily landed the odds at 1/3 ... despite ballooning left across the course' (*Racing Post* 20 September 1990). The OED recognises no such sense: the ballooning of cricket balls or footballs is recorded from 1904, but the closest sense to the racing one is an aeronautical usage, when an aeroplane bounces on landing and rises up into the air again; e.g., from 1949, 'The aircraft ballooned when the wheels hit; it shot up thirty feet and seemed to hang suspended.'

bandage   A protective wrapping for a horse's leg, often worn by hurdlers and chasers. A bandage can also be wrapped round the tail to keep the hair in place. 'Four weeks ago he told his stable staff that the patched-up Australian import – heavily bandaged again on Tuesday – would be their first winner together" (*Racing Post* 20 September 1990). The OED, which identifies the word as originally a term from surgery (16th C.), gives examples only of the bandaging of humans.

banker   A supposedly certain bet. A development from *bank upon*,

'to count or rely on with confidence or assurance'. The nearest
the OED comes to defining such a sense is to identify its use in
football pools betting, where the banker is the one 'result which
one forecasts in a series of entries.' This sense does occur in
racing, in combination bets like *jackpots* and *placepots*, but its
more common usage is to describe the one horse on the *card* upon
which one can bet with confidence.

bar   A preposition meaning 'except', probably derived from the
verb *bar* in the sense 'to exclude from consideration, set aside,'
The betting usages are *bar one*, as in '5/1 bar one', meaning that
all horses in the race, with the exception of the favourite, are
being offered at a price of 5/1 or better (also *bar two*, etc.); or,
more simply, *bar* on its own, as in '20/1 bar', meaning that all
the other horses whose prices have not been given are on offer at
20/1 or better. The OED's first attestation is from Hotten's 1860
Dictionary of Slang, where he identifies it as 'in common use in
the betting-ring: "I bet against the field bar two."' See *baa*.

barb   From French *barbe*, *Barbarie*: a horse of the Barbary breed
imported from Barbary and Morocco, from which the British
thoroughbred developed. In 1658 William Cavendish, the Duke
of Newcastle, gave this advice to would-be racehorse breeders:
'Your stallion by any means, must be a *Barb*...For a *Barb* that
is a *Jade* will Get a better *Running Horse* than the best Running
Horse in England.' One of the three sires from which all modern
thoroughbreds have evolved was known as the Godolphin Barb.

barrel   The body of a horse: not recorded until the beginning of
the eighteenth century. Clearly the similarity in shape influenced
the usage.

baulk   Or *balk*. The verb, meaning 'to miss or omit intentionally'
(15th C.) is derived from the noun meaning 'a ridge left in plough-
ing; a miss, slip.' A horse *baulks* when it *jibs*, refuses to go on or
refuses to take a jump.

bay   From Latin *badius*, via French *bai*: the reddish-brown colour
common in *thoroughbreds*, marked in the *card* with the abbreviation *b*. A *bay* can vary in colour from a dull red to near chestnut,
but is distinguished by its having a black mane and tail and,
usually, black on the legs; so it may be more accurate to describe
bay as a pattern rather than a colour. The word occurs in Chaucer
(1374), and may be punned on in Shakespeare's Sonnet 137 when
he calls his dark lady, ostensibly comparing her to the sea, 'the
bay where all men ride'.

beat   Backers talk of *beating* a *price*, or beating *S.P.*, when they
get better odds than those now, or finally, on offer.

behind   To keep a hard-pulling horse *in behind* another horse in a race is one of the acts of good jockeyship (see *cover*): 'The ground was plenty firm enough for him, but I sat in behind and let them cut their throats. They were going far too fast' (*Sporting Life* 7 June 1990).

behind the bit   This phrase describes the behaviour of a horse when it seems to be frightened of the *bit¹* and shakes its head to try to release the pressure. This is the opposite of *pulling¹*.

bell   Still occasionally found in the title of a race – e.g. the Lanark Bell – this recalls the traditional prize of a bell for the owner of the winning horse, before *plates* became the common prizes. The best races were known as *bell-courses* (1617). This may be one of the sources of the phrase 'bear away the bell', meaning 'to carry off the prize'.

bet   The derivation is uncertain: perhaps it is a shortened form of *abet*. The OED's definition of the word's meaning deserves reproduction in full:

> The backing of an affirmation or forecast by offering to forfeit, in case of an adverse issue, a sum of money or article of value, to one who by accepting, maintains the opposite, and backs his opinion by a corresponding stipulation.

The word's first certain attestation is from 1592: 'Certaine old sokers, which are lookers on, and listen for bets, either even or od.' An *even bet* occurs as early as 1624. The verb is first recorded in the 1590s, in Shakespeare's *2 Henry IV* (3:2:44), where the reference is to an archer in competition with others: 'John of Gaunt loved him well, and betted much money on his head.' Obviously horses were bet on at least as often as archers, but the signs are that 'bet' itself was a relative latecomer in the language of racing. In James Shirley's play *Hyde Park*, for instance, written in 1632, Act Four is largely taken up with the horse races at the park and the betting on them. The following formulations are used, rather than 'bet' (my italics):

I would *lay* the world upon my mare; she shall
Run with the devil *for* a hundred pieces.

Will you *go* half? I'll *go* it all, or anything.

Forty pounds to thirty! Done, done! I'll *take* all odds.
My lord, I *hold* as much.

Shall we *venture* nothing o' the horses?

That cuckoo was a witch, I'll *take* my death on't.

Even today 'bet' tends to be the least interesting of betting terms – *lay* and *take*, as in the quotations above, telling much more about the history and development of betting on horses.

The general term for one who bets is *bettor* or *better*. Neither is satisfactory: the first looks and sounds clinical, the second gets confused with the more common word which is spelt the same. Hence the more general use of *backer*.

For *multiple bets* see *multiple*.

better   *Better going* describes a change from firm to *good* ground, or even from good to good-to-soft. 'She was beaten six lengths into third by Local Derby here next time and this better ground could help her' (*Sporting Life* 7 September 1990).

betting boots   Not in the OED, but its usage is common enough: 'It's time to get your betting boots on', i.e. it is time for some serious betting. In fact, the term originally described the footwear of some bookmakers who, needing to be seen by the crowds milling round the *joint*, would wear specially built-up boots.

betting shop   A term in common use since the 1961 Betting and Gaming Act, which licensed the opening of betting offices to cash customers; but the history of the term goes well back into the nineteenth century. The OED quotes, from 1852, '"Commission Office", "Racing Bank",..."Betting Office" are the styles of announcement adopted by speculators who open what low people call Betting-shops.' The *leviathan* bookmaker Davies was the most successful organiser of such establishments, anticipating the achievements of the major combines in the twentieth century: see the quotation under *list*. In August 1853 Parliament passed an Act for the Suppression of Betting Houses, aimed at preventing 'the injury and demoralisation of improvident persons by the opening of places called Betting Houses and Offices' (Sidney, 51). The consequence was that a thriving *off-course* cash betting industry was driven underground. For over a hundred years, until the 1961 Act, cash betting could only be done legally at the racecourse, bookmakers' offices being solely for the use of credit clients.

bice   Racecourse slang for 'two', i.e. 2/1 (from French *bis*?); most often heard in *bison*, short for 'bice and a half', i.e. odds of 5/2 (= 2½/1).

big[1]   When a horse jumps a fence deliberately, with an excessive clearance, it is said to *jump big* (cp. *balloon*). This is undesirable because some momentum is lost so that the horse is slowly away from the fence. For obvious reasons *full[2]* horses tend to jump big, hence the preponderance of geldings in steeple-chasing.

big[2]   Horses *look big* when they seem not to be race fit.

birthday   See *age*.

bison   See *bice*.

bit[1]   The mouthpiece of a bridle, from the verb *bite*; but, as the

OED explains, 'it is not clear whether the word in this sense signifies that which the horse bites, or that which bites or grips the horse's mouth.' The first recorded example is from *c*.1340. Bits come in many shapes and sizes, with many names, but in racing varieties of *snaffle* are invariably used. *On the bit* means that the horse is on a short rein: 'All work except trials or semi-trials . . . is done "on the bit". This means that the horse is being ridden on a tight rein and is not galloping flat out' (Hislop, 35). *Off the bit* means that the horse is on a loose rein: 'The 6/4 favourite . . . cruised up to challenge approaching the last furlong, but found nothing off the bit and faded to finish fourth' (*Sporting Life* 19 May 1990). *Up to the Bit*, like *into the bridle*, means that the horse is running as fast as is allowed by the degree of restraint being imposed upon it. See also *behind the bit*.

bit² To *have a bit on* is to bet on a horse (Partridge, 1894). The 'bit' here usually means a lot of money, not a little. The OED identifies the use of 'bit' in understatements, beginning with the phrase 'a bit of', from the eighteenth century.

black *Black* thoroughbreds, although not unknown, are rare: most horses which appear to be black are actually *brown*. The last official black horse to win a *classic* was Charlebelle, who won the 1920 Oaks.

blackleg First recorded in 1771 as 'a turf swindler'. Thackeray, in 1858, writes of 'noblemen and black-legs brawling and betting in the Cockpit.' The OED says that, as with other slang expressions, the origin of whose name is lost, 'of the various guesses current none seems worth notice.' Three of these guesses (quoted by Partridge) are: (i) such men commonly wore boots (ii) in imitation of game-cocks, whose legs are always black (iii) a play on the appearance of 'the rook'. The strike-breaking sense of the word does not occur until the middle of the nineteenth century. See *leg*.

black type In *pedigrees*, *black type* stands for a win or a place in a *group* or *listed race*. Trainers will enter horses for such races in the hope of 'getting some black type' and therefore raising the horse's value at stud: 'Flower Girl . . . was gaining the black type her owner-breeder Bill Gredley had hoped for' (*Sporting Life* 28 May 1990).

blanket The OED defines a *blanket finish* as 'a finish of a race in which the contestants are so close together that they could be covered with a blanket.' In racing the phrase is only used when four or more horses are concerned. The idea of covering the finishers with a blanket appears in *The Sporting Magazine* in 1793 – 'Of the nineteen that started, the judge could only place the first four, for not only those, but four or five others, might have been nearly covered with a blanket' – but the phrase itself does not occur until the twentieth century.

blaze   Probably derived in some way from the Old Norse *blesi*, perhaps by way of Northern dialect usage: the word is first attested in the seventeenth century. The OED's definition, 'a white spot on the face of a horse or an ox', underestimates the size of the mark; in fact, a *blaze* is a white mark covering most of the horse's forehead and going down the face, between the eyes, often as far as the muzzle.

bleeder   A horse which has a tendency to break blood vessels in a race: 'Last year she was a chronic bleeder and I had to give her ten months off. It seems to have done the trick and she no longer breaks blood vessels' (*Racing Post* 6 June 1990). See *lasix*.

blinders, blinds   See *blinkers*.

blinkers   Sometimes known as *blinds*, and in America as *blinders*: 'The last time Orchard's Pet wore blinkers he finished a close second . . . and is now back sprinting with the blinds back on' (*Sporting Life* 30 May 1990). The word is obviously derived from the verb *blink*, although the origins of that word are unknown. Its original sense is 'to deceive' or 'to elude', and there may be an element of this in the racing sense, *blinkers* being, most often, a device to make a horse run better than it wants to – hence their popular name, 'the rogue's badge'. In their simplest form blinkers are screens attached to the bridle which force the horse to look directly ahead. Thomas Hardy is the first writer to extend the word into the general language: in '1967', written in 1867 (*Time's Laughing Stocks*), he writes of 'this blinkered time'. See *hood*; *visor*.

blister   To *blister* a horse is to apply a counter-irritant solution which causes an inflammation, the blood being drawn to a damaged area to help its repair. The OED recognises no such specific usage, but under *fire* it includes this quotation, from 1869: 'They'll be most of them "blistered" or "fired", and turned out!'

blood   *Blood-horse*, the name by which the *thoroughbred* is known, is now more commonly used in America than Britain. The OED's first attestation is from 1794, with nineteenth-century examples of its being shortened simply to *blood*. *Pedigrees* are traced through *blood lines*.

bloodstock   *Bloodstock*, meaning 'thoroughbred or pedigree horses collectively', occurs first, as *blood stock*, in 1830. *Tattersalls'* sales of racehorses are known as Bloodstock Sales.

blot   A *blot* on the *handicap* is a horse which is exceptionally well *in[1]* at the weights.

blow From Old English *blawan*, cognate with Latin *flare*, 'to blow'. *Blow*, since the sixteenth century, has had specific references to a horse's breathing: *blow short* described broken-windedness (1523), and *blow* by itself was used to describe a horse's breathlessness (1651). In racing, a horse *takes a blow* when it is given a breather in a race – the jockey speaks of 'getting a blow into it'. It *blows up* towards the end of a race when it runs out of breath because it is not quite race fit. 'The Green Forest cold finished sixth on his seasonal debut... where he ran well before blowing up after six furlongs' (*Racing Post* 19 June 1990).

blower In pre-celullar-telephone days the *blower* was the telephone service between bookmakers' *off-course* offices and the betting enclosure on the course. Money for such and such a horse 'came down', or was 'sent down' the blower.

blowout A light piece of exercise to keep a horse fit: 'Applecross and Madame Dubois had blowouts for their run in the Park Hill stakes today' (*Sporting Life* 12 September 1990). Not in OED.

blue As a verb, also spelt *blew*, meaning 'to spend or get through (money) lavishly or extravagantly', *blue* is first attested in 1846. It soon had, understandably enough, frequent racecourse usages. The OED quotes, from 1884, '5/1 He took to horses, and blewed the blooming lot in eighteen months'; and Partridge, who quotes the conjecture that this sense is derived from the idea of 'sending into the sky', cites this verse from *The Sporting Times* in 1889:

Isabel and Maudie knew the Turf and all its arts –
They had often blewed a dollar on a wrong 'un –
And Isabel one evening met a mug from rural parts,
An attenuated Juggins, and a long 'un.

In the twentieth century *blue* is used by bookmakers to mean a losing race: the clerk writes *B* on a losing book.

blue ribbon A blue ribbon, made of silk, is first recorded as a badge of honour in 1651. The Derby is known as the *Blue Ribbon*, or *Blue Riband*, after a famous remark by Disraeli to Lord George Bentinck. Bentinck, after years of involvement with racing, had suddenly sold all of his horses and his stud because of his realisation that his political duties needed all the time at his disposal. Two years later one of his former foals, now the three-year-old Surplice, won the Derby, the great race which he had never won, at the same time as his political efforts seemed to have come to nothing. 'All my life I have been trying for this, and for what have I sacrificed it?' he said to Disraeli, who had encountered him alone and agitated in the House of Commons library; and, in response to Disraeli's commiserations, he protested, 'You do not know what the Derby is.' 'Yes I do,' replied Disraeli, 'it is the Blue Riband of the Turf.'

blunder   From Middle English *blondren*, perhaps from Icelandic *blonda*, 'to doze'; *blunder* normally describes a mistake in steeple-chasing, when a horse hits a fence hard, but does not *fall*. A bad blunder often leads to an *unseated* rider. For an example of its use, see the quotation under *any price*.

board, boards   Short for the bookmakers' boards on which horses' *prices* are displayed: 'Merry Widow is showing 6/1 on the boards.' To bet *off the boards* is to be a bookmaker showing prices in *Tattersalls*, or one of the cheaper *enclosures*, as opposed to betting *off the card*, i.e. on the *rails*. A horse is 'wiped off the boards' when it has been so heavily backed that bookmakers have shortened its price dramatically.

board-boy   A racecourse menial employed by a bookmaker to stand all through the races, holding the board straight: the arrival of a tripod fixture for the board, early in the twentieth century, rendered his occupation redundant.

boat   Slang for a large, unwieldy horse: 'Some have accused Mukdaam of being a bigger boat than the QE2, but he keeps on galloping' (*Sporting Life* 20 June 1990).

bolt   Derived from Old English *bolt*, a cross-bow arrow, the verb has a variety of senses connected with the idea of 'sudden or hasty motion or application of force'. The meaning 'to rush suddenly off or away', used of men or beasts, is first attested in 1611, and the special application to a horse, 'to break away from the rider's control', is not found until the nineteenth century. In racing, horses most frequently *bolt* before the race itself, when they break free from the *lad*'s hold, when they are taken out on to the course, or when they get to the start. During the race, a horse which *pulls¹* so hard that the jockey has no control over it may be described as having bolted. When a horse wins easily, it may be described as having *bolted in*, or *bolted up*.

bone   *Bone in the ground*, originally a hunting term, describes *going* which is frost-hardened, even under a soft surface. The OED's first attestation is from 1906: 'The night's frost had left a great deal of "bone" in the ground.' When there is bone in the ground, racing is unlikely to take place.

book¹   To *make a book* on a race originally described the practice of keeping a record of bets made with different people on a race. Piers Egan describes a notebook kept by a nineteenth-century betting man:

> The art of betting on race-horses is considered a complete science; but without a person keeps a *book*, and attends daily to the rise and fall of the 'Sporting Stocks', and shifts his ground

according to the alteration of the odds, the going down of some, the first favourites, and the rising of others, so as to obtain a point or two the best of it, he is very likely to make but a 'sorry affair' of it altogether. (Egan, 184)

Egan's 'keep a book' soon became 'make a book', a practice which meant that the 'book maker' contrived to put himself into the position of being certain to make a profit, whatever the result of the race. By doing this consistently, the shrewdest backers evolved into the bookmakers of today, and nowadays the making of a book refers entirely to the bookmaker's taking of bets on a race – essentially, the fixing of a *price* for each horse. The American expression is 'make book'. For the book actually used by book-makers on the racecourse, see *field book*.

book²   *The Book* describes the General Stud Book, founded in 1791 by James Weatherby, published at regular intervals, giving details of all pure bred mares and their progeny, and the sires of their offspring. Only animals *in the book* are allowed to race on licensed racecourses.

book³   *Book* is used as a shortened form of 'the form-book' – not any specific *form* guide, but a way of referring to a horse's racing experience: 'On the book, Pashto should again finish in front of Tomahawk' (*Sporting Life* 19 September 1990).

bookmaker   An obvious development from the practice of making a *book¹* on a race, *bookmaker*, as someone who takes bets from the public, is first attested in 1862; shortened, affectionately, to *booky*, or *bookie*, in the 1880s. In discussing the various forms of the –*y* suffix, the OED comments that '*Bookie* for *bookmaker* is a formation of a rare type; cp. *nighty* for *nightdress*.' An earlier term for bookmaker was *fieldsman*. Jon Bee's description of fieldsmen shows the bookmaker just beginning to emerge: 'Those who make it a rule to give odds against the favourite, or any particular horse; they are considered very knowing.'

boot¹   Jockeys use their legs as much as their arms in a race, hence the phrase to *boot home*, that is, to ride a vigorous winning finish.

boot²   *Boots*, made of various materials, are designed to protect and support a horse's legs: often worn by *chasers* and *hurdlers* (1812). They offer more protection than *bandages*.

booty   To *play booty* is 'to play badly intentionally in order to lose the game' (16th C.). By the nineteenth century the phrase had taken on strong racing associations. The OED quotes, from 1813, 'I gave a jockey a handsome premium to play booty.' Patrick Chalmers, writing in 1939, describes the Prince Regent's support for his jockey Sam Chifney, 'whom he held to be innocent of riding "booty" (as it was called)' (*Racing England*, 39). *Booty* itself derives from Teutonic forms meaning 'exchange, barter', and the OED explains its use in this phrase as describing a confederacy in which the conspirators agree to cheat: one 'plays into the hands of confederates in order to share the "plunder" with them.'

bore See *bump*.

bottom Jon Bee defines *bottom* as 'spunk or lastingness under fatigue; as, a horse going a long and penible journey.' The OED quotes, from 1790, 'what is called in the language of the turf, bottom.' There is an echo of this when trainers and jockeys speak today of 'getting to the bottom of a horse', that is, discovering what he is ultimately capable of. The sense seems to derive from uses of 'bottom' to mean 'the fundamental character', and 'a foundation, basis, footing'.

box¹ in the sense of 'a separate apartment or stall for a horse... in a stable or a railway truck', the OED's first attestation of *box* is surprisingly late – 1846. Today, of course, it also describes the road vehicle which transports horses to the races – *horse-box*. A *loose box* is a stall large enough for a horse to move around.

box² On the racecourse the *judge's box* is set directly in front of the winning post. In the past it was clearly a moveable item, at Newmarket at least, where many different courses were used. Surtees describes how, after one race, 'the next proceeding is the wheeling of the judge's box, and removal of the old stakes and ropes to another course' (Surtees, 88).

box³ To be *boxed in* is to be surrounded by other horses, often against the rails, so that one cannot get out to make a *run*. This is common in big fields, but not as rare as one might think in three- or four-horse races. The OED does not recognise this meaning – although it does identify the use of 'box' to mean 'to confine ... in uncomfortably narrow limits' from 1710 – but *box in* is in common use today in athletics as well as racing. 'Michael Roberts found himself boxed in on Farmin at Newbury three weeks ago and the colt must rate as an unlucky loser' (*Sporting Life* 7 September 1990).

box⁴ To *box*, or, more often, *box carefully*, was nineteenth-century bookmakers' slang for ensuring 'that one's betting liabilities do not exceed one's cash in hand' (Partridge): perhaps an extension of the idea of *hedging*. I suspect that this, and not the sport of boxing, is the origin of the phrase 'box clever', although the OED disagrees.

boys *The boys* is racecourse slang, dating from the mid-nineteenth century, describing the bookmakers and their associates. This is Partridge's definition, but the OED is less kind, giving the meaning as 'the thieves and swindlers who frequent racecourses'. Perhaps

these are only two different ways of describing the same thing,
given the conditions of nineteenth-century racing. *Boy*, in a negative sense, goes back at least as far as the 'angry boys' and 'roaring
boys' of Elizabethan and Jacobean London. Cp. *spiv*.

brackets   *Brackets* indicates winning performances of horses as
listed in the index to the *Racing Calendar*: from the practice of
putting parentheses around each winning performance, begun in
Ruff's Guide to the Turf in 1847:

> The horse ran six times in his 2-yr.-old season, 1858, and won
> the Triennial Stakes at Ascot; started twelve times as a 3-yr.-old
> and won once; and fifteen times as a 4-yr.-old without earning
> brackets. (Osbaldeston, 241)

break¹   The *break* is the start. A horse which *misses the break* is
one which starts after the others, not necessarily a handicap since
a jockey may deliberately miss the break so as to be able to *settle¹*
a free runner behind the field.

break²   In the sense of taming a horse, *break* is first attested in
1474. In earlier centuries the verb was commonly used to describe
the education of human beings too: e.g. from 1519, 'It is better
to breake a mannys owne people in warr than to hyre straungers';
or, from Shakespeare's *Taming of the Shrew*, 'Why then thou
canst not break her to the lute?' In later centuries it could be used
for other animals: e.g. from 1824, 'Whose dog hath he broken?'
Today we would use *tame* for animals, *educate* for humans, and
keep *break* for animals which we ride, which, to all intents and
purposes, means the horse. The most concise summary of the
philosophy of breaking is Goldschmidt's: 'The requirements in
successful breaking are threefold – safety to man and beast, rapid-
ity, and, as far as possible, permanency' (Goldschmidt, 1).

break³   A horse's *action* is said to *break* when it changes from one
gait to another. The origin is American, and the word is commonly
used in trotting races when a horse changes gait and therefore
has to drop back to the rear of the field.

break down   A horse *breaks down* in a race when it goes lame,
normally by straining the suspensory ligament which supports
the fetlock joint; first attested in 1831, 'A slight injury . . . is called
a sprain of the back sinews or tendons; and when it is more
serious, the horse is said to have broken down.' This usage was
extended to engines and then to road vehicles.

break out   When a horse *breaks out* it begins to sweat: breaking
out commonly describes excessive sweating after previous drying,
a sign that something is wrong with the horse or that it has been
seriously overworked. This sense is not in the OED.

breathe   The verb *breathe* was commonly used to describe the exercising of animals and men. The OED defines its meaning as 'to excite the respiratory organs of: hence...to exercise briskly.' Its first attestation of the verb, from 1567, is 'you breath your foming steede', and of the past participle *breathed*, the second example, from 1525, is 'Rode forthe an easy passe to keepe their horses well breathed'. Well into the nineteenth century *breathing* was used to describe the training of horses: Jon Bee describes it as 'running at half speed (Turf and ring)'; and for an earlier example, *well-breathed* is the approbatory term which describes the favourite horse of the singer of a racing song in James Shirley's *Hyde Park* (1632):

> Lusty George, and, gentlemen, hark yet,
> To winning Mackarel, fine-mouthed Freak,
> Bay Tarrall, that won the cup at Newmarket,
> Thundering Tempest, Black Dragon eke.
> Precious Sweet Lips, I do not lose,
> Nor Toby with his golden shoes;
> But if I be just, all honour must
> Be given to well-breathed Jilian Thrust.

breeches   Jockeys' trousers. Originally breeches differed from trousers by extending only as far as just below the knee. From Old English *brēc*.

breeze   *Breeze, breeze up*, and *breeze down* are used to describe an easy exercise canter for a horse. At Breeze-Up sales young horses are put through their easy paces for prospective buyers to observe their *action*: 'We bought what we saw and liked at the Breeze-Up and the colt has been working well at home' (*Sporting Life* 4 July 1990). The OED identifies no such usage, but 'breeze-up' is recorded as a nautical term, from the nineteenth century, describing the freshening of a wind; and 'breeze' as a verb, meaning 'to move or proceed briskly' has become common in the twentieth century, as in 'breezing along with the breeze'. 'Geoff was to breeze his first-time partner a couple of furlongs to determine whether we paid the fine for withdrawal and sent him home – or sent him to post' (O'Sullevan, 258).

bridle   From Old English *bregdan*, 'to pull, twitch', the verb meaning 'to curb, check, restrain', occurs in the ninth century; and the noun, meaning 'the head-gear of the harness of a horse', in the eleventh. A horse *goes into the bridle* when he takes hold of his *bit[1]*; *keeping him up into the bridle* means that the jockey lets him go at 'the full speed allowed by the degree of restraint in which he is held by the bridle'. A horse comes *off the bridle* when no more restraint is imposed, usually at the end of the race when he is making his effort: 'Vincent O'Brien's colt...has a lot of ability and won the Tetrarch on the bridle here three weeks ago' (*Sporting Life* 19 May 1990); 'A fantastic racehorse. When he is cantering he has the older horses off the bridle' (*Sporting Life* 21 June 1990).

bring down   A horse is *brought down* when another horse impedes it and causes it to fall: most common in *chasing* and *hurdling*, when a fallen horse brings down another, but horses may be brought down on the flat too: 'Miss A Turn: reluctant to start, always behind, brought down bend after 7th' (*Racing Post* 29 May 1990).

bring on   *Bring on*, meaning 'advance the growth and development of', is a common racing idiom: skilled trainers bring on young horses gradually; races bring on horses to full fitness. The OED had originally described this sense as obsolete, but its supplement notes it as still current and quotes, from J.A. Worrall's *English Idioms* (1932), 'His trainer brought on the horse in fine style.' *Bring along* is used in a similar way.

brown   Covers a much narrower range of colour when describing horses than in general usage. It describes horses which are black, or nearly black, except that they have lighter areas on the legs, and around the muzzle and eyes: marked in the *card* with the abbreviation *br*.

brush   *Brushing* describes one of the consequences of a faulty *action*, when a horse grazes itself by striking its fore or hind leg with the opposite one inside the fetlock joints: first attested in 1691. See *plait*.

brush-pricker   A piece of leather studded with bristles, fitted around the mouthpiece of the bit: its purpose is to discourage a horse from *hanging*. The 'brush' element in this compound probably comes from the pricker's appearance.

buck   To *buck*, or *buck-jump*, is not recorded until the nineteenth century. It describes a horse's vertical leap into the air with its back arched. The 'buck' element refers to the male deer which performs a similar jump. Bucking is not necessarily a bad sign:

> When I got up on my horse he gave a buck and a kick, at which I was delighted. He had never done that before with me, and I took it as a really good omen, an indication that he was feeling 'good and well'. (Donoghue, 197)

bummer   Slang for 'a severe pecuniary loss' which originated on the racecourse *c.*1870-1914 (Partridge).

bump   *Bumping and boring* is a catchall phrase for the kind of *interference*, usually in the closing stages of a race, in which one horse collides with another. *Bore*, in this sense, can be traced back to the seventeenth century: the OED cites, from 1677, 'He bor'd him out of the saddle fair.' Horses are said to *catch a bump* when they meet with slight interference in a race.

bumper   *Bumper* used to mean an amateur rider, perhaps because such riders bump up and down in the saddle, or because they do not always steer a straight path; probably the former, because *bump* was a slang term for a casual ride: 'In spite of that persistent sinking sensation, I was thankful that, at any rate, I had got as far as "having a bump round" ' (Sassoon, *Memoirs of a Fox Hunting Man*). Today *bumper*, or, more fully, a *bumper's race*, is a flat race for four-, five-, and six-year-old would-be *hurdlers* and *chasers* which have had no other racing experience than running in bumpers. As entertainment they leave a lot to be desired; as a betting medium, even more. Officially, these races are known as National Hunt flat races.

bunch   Horses *bunch* when they crowd together, often when going round a bend, at which the desperate cries of jockeys calling for room can be heard: 'The stewards held an inquiry into Bastiman's fall and found it was due to general bunching' (*Sporting Life* 16 June 1990). The use of 'bunch' to describe the crowding together of animals is originally American: from 1885, when hogs are described as standing 'bunched around at the root of the tree'. Americans are more likely to describe as a *bunch finish* what the British call a *blanket* finish.

burnt fingers   Proverbially suffered by backers when short-priced favourites get beaten, or, less often, by bookmakers when they make a mistake: 'some bookmakers were so convinced that Tudor Beacon had prevailed that they paid out over this horse before the weigh-in and burned their fingers' (*Sporting Life* 30 May 1990).

burst   To *burst* a horse is to ride it so hard that it *blows up*: 'The jockey charged off in front, raced wide, and just burst the horse – and it fell in a heap' (*Sporting Life* 15 May 1990).

bury   In *chasing*, a jockey is *buried* after a bad fall, particularly when the horse hits the fence hard and catapults him into the ground – even more so if the horse falls on top of him. A jockey *buries* his horse when he completely *covers* him up in a race: 'Tebbutt, mindful of the fact that the four-year-old does not like to hit the front too soon, buried his mount behind Silly Habit' (*Sporting Life* 21 September 1990).

business   A horse which *does the business* is one which wins. The other phrase is to *go about its business*. When a horse does this, it begins to make its final effort in a race: 'He certainly knew what to do when Reid asked him to go about his business approaching the final furlong' (*Sporting Life* 30 May 1990). The OED records neither of these phrases in these senses, but does note 'business' as once being used to describe work done by a horse, in 1739: 'a horse which eats only a moderate Quantity of Food, will do as much business... as one that eats continually' (although I suspect a euphemism here). The *business end* of a race is the last furlong or two, when all the hard work is done.

bute   *Bute* is phenylbutazone ($C_{19}H_{20}N_2O_2$), so called as a shortened form of its trade name *butazolidin*. Given by vets to ease musculoskeletal disorders, bute helps strengthen the weakest part of a racehorse, its legs. In Britain, and in some states of America, it is regarded as a forbidden substance, but other American states permit it. Two debates focus on its use: whether it is right to run unbutified horses against those on bute, given the distinct advantage which the latter have; and, leading on from this disadvantage, whether British horses should be treated with bute when running in America, and, if they are, whether they should ever be allowed to race in Britain again. Cp. *lasix*.

buy money   One *buys money* when one backs a horse which is heavily *odds-on*, investing, say, £1000 to win £100. The imposition of betting *tax* nearly made this practice die the death, but its recent lifting from *on-course* betting has seen its revival in the last few years. The OED identifies the phrase as racing slang, its first attestation being from 1906.

buzz, buzzer   A *buzzer* is a horse for which there is a lot of support in the betting market: 'Laying S.P. consequently implied laying the shortest price for the "buzzers", or fancied horses' (Sidney, 122). It is probably derived from *buzz*, 'a busy rumour'. On the racecourse a buzz is, paradoxically, not as strong as a *whisper*: 'As always, there was a buzz about a number of debutants in the race, including the 4/1 joint favourite Red Bishop, who finished third' (*Racing Post* 19 September 1990).

by[1]   Horses win *by* a certain *distance[2]* (but see *win*).

by[2]   Every horse is said to be *by* a certain sire: thus, 'Doodlebug, a colt by Bombshell'. This is a short form of *got by*. Cp. *out of*.

bye   A *bye-bet* is one in which a horse is backed to beat another, no matter where they finish in a race: first attestation, 1886. Bye betting was common in cock-fighting: the OED quotes, from 1859, 'Eleven a-head on the main and byes seven' (the 'main' was the main cock-fight). To *run a bye* was a term used in coursing to describe the practice of running one dog against another who was not in the contest. This took place when there was an odd number of dogs in the draw, and rather than give the dog a bye it was required to run so that it had no fitness advantage over the rest of the field. From this usage 'run a bye' took on a racing sense, to describe the running of a horse in a race with no intention of putting it under pressure to win: 'Pull her! Who talked of pullin'? She'll run a bye, that's all. We shan't ever know whether she could a' won or not' (Galsworthy, 'Had a Horse').

C *With the c*: bookmakers' slang for horses on their list which are marked with a *c* for 'careful'; i.e. horses to look out for in the betting exchanges.

cab To *call a cab*, or *hail a cab*, describes the gesture of a jump jockey when his horse pitches forward at landing and he is forced to lean back, or to the side, with one arm outstretched to keep his balance, thereby looking, to those of an unsympathetic nature, as if he were signalling a cab driver to stop.

calendar The *Calendar* is 'The Racing Calendar', founded in 1727, with the aim of giving (according to its title page):

An Historical List or Account of all the Horse-Matches Run, And of all the Plates and Prizes run for in England (of the Value of Ten Pounds or upwards) in 1727, Containing The Names of the Owners of the Horses, etc., that have Run, as above, and the Names and Colours of the Horses also, with the Winner distinguished of every Match, Plate, Prize, or Stakes; The Conditions of Running, as to Weight, Age, Size, etc., and the Places in which the losing Horses have come in . . .

The founder of the Calendar was John Cheny. His intended readers were gentlemen who would welcome the opportunity 'in the midst of winter' of 'diverting themselves with a Prospect, as it were, of the Sport of each past Year,' with the eventual aim of making a profit from their betting:

From hence 'twill be always discoverable what old Horses are dropping, and how they decline and go off; what young Horses are every Year coming up; and by what steps they advance and improve. Which must render Gentlemen capable of reducing their Calculations nearer to perfection, and consequently of matching or betting with greater advantage.

In 1773 the Calendar came under the control of the *Weatherby* family and became, thereby, the official organ of the *Jockey Club*.

call[1] To *have the call*, or *hold call*, is to be in the lead in a race; an extension of its figurative use to mean 'to be in chief or greatest demand' – 1840, 'Youth has the call.' The source is the card game Long Whist, where those partners who have the call have the right to nominate trumps. 'Judicial Hero then had the call from Adrie Bridge who drifted right across' (*Sporting Life* 4 August 1990).

call[2] To *call* a race is to commentate on its running, either on the

39

racecourse or for a broadcast. This usage connects two senses of
the verb, to utter loudly and to name, and may well be the origin
of the expression 'a close call', a piece of American slang which
entered the language in the 1880s. Peter O'Sullevan, the greatest
of all British commentators, titled his autobiography *Calling the
Horses*.

call on   To *call on*, or *call upon*, meaning 'to require or urge to
exert itself further', has a general application now, but was originally a technical term in racing. The OED's first attestation is
from 1850: 'In the last few strides, where sudden and increased
exertion is called for, and the horse is, in technical phrase, "called
upon".'

call over   The *call over* was the bookmakers' former practice of
calling over, at regular intervals in the weeks before a race, the
list of runners with their *ante-post* prices. The practice probably
began in the early years of the twentieth century: the OED's first
attestation is from 1927, 'That all such bets transacted at the club's
"call-over" would be free of tax to the backer.' The club in question was the Victoria Club, founded in 1860 at Chatham Place,
Blackfriars, as a betting and gambling club. From 1872-1961 it
was located near Covent Garden, and during this time the call-over
was instituted:

> A Chairman was elected; a most respected layer who held this
> office for many years in the writer's memory was Ike Morris,
> and he simply 'called out' the names of the runners for the
> race for which the meeting had been convened. The calling
> was done from a table or from a type of lectern and the calling
> invited 'offers about the horse called' from the assembled mem-
> bers of the Club. The offers and the amounts to which they
> were taken were recorded and after the entire field had been
> Called Over the market prices for that race, for that day, were
> estimated from the recorded transactions. A most businesslike
> ritual altogether. (Sidney, 81)

canadian   See *multiple bet*.

canter   Comes from Canterbury: a *Canterbury pace*, as in 'Have
I practic'd ... my smooth Ambles, and Canterbury paces?'
described the *pace* of mounted pilgrims. This first attestation, in
1636, is surprisingly late, given that the pilgrimages were
medieval affairs. Before *canter* was used in this sense, however,
the common term for such a pace was 'false gallop' (see *gallop*).
The shortened form *canter* is not attested until early in the
eighteenth century.

  Since a canter is relatively slow, a horse which wins very easily
is said to win *in a canter*, in a *common canter*, or even in a *hack*

canter. A hack canter is the slowest type of canter, little more than a trot; *steady canter* and *sharp canter* are respectively faster. An *extended canter* describes a free-going pace with the horse well under control. A *false canter* describes a horse cantering, but with its legs going in the wrong sequence. The proper sequence in a canter is three-time, in which the hoof beats are heard in this order: near hind, near fore and off hind together, off fore; or, off hind, off fore and near hind together, near fore.

Used as a verb, *canter over* describes one horse's great superiority to another or others: 'He looks potentially high class on occasions, as, for example, when he cantered over Serious Trouble at Pontefract' (*Racing Post* 29 May 1990).

card   The programme of races at a meeting, as given on the *race-card*: 'Haydock's card opens with a seller.' To *go through the card* is to select the winner of every race, or, in a jockey's case, to ride all the winners. The *correct card*, often written *k'rect card*, meant 'the right thing to have or do' (Partridge, *c.*1860). The original OED volume C, published in 1888, just gets in the sense of 'card' as 'a programme, official or not, of the "events" at races, regattas, and the like', offering one illustrative (unattributed) example of 'modern' speech: 'Here's the c'rect card, sir!' A later example, in the Supplement, taken from 1903 and referring to cricket, describes the setting up of a 'printing tent' at Lord's, so that 'the public, for the first time, could secure a "correct card" of the game.' It would seem, therefore, that there were originally unofficial cards of races for the public, to be replaced with official race-cards, produced by the course, offering the final *declarations* of runners, details of weights carried, ownership, race *conditions*, prize moneys, and *colours* – with, in the middle of the nineteenth century, some rivalry between the official (correct) cards and the unofficial.

An *across the card* bet, normally a *double* or a *treble*, is one in which horses are backed in races starting at the same time (or within a short space of time) at two (or more) separate meetings. For *off the card* see *rails*. See, also, *mark*[2].

careless   *Careless riding* is an offence against the Rules of racing and, if it causes *interference*, may lead to a horse's disqualification, or its being placed behind the horse or horses interfered with, and to the jockey's suspension. Careless riding is defined by the *Jockey Club* as failing to take all reasonable steps to avoid causing interference, or causing interference by misjudgment or inattention. *Careless* originally meant 'free from care' (= 'carefree', archaic since 1650) or 'unconcerned', with the prevailing modern senses only developing late in the sixteenth century. In racing, careless riding is carefully distinguished from the more serious offence of *reckless* riding.

carpet Racecourse slang for three, particularly odds of 3/1. *Double carpet* is 33/1. The origin is rhyming slang: 'carpet bag' = 'drag', a nineteenth-century term for a prison sentence of three months' hard labour.

carry¹ The verb may be used, as with people, to describe the way a horse bears itself. The OED quotes, under the definition 'to hold (the body, head, etc.) up in a certain way', from 1724: 'Stolen... a Mare... does not carry her tail well'; and, as an example of the verb's absolute usage, from 1829: 'A horse is said to carry well, when his neck is arched, and he holds his head high.' Jon Bee offers an expansive description of the verb's possible uses:

'To carry well', a horse should have his neck well set, large in his shoulder; *bent*, if small-headed, if not straight, but not too long: the tail is concerned in the animal's *carrying* well. To *carry high* or *low*; the head being too much elevated, or somewhat depressed. The former arises from weak fore-quarters; the latter from large head and neck too long.

carry² A horse is *carried out* in a race when forced off the course by another horse which is riderless or out of control. In a less extreme case, a horse may be *carried wide* by another, particularly at a bend when a horse goes wide and forces another horse outside it to go wide too.

carry³ *Carry weight* refers to the carrying of 'such additional weight as equalises the competitors': in 'John Gilpin', 'He carries weight! He rides a race!' Today we would more likely refer to such a horse carrying *lead*.

cart, carted *Cart* was nineteenth-century slang for a racecourse, which Partridge suggests may be derived from the phrase 'the correct card' (see *card*). To *walk the cart* meant 'to walk over the course' (Partridge, *c*.1870). Perhaps 'cart' in this sense is the origin of the common racecourse usage to be, or get, *carted*, meaning to be thrown off a horse. A jockey gets carted when he is thrown off on the way down to the start.

The phrase 'in the cart', meaning 'in the wrong' or 'in a fix', may come from the cart in which criminals were taken to execution, but its earliest uses seem to be connected with racing, as in the OED's two examples from 1889; one from a Dictionary of Slang: 'An owner is said to be *in the cart*, or *carted*, when his horse is prevented from winning by some fraud on the part of those in his employment'; the other is from the *Evening Standard*: 'In two races... Sir George Chetwynd – to use a vulgarism – had been "put in the cart" by his jockey.'

cast   In Old English the common verb for 'throw' was *weorpan*; this was superseded in Middle English by *casten*, itself now generally replaced by *throw*, but still surviving in scores of words and expressions (castaway, cast an eye, cast a spell). One such is the phrase *cast in his box* to describe a horse's inability to rise after it has lain on its back in its stall. This occurs because it rolls over so near to a wall that it cannot get its legs out. The horse's consequent panic may lead to injury, external or internal, so that *getting cast* is often a reason for a horse's withdrawal from a race. 'Cast', in the sense 'to throw a beast on its back or side', is first attested, with reference to sheep, in 1577.

castor   See *chestnut*.

catch hold   A horse is said to *catch hold* when it *pulls¹*; i.e. it takes hold of the bit.

catch-weight   *Catch-weights* were races for which there was no *weighing* in or weighing out; i.e. horses carried whatever weight their owners wished – or could get. They were also known as *catch as catch can* races. When racing became properly organised, the practice was restricted to National Hunt racing and private matches. In *The Taming of the Shrew* Kate plays on the phrase when she counters Petruchio's taunt that he will not 'burden' her because he knows her 'to be but young and light', with the reply (2:1:204): 'Too light for such a swain as you to catch, / And yet as heavy as my weight should be.' Jon Bee defines it as 'any weights, the first jockies to be met with – no going to scale.'

cavesson   See *noseband*.

cavort   Perhaps a corruption of *curvet*, 'the leap of a horse in the *manège*' (1575), *cavort* came into the language from America in the mid-nineteenth century to describe the prancing around of a frisky horse.

cert   A contraction of *certainty*, first attested in 1889, 'I hear Pioneer is a cert. for the St. James.' Soon intensified to *dead cert*.

chalk jockey   A jockey, usually an amateur or an *apprentice*, who rides so infrequently that his name has to be chalked up on the *number-board*, there being no painted slat with his name on it. Partridge dates the phrase from *c*.1870.

championship   *Championship races*, until the end of the 1989-90 season, were the best kind of jump races. Formerly known as Grade One races, from 1990-91 the Grade One designation was restored, but with more races elevated to this standing.

change¹   *Change hands* is defined by the OED according to the quotation which it offers as the first attestation, from 1753: 'To change a horse or change hand is to turn or beat the horse's head from one hand to the other, from the right to the left, or from the left to the right.' Today, however, a jockey is normally described as changing his hands when he lengthens or tightens up the reins.

change[2]   A horse changes legs when it has been *leading* with one leg and changes to the other. This often happens when it finds itself on the 'wrong' leg coming round a bend, when the *going* does not suit it, or, more generally, because it is feeling some kind of discomfort:

> Charlton believes Quest for Fame might have been carrying the injury before his Irish effort. He said: "The race probably brought it to the surface, but it would explain why he was changing his legs in Ireland." (*Sporting Life* 4 July 1990).

chase[1], **chasing**   That the sport of *chasing* should be so called seems quite reasonable, given the original hunting senses of the verb *chase*, from Old French *chacier, chasser* – 'þe hert to chacen and þe hinde' – and the noun, *the chase*, 'the occupation or pastime of hunting wild animals for profit or (more usually) sport' (1330). The racing of horses over a course of obstacles developed from the hunting field, and the use of *chaser* to describe a hunting horse occurs as early as 1300, 'palfrei, chasur, no no stede'. However, once we consider how the *steeplechase* evolved from the *wild goose chase*, then we can see that 'chase' is not simply a loose synonym for riding over a course of fences, but actually describes quite literally the kind of pursuit involved in early steeplechasing. As detailed in entries under those words, it seems likely that the first such races took the form of chase the leader, one rider going off in front, choosing his *line*[1] over country, with the rest of the field required to follow him closely.

chase[2]   To *chase along* a horse in a race is not to pursue it but to urge it on. The phrase usually describes a jockey's efforts in the early or middle stages of a race when he is trying to get the horse to keep, or improve, its position. Not in the OED, but the expression is common enough in racing on the Flat and over jumps: 'Headrest: chased along to keep in touch halfway, never near to challenge' (*Sporting Life* 8 September 1990).

chestnut[1]   A common colour in *thoroughbreds*, *chestnut* describes different varieties of yellow, from golden to liver. First attested, as 'chestnut-coloured', in 1636. A true chestnut has a chestnut mane and tail. Marked on the *card* with the abbreviation *ch*.

chestnut[2]   'The hard knob in the skin of a horse at the inner side of the fore-legs' (1859); also known as the *castor*, and, in America, as *night-eyes*. The OED's first attestation offers this bizarre formula: 'To tame the horse, sometimes using the chestnut of his leg, which they dry, grind... and blow into his nostrils.'

Chifney   The jockey Sam Chifney (1753-1807) gave his name to the *Chifney bit*: a bit whose upper part swivels on the mouthpiece, independent of the lower part. Its purpose is to correct the vice of rearing, being used to lead horses which have this fault. The OED, which spells it Chiffney, gives its first attestation from 1834.

Christian   Until the mid-nineteenth century *Christian* was commonly used to distinguish humans from brutes: e.g. from *Tom Jones*, 'fitter food for a horse than a Christian'. A slang sense developed from this, making 'Christian' mean 'a "decent", "respectable", or "presentable" person', and it became possible to describe a racehorse as a Christian when he proved himself to be well-behaved, honest, and reliable: '"I've never trained a kinder horse. There isn't a bad bone in his body, he's a Christian," added the trainer' (*Racing Post* 21 April 1990). This extension of the word's usage is not in the OED.

chuck   A horse is *chucked in* when it is given an unexpectedly low weight in a *handicap*. A variant of *thrown in*, 'chuck' offers more of a sense of the handicapper's recklessness, in line with the OED's definition of the verb as describing a throwing 'of heavy things... with ease or contempt'. Alternatively, *chucked out* is occasionally used as a synonym for *thrown out*, when a horse is disqualified by the stewards after an *enquiry*.

cinch   A supposed certainty. The word is by no means confined to racing, but its origins, from the Spanish *cincha*, 'a girth', via American usage, points to a horse, if not horseracing, connection; as does the OED's first attestation of the word in its general meaning, from 1888: 'The racehorse owner who has a cinch bottled up for the big race.'

claim, claimer   Both words are used to describe jockeys and races. A *claiming jockey* – or *claimer* – is one who claims a weight *allowance*. The amount claimed is related to the number of winners the apprentice jockey has ridden: 'Reg Hollinshead's lad followed up his Doncaster double... by landing another two winners at Edinburgh yesterday, resulting in his claim being cut to 3lb' (*Sporting Life* 3 July 1990). A *claiming race* – or *claimer* – is one in which every horse which runs, according to the framed *conditions* of the race, may be claimed by a buyer for a price related to the weight it carries. The attractive feature of such races is that they are designed to allow the trainers to frame the *handicap* themselves, their horses being allowed, say, to carry one pound less for each £1,000 by which they lower the claiming price: 'This claimer proved particularly useful for the racecourse, generating a profit of £8,347 for the course after six claims had been lodged for four of the horses' (*Sporting Life* 3 July 1990). Just as in a *seller* a horse may be 'bought in', that is, retained by the owner bidding for his own horse, so in a claimer a 'friendly claim' may be lodged so that the horse is retained. In each case the racecourse gets the same proportion of the price as it would have got from a sale to an outside bidder or claimer.

classic A *classic* is one of the five races framed to test the best of the three-year-olds: the One Thousand Guineas and Two Thousand Guineas, for fillies and colts respectively, over a mile at Newmarket early in the season; the Derby and Oaks, over a mile and a half at Epsom, in early June or late May – the Oaks is for fillies, the Derby is open to colts and fillies; and the St. Leger, for colts and fillies, over a mile and three-quarters at Doncaster in September. The OED defines 'classic', from the French *classique*, and Latin *classicus*, as meaning 'of the first rank or authority', which gets its racing sense exactly; but the word is not used to describe these races until 1885, first of all in the phrase *classic races*. The shorter form, *classic*, is first attested in 1905. Like all words denoting excellence, attempts are frequently made to extend its range of reference – and should be stoutly resisted.

clear[1] Horses *clear* fences when they jump them successfully: a development of the sense 'to leap clear over; to pass over'. The OED's first attestation, from 1791, describes a horse which 'clears everything with his fore legs in capital style'; but it is worth noting that in chasing a horse clears a fence even if, in doing so, it takes a large chunk out of it.

clear[2] When horses *come clear* they draw away from the rest of the field.

clench See *clinch*.

clerk The *clerk of the course* is the official responsible for the general arrangements of a race meeting: first attested, 1835. The *clerk of the scales* is the official responsible for the *weighing-in* and weighing out of jockeys and for the *draw* for places at the start.

clever, cleverly In January 1989 the *Sporting Life* was criticised for using *cleverly* to describe the way a horse had won. As the complainant put it,

> 'Easily' might apply, or 'comfortably', but what has 'cleverly' got to do with it? Does cleverly mean that the horse won with a lot in hand ...or does it mean that it had nothing in hand but, because the jockey was able to hold him together, he won anyway?

The short answer is neither, although the second suggestion is closer, because to *win cleverly* means, as the OED defines it, 'to win neatly after a close contest, with rather more advantage than seemed likely' – a usage which goes back to the nineteenth

century. In 1887 one Hawley Smart wrote a novel *Cleverly Won,
A Romance of the Grand National*. Steve Donoghue explained the
jockey's purpose in winning cleverly like this:

> Mount William certainly came a rattle at me when he made
> his effort, but Silver Tag always held him comfortably,
> although she only won a head, cleverly. I may be asked, "Why,
> then, did you only win by a head on her if you won so comfort-
> ably?" The answer is: "The animal, a three-year-old filly, car-
> ried 8st 3lbs; why should she have been pressed to do more
> than was necessary?" (Donoghue, 45)

In essence, then, it is probably the jockey's skill which the word
describes. In steeplechasing, however, 'clever' does describe a
horse's quick thinking. If he is *clever at his fences* he is one who
seldom falls, even though he may make the odd mistake. This
sense is worth preserving because it looks back to the original
meaning of the word, which was 'deft or nimble of hands...
adroit, dexterous, or skilful in the use of limbs and in bodily
movements' (16th C.).

click See *forge*.

climb When a horse's stride *shortens* in an exaggerated fashion,
its knee-action becoming very high, it is said to *climb*. Steve
Donoghue tells the horrifying story of his suddenly realising that
his mount Seaforth had gone blind in the middle of a race:

> We jumped off together and Seaforth was going well, full of
> running, until about half-way through the race I suddenly felt
> him falter, and then he began to "climb", bringing his knees
> up to his chin at every stride instead of stretching out, and all
> at once I realised that in the excitement and exertion of the
> race his defective eye must have affected the sight of the good
> one, which had also clouded right over, and my horse had
> literally gone totally blind in the middle of the race.
>
> It was the worst predicament I was ever in.
>
> It took me all my time to hold him up and save him from
> falling on his head. Fortunately I was just alongside another
> horse and I quickly decided that my only chance of escaping
> disaster was to try to keep Seaforth exactly where he was, lying
> by the other so that he could at least *hear* the galloping hooves
> of the animal beside him and gain some little confidence from
> that. I sat as still as a mouse, not daring to move, and straining
> every muscle to keep the poor horse on his feet; it was sheer
> instinct that told me the winning-post was reached, and we
> actually won the race by a short head. (Donoghue, 124)

clinch A variant form of *clench* (1598), from the Old English verb
clencan: 'a fastening in which the end of a nail is turned over

over and driven back into the substance through which it has passed.' The *clinch* is the nail which fixes a horseshoe to its foot. The OED quotes, from 1725, 'Cut them off and clinch them, so the clinches may be hidden to the Hoof.' When clinches work free, the horse *spreads a plate*.

clinker, clinking   From the verb *clink*, to make a 'sharp, metallic sound', a *clinker* is a horse of first-rate quality: it makes the right sound to attract one's attention. The nineteenth-century jockey Bill Scott was heard to include in his prayers the sentence 'the Almighty be thanked, I've got a bloody clinker at last', over Sir Tatton Sykes, the horse on which he eventually won the St. Leger. *Clinking*, meaning 'first rate, remarkably good', is dated by Partridge *c*.1855, who quotes from the *Sporting Times* of 1887, 'Prince Henry must be a clinking good horse.'

clip, clipper   A rapid pace, usually in the phrase *a good clip*: 'Tiger Flower had a spin with Nadma while River God and Great Heights went a good clip together' (*Sporting Life* 25 March 1990). In this sense, *clip* is first attested in 1867, and was originally confined to horses. A *clipper* was 'a splendid or very smart specimen of humanity or horseflesh': Partridge dates it from 1835, an American usage, anglicised *c*.1845, from 'clipper' in the sense 'any fast-moving ship'; and, as a horse, influenced by the Dutch *klepper*. A *clipping pace* meant a very fast one.

close coupled   See *coupled*.

club   The *club*, or *members'*, is the *enclosure* on the racecourse where bookmakers are not permitted to lay bets. See *rail*.

coat   A horse's *coat* grows towards the end of September and again in the Spring. Phrases which describe a horse's appearance, relating to these changes, are to 'go in the coat', 'look well in the coat', 'be right – or wrong – in the coat', 'to change – or break – coat'. See *stare*.

cockle   Betting slang for ten; i.e. 10/1. From rhyming slang, 'cock and hen'.

cocktail   A term for a non-*thoroughbred* horse, the name probably referring to the practice of docking the tails of hunters and stagecoach horses – and, possibly, the origin of the drink, the mixing of the horse's parentage being the shared factor. There were cocktail races in the nineteenth century.

collar   *On the collar* describes a stiff racecourse, or part of a course, as in this sentence from W. Allison's account of 'Sceptre at Home', describing one of the *gallops*[2] which the famous Sceptre used to take in his stride: 'It is all on the collar and affords a very severe test when horses are sent along from end to end of it.' It is an odd phrase in that it seems to link 'against the collar' – defined by the OED as 'entailing continuous exertion or hard strain' – with some kind of recollection of the Latin *collis*, 'a hill'.

collect¹ Like the phrase 'collect one self' for humans, *collect* is used to describe the bringing of a horse 'into such a position that he has complete command of his powers, and is completely in hand' (1833). The word is used particularly in *chasing*, when a horse is collected before and after a jump:

> One of the finest pieces of riding I ever witnessed was in a steeplechase at Melton as long ago as the year 1864, when, happening to stand near the brook, *eighteen feet of water*, I observed my friend Captain Coventry come down at it. Choosing some ground and a clear place, for it was already beginning to fill with numerous competitors, he set his horse going, at about a hundred yards from the brink, in the most masterly manner, increasing the pace resolutely but gradually, so as not to flurry or cause the animal to change his leg, nearly to full speed before he took off. I could not have believed it possible to make a horse go so fast in so collected a form; but with the rider's strength in the saddle, and perfectly skilful hands, he accomplished the feat, and got well over, I need hardly say in his stride. (Goldschmidt, 67)

collect² In betting, *collect* is used as shorthand for winning a bet; i.e. collecting one's money: 'Moonshot's backers never had any doubt that they were going to collect.'

colours *Racing silks*, first recorded in 1762, when the *Jockey Club* issued its second order, that

> For the greater Conveniency of distinguishing the Horses in Running, as also for the Prevention of Disputes arising from not knowing the Colours worn by each Rider, the underwritten GENTLEMEN have come to the Resolution and Agreement of having the Colours annexed to the following NAMES, worn by their respective Riders. (Prior, 143)

In the list of names which follows, only the Duke of Devonshire's 'Straw-colour' is still seen on the racecourse.

colt The word's origin is uncertain: *colt* is used in Old English to describe young asses and camels. In racing, a colt is a male *thoroughbred*, ungelded, under the age of five (other horses are called colts up to the age of four). While still with its dam the colt is usually called a *foal*.

coltish, colty Describes either the immature appearance of a horse or its frisky, or even wild, behaviour. Most literally, it describes friskiness as a result of sexual excitement when a filly is around: 'Kawtuban has been very colty, and tried to cover everything in sight at the start previously. We threatened him with the knife – it seems to have worked' (*Sporting Life* 23 May 1990).

come   A horse *comes* when it accelerates in the final part of a race. To *come again*, that is to accelerate when it had seemed to be losing pace, is the sign of a game horse. The OED's first attestation of the phrase is American, from the *Baltimore Sun* in 1946: 'Many of the supporters ... were ready to throw away their tickets when the odds-on favourite gave up the command, but cheered loudly when he "came again" to win going away.' The American style of racing, where good horses try to *make all*, instead of 'coming from behind', means that coming again is more common there than in Europe.

come back   The general sense of a competitor in a race 'coming back' to his field is first attested in racing: from *The Times* in 1885, 'Half-way down the hill Royal Hampton began to come back to his horses.' More technically, when a horse *comes back* at a jockey it shortens its stride, lifts its head, and does not run on.

come in¹, come up   When a well-backed horse, usually the *favourite*, wins, it *comes in* or *comes up* (Partridge, 20th C.). The OED records no use of 'come in' in this sense, but perhaps it should be treated as a development of the meaning 'to be successful in a candidature' (1705). 'Come up' is more difficult to explain. Again the OED has no relevant definition: perhaps the source lies in the expression of having one's number up, i.e. being lucky at last.

come in²   A horse's *price comes in* when its *odds* shorten; e.g. from 3/1 to 2/1.

come undone, come unstuck   These two phrases in general use occur commonly in racing circles and may well have originated there. The OED's earliest attestation of *come undone* is from 1899, where a horse-racing metaphor is used: 'The Oban "boom" came badly undone ... But let us suppose Oban had won, what would the other owners with horses in the race have said about the handicap?'; and it quotes, from *Notes and Queries* in 1922, the explanation that 'when a fancied horse, thought to be a "good thing", fails to realise expectations, it is said to be "a good thing come undone."' Likewise, its 1928 example for *come unstuck* has a racing context: 'Soon after this I came unstuck over a horse which the Prince of Wales, later King Edward, had very kindly given me.' But the phrase is more literally used in *chasing*, when a jockey is *unseated* at a fence.

commission   An order to place a sum of money on a horse for someone else. Normally the *commissioner* does his best to get the longest price; indeed, this is often the reason for betting in this

way, owners and trainers preferring to use someone whose connection with the horse is less well-known. T.H. Bird tells of Lord
Eglinton, that:

> If there was one thing in the world he hated, it was a mystery
> being made about the merit of any horse he owned. He suffered
> for his candour as, when he wanted to bet himself, his commis-
> sioner often found himself anticipated in the market.

(*Admiral Rous and the English Turf*)

'Commissioner', in this sense, is first attested in 1860; but nearly
twenty years earlier, in 1844, Richard *Tattersall* discussed the
employment of commissioners before the Parliamentary Special
Committee on Gaming Laws:

> Is there much betting by commission? – *I should think a great
> deal; not by me.*
>
> Is it known when a person makes a bet, whether he makes it
> for himself or for somebody else? – *Generally speaking it is. I
> myself have small bets for people, but I always declare the person
> for whom I do it, and they take him, and not me.*
>
> Is that the practice generally? – *Generally; otherwise you become
> liable.*
>
> But it is not always the practice? – *Not always, of course; there
> are many men in the City who would not like to have their names
> known.*
>
> They would bet by commission, and their agent would not
> declare who they were? – *Certainly.*
>
> From your experience of the betting world, are you of opinion
> that large sums have been made, and that properties have been
> accumulated by parties who have followed the pursuit of bet-
> ting, as public betters, either by commission or by themselves?
> – *Very few; I know very few instances in my life where they have
> made money.* (Orchard, 289)

commit   In racing, *commit* describes the moment when the jockey
asks his horse to go for home in the final stages of a race: 'A
furlong out Eddery still had not committed.' This usage is a contraction of the reflexive use of the verb; i.e. to commit oneself to
a course of action.

company[1]   Horse, being pack animals, are happiest when running
with other horses; so a jockey may well give his horse some *company*, that is, *settle[1]* it alongside others, or another, in the first
part of a race. For an extreme example of giving a horse company
in a race, see the quotation under *climb*.

company[2]   Refers to the class of a race, from a *seller* to a *classic*,
as in the famous advice to keep yourself in the best company and
run your horses in the worst. 'The colt was having his first run

in selling company' (*Sporting Life* 16 June 1990).

complete   A horse *completes* the course when it jumps round it successfully: normally used when a horse has been remounted after a fall and has then finished the race. 'Wages of Sin: mistakes, always behind...tailed off when refused last, completed second attempt' (*Racing Post* 29 May 1990).

compound   *Compound* has been used since c.1860 to describe a horse's failure to maintain its speed. Partridge suggests that this sense is derived from the meaning 'to compromise'; however, the various ideas of settling and paying off debts which the word has had since the seventeenth century would seem an equally likely source: the horse is 'paying for' the effort it has expended. The OED's first attestation is from 1876, with reference to hare-coursing; and it quotes from *The Observer* in 1928, 'Once in the line for home, Goose Kiss did not remain at the head of affairs, for he compounded rapidly.'

condition[1]   A technical term, describing a horse's fitness, defined by the OED as 'proper or good condition for work, market, etc'; but its use to describe a horse's appearance and readiness to run is a little more complicated than this definition implies. *Condition* is put *on* a horse by careful training and then by racing: 'She was probably not so forward in condition as either the winner or second, both of whom enjoyed the advantage of a previous outing' (*Sporting Life* 6 September 1990). A fully fit horse is said to *carry condition*: this means that it should be well muscled, firm to the touch, with the skin freely moveable over the ribs. It is possible, however, for a horse to carry too much condition, in which case it has been over-trained. The OED's first attestation of the technical sense is from 1849: 'If the nourishing property of the hay has been impaired...the animal will...lose condition.' This sense goes back to one of the word's original meanings, 'state of being': from 1340, 'A man waxes olde and chaunges his complexcion and his maners and his condicion.' Compare the phrase 'out of condition', meaning 'unfit'.

condition[2]   A *conditions race* is a non-*handicap*, governed by a *condition* or set of conditions, such as the entry being limited to horses which have not won a race of a certain value. However, every race that is run, handicap or not, has one or more condition attached to it. To take an example from a typical day's racing, the *card* for the Wednesday of the 1990 May meeting at York had the following conditions attached to its races:

The Dalton Stakes, 'for two-year-olds only'.

The BBA Middleton Graduation Stakes, 'for three-year-fillies only which, at starting, have not won more than one race'.

Homeowners Sprint Handicap, 'for three-year-olds and up, rated 0-110' (i.e. no horse with a handicap *mark* over 110 is allowed to enter).

The William Hill Dante Stakes, 'for three-year-olds only'.

The Mail on Sunday Three-Year-Old Series Handicap, 'for three-year-old fillies only, rated 0-100'.

The Wilkinson Memorial Stakes, 'for three-year-olds only, maidens at starting, which did not run at two-years-old'.

The verb used to describe the making of conditions is *frame*. The examples from York are fairly straightforward, but in some races conditions are framed in great detail. This example is of the framing of an *Auction* stakes, run at Newbury in May 1990:

For two-year-olds only, maidens at starting, which were sold as yearlings by public auction (under the hammer) at sales administered by Tattersalls Ltd, Tattersalls (Ireland) Ltd, Goffs Bloodstock Ltd, Ascot Bloodstock Sales, or Doncaster Bloodstock Sales Ltd, or as two-year-olds at any of the following 'Breeze-Up' Sales, Doncaster 22 and 23 March 1990, Lingfield 12 April 1990, Newmarket 17, 18, and 19 April 1990, and Ascot 9 May 1990, for 30,000 guineas or less (the first sale to govern the price if sold more than once).

Possibly the oddest race conditions ever framed were for a £50 Plate to be run for in 1805 at the Tralee meeting in Ireland. Given by the lawyers of County Kerry, the plate was open to:

Horses the property of Gentlemen who must have, prior to the first day of the Meeting, actually expended in fair adverse litigation the sum of £200. Horses of persons who have expended £1,000 allowed 3lb. (Prior, 181)

As you might have guessed, the race ended in an objection, not settled until a final ruling by the stewards of the Turf Club.

conditional A *conditional jockey* is one who may claim an *allowance*; a *conditional race* is one in which only such jockeys may ride.

conformation The shape of a racehorse, its proportion and symmetry: attractive to racing people because of the sense that there is an ideal size and shape to which all *thoroughbreds* more or less conform. The word was used, in the seventeenth and eighteenth centuries, to describe human anatomies. The OED's first attestation is from 1646: 'Many wayes of Coition, according to divers shapes and different conformations.' Now it is one of the prize terms of judges of horseflesh, but this usage is not distinguished as a special sense in the OED. R.C. Lyle tells this story of the royal trainer Richard Marsh:

There was no finer judge of a horse in all Newmarket than Mr Chaplin, commonly known as 'the Squire'. One day he made one of a party being shown round the stables at Egerton House by King Edward.

As the royal party strolled past the boxes, looking at each occupant in turn, Mr Chaplin remarked, "There is no such thing in existence as a horse absolutely faultless in the matter of conformation."

Marsh, who overheard the remark, said, "There is a horse in the stable now which cannot be faulted."

"Oh, nonsense," came the reply, "there's no such thing as a horse that cannot be faulted."

"Well, Squire," said the trainer, "I will bet you a fiver you cannot fault this horse."

"Done with you, Marsh. I'll bet you a fiver. But who is to be judge between us."

"You can be your own judge."

Shortly after this conversation the party arrived at Diamond Jubilee's box.

"Here is your perfect horse," said Marsh to the Squire.

Mr Chaplin stood for a long time running and re-running his eye over the colt, until the King and his other guests, in spite of their interest in the bet, were constrained to go on. Quite a number of the remaining horses had been looked at, before the Squire caught up with the party. In his hand was a five-pound note, and without a word he pressed it into Marsh's, much to the amusement of the King and his guests. (Brock, 162)

connections   The owners and trainer of a racehorse. *Connection* is a latecomer into English, not being found in either Shakespeare or the Authorized Version of the Bible. The OED does not recognise this racing sense, but it is now in very common use, as an extension of the sense 'a personal relation of intercourse, common interest, or action':

> Swift Sword's 25/1 success was as much a surprise to connections as that of Flight Fantasy in the Rose and Crown Handicap. The...mare started at 20/1, but paid 105/1 on the Tote, much to the chagrin of owner's wife Madeline Leslie, who has a habit of cashing in on longshots but on this occasion kept her money in her pocket. (*Sporting Life* 23 May 1990).

contingency bet   A bet, such as an *any to come*, in which the amount of money staked on a selection depends upon the *returns* available from earlier selections.

cop   When a bookmaker wins on a race he has *copped* and his clerk marks the foot of a profitable page with a *C*. The word derives from North-country slang, an adaptation of the Old

French *caper*, 'to seize'. Compare the slang expression 'cop the lot'.

corkscrew In *chasing*, a horse *corkscrews* a fence when it twists its body as it jumps it. The OED's first attestation of 'corkscrew' as a verb is from Charles Dickens's *Pickwick Papers*: 'Mr Bantam corkscrewed his way through the crowd.' See *screw*.

coronet The lowest part of a horse's *pastern* just above the hoof, so called from the shape and the growth of hair around it. First attestation 1696.

corpse 'A horse entered in a race for betting purposes only' (Partridge, *c*.1870). By entering such a horse, unscrupulous owners were able to get better *prices* about horses which were going to run. Cp. *dead one* and *dead meat*.

cough, coughing A symptom of illness, notably equine influenza, the *cough* is dreaded by trainers because of the way it sweeps through a stable: one week's rest for each day of *coughing* is the recommended recovery period. This usage recalls the original sense of the word in English, when 'the cough' described general respiratory disorders. The influenza itself is nothing new. The *Racing Calendar* for 1798 records

An epidemical Distemper in Horses of every description broke out this Spring, and appears to have affected the racing stables in every part of the kingdom to a considerable degree for nearly two months, commencing a short time previous to Epsom races.

The striking difference between the Autumn and Spring performances of several horses that were suffered to start with the Distemper upon them may in a great measure be attributed to this circumstance. (Prior, 177)

country Steeplechasing began as a form of racing over natural fences and ditches, with only a man-made *straight*. One relic of those days is that chasers are said to be going out *into the country* when they leave the straight and the *stands* to go out on a circuit of the course. The OED does not recognise this sense, but records a usage in cricket, from 1884, where 'country' is 'applied to parts of the field a long way from the wickets.'

coup From Old French *coup*, 'a blow', the word came into English in the fourteenth century as *coupe*, disappeared from the language, and then returned with its French pronunciation at the end of the eighteenth century. In racing a *coup* is a successful – or attempted – blow against the bookmakers, when a horse is heavily backed at a good *price* by people in the know. Some stables are famous – or notorious – for *laying out* horses to *land a coup*:

P.J. Finn ... showed that his judgment is spot on by bringing

off the biggest coup of the year at the Leopardstown Bank
Holiday meeting... Silken Fan... had finished only eighth on
his two previous outings this season and, although he had lost
ground at the start in both of them, there was no reason to
suppose he had the slightest chance in the ten furlong Cara
handicap. But on the morning of the race the money started
to go on in the Dublin offices... He was still an 8/1 chance
when the course bookies chalked up their prices in the afternoon. Finn's men took them to the cleaners, putting on as
much money as the layers would accept... Silken Fan started
9/4 favourite and beat Masai Warrior a neck. Course bookmakers... calculate that Finn's masterstroke cost them £400,000.
(*Sporting Life* 21 June 1990).
Goodwin Brothers offer a more succinct definition of a 'coup':
'The success of a horse concerning the racing capabilities of which
the public know nothing' (125).

coupled[1]   *Coupled* describes the joining – i.e. coupling – of a
horse's back to its hind quarters: first attestation 1641, in the
phrase *short coupled*. A *close coupled* horse has a compact body,
with deep, well-sprung ribs and no slackness in the loins.

coupled[2]   In France, and other countries, horses are *coupled* in
pari-mutuel bets if they are in the same ownership, even if they
have different trainers: whichever of the two horses wins, the pay
out is the same. The advantage of this practice is that it effectively
prevents an owner from 'arranging' for the less fancied of his
runners to win at correspondingly rewarding odds, to the anger
of the duped public. The disadvantage is that if one fancies the
outsider one gets only a relatively short price on it.

course   The OED lists three traditional racing senses for *course*:
first, 'the action of running, a run, a gallop on horseback', the
word's original sense, now obsolete; second, 'a race', citing from
1489, 'tomorowe shall be the courses of the horses'; and third,
'the ground on which a race is run' (13th C.), the surviving usage,
whether as *racecourse* or as *course* on its own. In Britain every
course has its own characteristics, hence the saying 'horses for
courses', meaning that certain horses are better suited by one
course than are others. A *course winner* is a horse which has previously won a race over the course; a *course and distance winner*
is one which has done so over the same *distance*[1] as the race in
which it is now engaged. The idiom 'stay the course' probably
recalls the earlier sense 'a race', although its first attestation is as
late as 1885, in the *Daily Telegraph*'s conjecture as to whether a
horse has the 'ability to stay the course'. While the idiom has
gone into the general language, it is seldom used in racing today,

the simple verb *stay* being sufficient. The *course enclosure* is the cheapest *enclosure* from which to watch the races: often an area in the centre of the course, opposite the stands.

cover   A stallion *covers* a mare when he copulates with her: first attestation 1535, rarely used about other animals.

cover up   In Flat racing, to *cover up* a horse, or *keep it covered up*, is to keep it surrounded by other runners, the best way to ride a hard *puller¹*:

> He does not want to see a lot of daylight and the last time he ran here he was on the wide outside and was always hanging in, but John Lowe was able to keep him covered up nicely today. (*Sporting Life* 6 September 1990)

In *chasing*, the phrase describes the tactic, surprisingly preferred by some horses, of keeping them in behind another horse so that they cannot see the fence they are about to jump. Neither of these senses is noted in the OED.

coward   Like a *rogue*, a horse which will not try in a race. The OED's first example of its use with reference to a horse is from 1880: 'Don Juan...ran a coward throughout, and Dinna Forget landed her backers with ease.' This is the third (chronologically speaking) use of the word to describe an animal: it was first used as a familiar name for the hare (1481); and then, closer to racing, for 'a cock which will not fight' (1684). The hare sense takes us back to the word's etymology, from Old French *coart*, derived from *coe*, 'a tail'. A coward may be one who turns tail or one which puts its tail between its legs. In racing the tail is, coincidently, one way of spotting a coward: a suspect horse may *thrash* its tail when it comes under pressure.

cow-kick   A forward kick given by a horse's hind legs. It can badly injure a jockey who is dismounting, not least because it is so unexpected:

> To correct a kicking horse one must seize the moment that his hind legs are coming off the ground and jerk the bit up in his mouth, as with a bucking horse. Cow-kicking – that is, striking out with one hind leg – is more difficult to deal with; we are unable to anticipate him because we cannot detect a horse's intention. Often we cannot even tell, from his back, that he has cow-kicked. (Goldschmidt, 94)

crab   Stable slang: to *crab* a horse is to criticise the *conformation* or appearance of a horse which is for sale (19th C.). Originally the word was a falconry term, meaning 'to scratch, claw, or fight with each other'. In this century the sense has widened: the OED gives examples of crabbing cars, politicians, and the heat (this last from *The Great Gatsby*), and in racing the word is commonly used in the sense of crabbing a horse's *form*, that is, finding reasons why, for example, the favourite will not win. 'It is difficult to crab Michael Stoute's filly as she ran Salsabil to ¾ of a length in the Thousand Guineas' (*Sporting Life* 20 June 1990).

crack¹   *Crack*, in its adjectival sense, meaning 'pre-eminent', as in a 'crack regiment', probably comes from the noun *crack*, meaning 'that which is the subject of boast or eulogy; that which is "cracked up",' whose first use seems to have been to describe a good racehorse. In Shirley's play *Hyde Park* (1637) a jockey is told that 'the crack o' the field's against you'. So, to call a horse a 'crack miler' has a venerable tradition behind it.

crack²   As a verb, *crack* describes a collapsing under pressure. The OED traces this sense back to the idea of a bank 'breaking', giving this example from John Dryden: 'The credit not only of banks, but of exchequers, cracks when little comes in and much goes out.' By the late nineteenth century, when the *C* volume of the OED was completed, this sense was described as being found 'now only in racing slang', with an example from 1884: 'The first named ... "cracked" some distance from home.' This sense is still common in racing, but has expanded to include not only other sports – athletes and football teams crack under pressure – but many of the other crack-ups of modern life.

crack³   Backers *crack into* a horse when they bet heavily on it, forcing its price to *shorten*.

cramped   A *cramped action* occurs when a horse fails to stride out freely: often because the *going* is unsuitable.

crane   A nineteenth-century hunting term, sometimes used in chasing, to describe a horse's refusal to jump, stopping to look over the fence before it attempts to jump it. The OED's first attestation is from Byron's *Don Juan*: 'He clear'd hedge, ditch, and double post, and rail, And never craned.'

crock   A broken-down horse: first attestation 1879. The word originally described an old ewe, and is of Scottish origin; but there are cognate forms in other languages, like the Norwegian *krake*, 'a sickly, weakly, or emaciated beast', or East Frisian *krakke*, 'a broken down horse, house, or old man' (!): all are apparently related to the verb 'crack'. Like *nag*, the word's use in racing is usually to express disgust at the slowness of any horse which one has backed and which has been beaten.

crop the field   See *field*.

cross   A horse *crosses* another when it runs across and into its path: *crossing* is a common reason for disqualification. See the quotation under *jostle* for an early example of its use. The OED does not recognise this as a special sense, although it does, for instance, give two distinct uses of the verb in cricket.

croup   From French *croupe*, the *croup* is the horse's rump, specifically the upper line from its loins to the root of its tail: first attestation 1300.

cup   In the second half of the seventeenth century silver bowls and cups largely replaced *bells* as the prizes for prestigious races. The OED's first example for its definition 'an ornamental cup or other vessel offered as a prize for a race or athletic contest' is with reference to horseracing, from 1640: 'Does the race hold at Newmarket for the Cup?' (cp. *plate*). Today *cup* survives largely in the titles of – and as prizes for – long distance races on the Flat, so that a *cup horse* is one capable of running in top *company* in races of a mile and three-quarters and more. The Holy Grail theme of James Joyce's *Ulysses* is related to the novel's action all taking place on Ascot Gold Cup day.

curb   From French *courbe*, ultimately Latin *curvis*, 'bent, crooked': curb is 'a hard swelling on the hock or other part of a horse's leg' (1523). Curbs are caused by a thickening of the tendon or ligament on the back of the hock: *curby hocks* are hocks which suffer from – or look likely to suffer from – such a complaint. 'I would have run him over six furlongs at the July meeting but he sprung a curb' (*Racing Post* 7 September 1990).

curry   From Old French *correier*, 'to put in order, prepare, arrange', *curry* means 'to rub down or dress a horse with a comb' (1290). The form *curry-comb* is first attested in 1573.

cut¹   A horse which is *cut* is one which is castrated, a gelding (1465): 'Swift Sword ran desperately first time out, we couldn't believe it so we had him cut and we have not done much with him since then' (!) (*Sporting Life* 23 May 1990).

cut²   Many horses prefer some *cut* in the ground: a common racing term, meaning that the *going* is soft enough for the horse's hooves to print in. 'Seven furlongs to a mile is her best trip, and the bit of cut has helped' (*Sporting Life* 6 July 1990).

cut³   A blow with the whip. The OED cites, from 1715, 'I took him a cut across the shoulders.'

cut⁴   A horse *cuts* itself when it strikes the inside of its fetlock with the opposite hoof: first attestation, 1660.

cut⁵   To *take a cut* at a fence is to jump it fearlessly and somewhat dangerously. This may be a development of *cut³*, the image being one of the horse driven from fence to fence by an aggressive rider.

cut⁶   Bookmakers *cut prices* like any other trader, except, of course, it is demand, not lack of it, which has this effect. At least once a potential confusion with *cut¹* must have had some readers of the *Sporting Life* momentarily puzzled. Its headline, 'Old Vic

Cut' (5 September 1990) referred to the horse's price for the Prix
de l'Arc de Triomphe shortening from 4/1 to 7/2, and not to the
prospects of a billion-dollar prospect at stud being gelded.

cut up Fields *cut up* when an originally large *entry* for a race is
drastically reduced because only a very few are *declared* to run in
it. The OED does not seem to recognise this sense, but it does
identify two other uses of the phrase with relevance to racing.
One is the sense 'to "behave" (badly, etc.) in a race or competition', as in an expression in general use like 'he cut up rough'.
The first attestations, from 1883, include 'Export again cut up
wretchedly in the Barwell Stakes.' A later slang usage is 'to conduct or manage (a contest) fraudulently': among the first attestations, from 1923, is 'I read in newspapers now that more than
half the races under National Hunt rules are cut up, and that
jockeys and trainers are out to rob the public.'

Daisy cutter 'A horse which in trotting lifts its feet only slightly from the ground.' The first horse attestation, from 1791, antedates its use in baseball and cricket by a hundred years.

dam The *mare* or mother of a *foal*, the correlative of *sire*. The word is a variant form of *dame*, frequently written *damme* from the fourteenth century, the short *a* of the French pronunciation being retained. See *out of*.

danger The *danger* is the horse which most threatens one's selection for a race: 'Then the Yanks got wise to it, and ran a few down the course, and someone backed the "danger" for them with the result that the ring nearly always lost' (Frank Johnson, *The Turf Crook*). The OED's nearest definition to this sense is 'an instance or cause of danger', as in 'a positive danger to the peace of Europe' (1884).

dangerous *Never dangerous* in a form guide means that the horse never threatened the leaders at any stage in a race. However, it would be uncommon to use *dangerous* in the opposite context: much rather, one would describe the horse as 'a danger' – see above.

dark horse The OED defines a *dark horse* as one 'about whose racing powers little is known'; hence its figurative extension to describe 'a candidate or competitor of whom little is known'. Its first recorded racing use is by Disraeli in 1831: 'A dark horse, which had never been thought of... rushed past the grand stand in sweeping triumph' – as so often, a political situation is given a complete racing image. The phrase's derivation is problematic. The OED seems to relate it to 'dark' in the sense 'concealed, secret'. But it may that what is concealed is not so much the horse's form as its parentage: 'Moonraker is what is called a "dark horse"; that is to say, neither his sire nor dam is known' (Egan, 164).

dash Originally an American term for a 'race run in one heat', it is now the general term for a *sprint* race in America, only occasionally used in Britain. 'This time it is a three-quarter dash, and as the horses approach...' (Goodwin Bros., 73). This sense is an extension of such meanings of 'dash' as 'a sudden impetuous movement' (1809) and 'spirited vigour of action' (1796), themselves going back to an early use of the verb to mean 'to drive impetuously *forth* or *out*'. The OED's first attestation of this sense

61

sense is: 'Then th' englyshmen dashed forth their horses after the frenchmen.'

daylight   Used by jump jockeys to describe a safe jump: the *daylight* in question is the gap between the horse and the fence it jumps. Otherwise, *daylight* means that the horse has nothing directly in front of it: a desirable state of affairs within the final furlong, but not so attractive earlier in a race when most horses prefer to be *covered up*. 'Christy Roche reported to Prendegast that the filly was always seeing too much daylight' (*Sporting Life* 21 June 1990).

dead, dead one   *Dead* is generally used today to describe a horse which has no more to give in a race and is dropping out of contention: 'He loves passing "dead" horses, and he got a lovely run through on the inside here' (*Sporting Life* 12 June 1990). However the chief use of the word in earlier racing slang was to describe a racehorse which was 'not intended to win; fraudulently run in such a way that it cannot win'. The common expressions were *dead one* and *dead 'un*. The OED's first attestation is from 1864: 'A horse which has been regarded occasionally as a dead one has proved lively enough to beat the winner of the Two Thousand.' This sense is not itself dead: the *Sporting Life* reported a bookmaker as saying, about support for the Derby favourite, in spite of doubts about its running: 'You don't lay dead horses at 5/1 at this stage of the game' (15 May 1990). See *corpse, dead meat*.

dead-heat   A *dead-heat* occurs when two horses cannot be separated by the judge and both are deemed to have won – or, to have finished in the same place, it being possible to dead-heat for second, third, etc. Dead-heats used to be more common in the days before *photo finishes*, for obvious reasons. A *triple dead-heat* occurs when three horses cannot be separated: this almost never happens. In 1880 the Astley Stakes, at Lewes, ended in a triple dead-heat between Scobell, Wading Nun, and Mazurka, with two other horses, Cumberland and Thora, dead-heating for fourth place, only a head behind the first three. At Newmarket in 1855 four of the five runners in a race dead-heated at the Houghton meeting. Where does the term come from? The OED, whose first attestation is from 1796, relates it to the use of 'dead' in the senses 'applied to the absolute or utmost exertion of strength' and 'absolute, complete, entire, thorough, downright.' It may be better to put it into its context of the early days of racing, when races were run in heats, the same horses running against each other several times in a day. The horse which won most heats won the prize. A heat in which there was no outright winner would be discounted, hence regarded as 'dead': 'Sea-Song and Deuce of Clubs

twice dead-heated in a race at Sandown in 1888. In a third run-off
Deuce of Clubs won by a neck. Now dead-heats are not run off,
but the stakes are divided' (Brock, 197). With regard to the history
of the word, there is an unusual, and apparently unique seventeenth-century use of *dead* to mean dead-heat, in the works of a
minor poet, Francis Quarles (1635):

Mammon well follow'd, Cupid bravely led;
Both touchers; equal fortune makes a dead.

dead meat   Used by a stable to describe a horse which has no
chance of winning. See *corpse*, *dead one*.

declare   After *entry* in a race, at various stages the *connections* may
withdraw their horse by *declaring forfeit*, in which case the stakes
are lost. In the nineteenth century this was normally shortened
to *declare*, hence the OED's definition of its racing sense as 'to
announce the withdrawal of a horse from a race for which it has
been entered'. Its first attestation, from 1847, is 'Stakes of 10 sovs
each, 5 f[orfei]t, and only 3 if declared.' *Declare off* was a common
expression for withdrawing from a *match*, usually with the implication that the withdrawal was unsporting or unfair. This is an
extension of the use of the phrase to mean 'state formally that one
is "off" with a bargain or undertaking'.

If a horse is to run, then it must be declared a runner:
Blue Stag was a surprise acceptor for the Irish St. Leger...
Sangster said yesterday: 'The vet is examining Blue Stag today
prior to him going off to the States, and we thought it best to
declare him in case something went wrong.' (*Sporting Life* 19
September 1990).
Declare is also used in reference to other matters concerning a
race: *blinkers*, *visor*, etc. must be declared, and there are frequent
campaigns to make official the declaration of jockeys on the day
before a race. 'Starlight Flyer was running for the first time without blinkers – Moubarak had forgotten to declare them' (*Sporting
Life* 12 June 1990).

Derby   Founded in 1780: the premier *classic* race, run at Epsom
by three-year-olds on the Wednesday nearest to 1 June; once so
important that it was said that the whole sport of racing, with all
of its investment in bloodstock, exists for one piece of wood, the
winning post at Epsom. In 1784 the original distance of one mile
was extended to a mile and a half, the distance it remains. The
race is named after its founder, the twelfth Earl of Derby. The
name was soon extended to other sports – as in 'local derby' –
and, more significantly, to other races – as in the Kentucky Derby
– so that the real Derby is often known now as the Epsom Derby.
This shameful situation has been compounded by the *Jockey*

Club's permission for the race to be sponsored: the title 'Ever-Ready Derby' must be the prime example of bad taste in racing. Still, a famous story has it that the Derby was only so called because the Earl won the privilege of using his name for the race by tossing a coin with Sir Charles Bunbury.

destroy   A horse is *destroyed* when it is humanely killed: a usage harking back to the old sense of the verb, 'to put out of existence' (from 1300). 'High Story broke down and had to be pulled up. The four-year-old was later destroyed' (*Sporting Life* 14 June 1990).

dip   The *dip* is the most famous depression in racing, about two furlongs from the winning post at Newmarket:

Races can be won and lost by the use a jockey makes of the dip. If a horse can gallop smoothly down a slope, he can be rushed down the dip, thus gaining an impetus that will take him up the rise. If he cannot come down a slope well, he will have to be held up coming down the dip; as a result, he cannot be given so much to do from the dip as a horse who comes downhill well. (Hislop, 119)

A nineteenth-century slang term for the dip was the *choke-jade*, so named because 'it "chokes off" inferior horses' (Partridge).

dipped back   Describes a horse with an unusually pronounced dip in its back. Many horses develop a *dipped back* with age: in a younger horse it may indicate a constitutional weakness. Also known as *hollow back*.

disappointing   Describes a horse whose *form* deteriorates so that it no longer runs up to its capabilities: for examples of its use, see under *distance* and *quicken*.

dish   A horse *dishes* when it moves its fore-feet with a circular rather than straightforward motion – usually a sign that it does not like the *going*. Its first attestation is 1863: derived from the 'dish' shape of the movement.

distance[1]   The length of a race: e.g. the distance of the Derby is a mile and a half. Different horses are suited by different distances: 'He made the first two in each of his three runs last month, showing himself well suited to this distance' (*Sporting Life* 16 June 1990).

distance[2]   The margin between horses at the end of a race is described as a certain *distance*, no matter how short: anything from a short-head to thirty *lengths* can be a winning distance. In British racing the actual distances are, beginning with the shortest: a short-head, a head, a neck, a quarter of a length, a half a length, three-quarters of a length, a length, one and a quarter lengths, one and a half lengths, one and three-quarter lengths, two lengths, two and a half lengths, three lengths, four lengths, five lengths... When the gap cannot be measured – usually over twenty lengths – it is described as a *distance*: 'Mohawk won by a neck from Tomahawk, with Blackfoot eight lengths away third, and Wigwam a distance behind.' See the next entry.

distance³ The *distance* is a point just over a furlong from the finish – actually 240 yards out: 'Markofdistinction, a length behind in third, looked to be going as well as any at the distance and was a bit disappointing' (*Racing Post* 19 May 1990). This sense goes back to the early days of racing, when a horse which was beaten so far in a *heat* was said to have been *distanced* and was accordingly disqualified from racing in further heats. The OED's first attestation is from as early as 1674: 'A Horse-length lost by odds of Weight in the first Train, may prove a distance in the streight Course at last; for the Weight is the same every Heat tho his strength be not.' The reason for disqualifying a distanced horse was to discourage a jockey from giving his horse a very easy race in one heat with the aim of keeping him fresh enough to win the other two. '*Double-distanced* is the same thing, superlatively..."out of sight" expresses it as well' (Bee).

distress A horse is *distressed* when it ties up quickly in a race, showing distinct signs of acute discomfort in breathing or in *action*. This usage is a well-established, general one, first attested in 1586, 'my distressed eies', and 1597, 'poore distressed woman'; but its present use is somewhat archaic or affected, except for this racing sense which is still quite straightforward, almost technical. The OED gives a sense for 'distress' of ' "distressed" or exhausted condition under extreme physical strain', its second attestation, from 1836, being 'She showed some symptoms of distress and the backers of the field thought there was still a chance.' *Distress signals* describes a jockey's obvious arm and leg movements when trying to galvanise a horse which is dropping out of contention in a race:

> Lord George won the match, but apparently more by good luck than good horsemanship, for "The Druid" says, "Many a jockey-boy grinned derisively when he saw his lordship making all the running, and shaking and punishing his roarer, Captain Cook, right furiously, long after the colt had hung out signals of distress." (Thormanby, *Famous*, 65)

ditch-in The earliest specially prepared racecourses were known as *ditch-in*; i.e. they were enclosed with a ditch to ensure than no horse took, as had been the habit, a short cut: 'The following year, at Newmarket, Young Eclipse beat Tyrant, Ditch-in, giving him 4lbs' (Egan, 186). Jorrocks, arriving at Newmarket, observes its strange language: 'It is "Heath", "Ditch-in", "Abingdon mile", "T.Y.C. Stakes", "Sweepstakes", "Handicaps", "Bet", "Lay", "take", "Odds", "Evens", morning, noon and night' (Surtees, 82). The Newmarket ditch-in course – one of twenty-nine courses which have been used there – is still used for the Challenge Cup and the Whip, although both of these events are usually *walk-overs*.

do[1] To look after a horse. A stable *lad*'s job is to *do his two*: i.e. look after, feed, and prepare for the races two horses in the stable. 'Every lad wants to do a classic horse' (*Sporting Life* 5 June 1990).

do[2] Describes the minimum weight a jockey can get down to, with saddle and equipment. If he can *do* seven stone he is a light-weight; if he can only do eight stone seven pounds then he is limited to riding horses in the top half of the handicap: 'Miss Balding cannot... do less than 10st, but she is going to have another crack at the ladies' title' (*Racing Post* 19 May 1990).

do[3] In betting, to *do* one's money is to lose it. A more extreme form is to *do in*, meaning to bet recklessly. Bookmakers as well as backers may do their money: 'Said Dave, representing Albert Brown... "That's the first time I've lost for ages. In fact, I did £1,852 on the race"' (*Sporting Life* 23 May 1990).

do[4] To *do* a horse, or *do* one *up*, is to *nobble* it: 'He asked for a private chat and suggested that he could arrange "to do" the very hot Derby favourite' (Sidney, 25).

dock Originally 'the solid fleshly part of an animal's tail' (1340, etymology obscure): from this developed the sense of cutting short an animal's tail. Racehorses only have their tails docked in special circumstances:

> Venturist... had a bad infection in his back-end and, in saving him, vets had to dock his tail. However, despite looking more like something from a Stubbs' painting, it does not stop him galloping. (*Racing Post* 19 September 1990)

dodgepot Presumably derived from 'dodgy' and 'hotpot', a *dodgepot* is a horse which has failed to live up to its breeding and reputation: 'Some mostly well-bred "dodgepots" contested the Parker Steel Merlin Maiden Fillies' Stakes' (*Sporting Life* 14 September 1990).

dog A horse which will not give of its best: 'Is it going to be dry at Newbury?... Walled Garden's a dog on heavy going?' (Rattigan, *Separate Tables*). *Dog* is recorded as a general term of abuse from 1325, but the specific reference to horses not until well into the twentieth century, an example from 1945 identifying it as Australian slang for 'a horse difficult to handle'.

doll A temporary barrier on a racecourse, or on the gallops, to

mark out the track or to close off part of the course. The verb is
to doll off, or *doll out*. In heavy *going*, for instance, a certain fence
may be dolled off because of very slippery conditions on the take-
off or landing side. The word is first attested only in 1942, but
may be a variant form of *dool* or *dole*, derivation unknown, 'a
boundary or landmark, consisting of a post, a stone, or an
unploughed balk or strip of land' (1440). 'We do keep a strip on
the inside which we use for the Derby and then doll it out for
Thursday and Friday's meetings to have it fresh for the Oaks on
Saturday' (*Sporting Life* 17 May 1990).

dope   Derived from the Dutch *doop*, 'dipping, sauce', and *doopen*,
'to dip', *dope* came into the language in the last quarter of the
nineteenth century, originally in innocent senses, but soon
coming to mean 'opium, especially the thick treacle-like preparation used in opium smoking' (1889) and then extending its meaning to cover 'stupefying drugs and narcotics in general'. Its horse-
racing sense was soon established. The OED quotes, from 1900,
'they urge a liberal investment on the American horse, and confidentially impart the information that the animal is "doped"'. In
the nineteenth century, and into the beginning of the twentieth,
doping horses was not an offence, as this anecdote by John
McGuigan bears out, writing about racing in the 1890s:

> Jimmy Deans came again up to me and made excuses that
> Kelso course had been too sharp for Sporran, and that I would
> see a different result on the more severe course at Hexham,
> and he was giving him an injection. As a matter of fact Sporran
> did not finish in the first four, Bruff winning by 25 lengths.
> At that period doping was not illegal, and I fancy the late Geo.
> Menzies was one of the first to use what used to be called
> 'Jimmy Deans's speedy balls.' The Bishop Auckland vet...
> did quite a trade in these 'speedy balls' and rather prided him-
> self on having 'doped' horses before ever the Americans came
> over here and started wholesale 'doping'. In *The Sportsman*
> and *The Yorkshire Post* he wrote signed letters stating that he
> had made up and used 'dopes', and claimed that he could alter
> the form of horses for the better from 14lbs to 21lbs.
> (McGuigan, 54)

In Britain doping was outlawed by the *Jockey Club* in 1903, but
continued in America well into the century. See *bute*; *fake*; *lasix*.

double   For the chief betting use of *double*, see *multiple bet*. The
Daily Double was a popular *Tote* bet, involving the nomination
of the winners of the third and fifth races on the *card*. For *pull
double* see *pull¹*.

double-cross   Originally a racing term. Partridge defines it as

'winning, or trying to win, after promising to lose a race'. The
OED quotes, from 1848, 'all bets are off. It has...been
"rumoured" that a double cross was intended.' In this sense a
'cross' was 'a contest or match lost by collusory arrangement
between the principals' (1812), the phrase 'on the cross' being
the opposite of 'on the square'.

down   *Down the course* means that a horse is unplaced in a race:
to run a horse down the course is not to try to win with it – see
the quotation under *danger*. For other uses of *down* see *go down*
and *money*.

draw¹   The *draw* describes the horse's starting position: a *low
drawn* horse is one which started from a low-numbered *stall*, a
high-drawn horse starts from a high-numbered stall. 'Draw' is
used because, unlike greyhound racing, where dogs are allocated
specific traps, a horse's stall number is a matter of chance. The
OED records 'draw', meaning to 'obtain or select by lot' from
1709, the noun first appearing in Johnson's Dictionary, defined
there as 'the lot or chance drawn'. On many courses the draw in
races of distances from five furlongs to a mile is of great importance; but the effects of the draw may vary according to the *going*
and the positioning of the stalls. 'Traditionally, a low number in
the draw is a distinct advantage when the going is on the soft side'
(*Sporting Life* 21 September 1990).

draw²   Backers *draw* when they collect their winnings, a usage of
the verb which goes back to *The Merchant of Venice*: 'If everie
Ducat in sixe thousand Ducates were in sixe parts, and every part
a Ducate, I would not draw them, I would have my bond.' To
get a draw from a race is to get some money back from it – not
necessarily to win money, for the backer may, on an *each-way*
bet, for instance, draw less than he originally staked.

draw³   See *withdraw*.

drive   Possibly derived from an old use of the verb to mean 'to
ride hard on horseback', to *drive out* a horse is to ride it hard all
the way to the line. 'All Fired Up just had the edge until Adams
drove Sharp Anne into a narrow lead inside the last quarter of a
mile' (*Sporting Life* 1 September 1990); 'Peter Davies: led over
1f., hard ridden 3f. out, led 1f. out, driven out' (*Racing Post* 6
October 1990).

drop¹   A horse *drops* its shoulder when, usually in the *canter*, it
suddenly drops either shoulder and unseats the jockey.

drop²   A jockey *drops* his hands when he relaxes his hold on the reins
and allows the horse to coast home: compare *hands down*. If he
miscalculates and gets caught on the line, then 'dropping his hands'
becomes an offence for which he can be fined and suspended:

Those who had taken odds of 6/4 on about Golden Daffodil...
must have acquired a few grey hairs as Chinese jockey Raymond
Tsui had a far from smooth passage... He lost around five to
six lengths when having to switch his mount to the outside
over three furlongs out and then, when eventually hitting the
front in the final furlong, dropped his hands, allowing Vain
Prince to rally and get within a neck. (*Sporting Life* 6 July 1990)

drop³ In betting, *drop* is a slang term for losing money: first
attested in 1849, a development of 'drop' in the sense 'to part
with, give' (Partridge). 'But he was dropping money every day
on the track' (Hemingway, 'My Old Man').

drop-fence In *chasing*: a fence whose landing side is lower than
the take-off side.

drop out As in other sports, a horse will *drop out* of contention
when it has no chance of winning; but the phrase has a positive
sense too. A jockey will often try to get a horse to drop out in the
early stages of a race, that is to stay well behind the leaders, *switch
off*, and save its energy for the finish. 'Safety dropped himself
out from halfway at Pontefract last time so Pat suggested we try
him in blinkers' (*Racing Post* 20 June 1990).

dual forecast See *forecast*.

dual purpose A *dual purpose* horse is one which runs on the Flat
and over jumps; a dual purpose trainer trains horses to run under
both sets of rules.

duck A horse *ducks in* behind another when it is reluctant to go
by it in the final stages of a race. In *chasing*, a horse *ducks out*
when it suddenly *refuses* and runs out to the side of the fence
instead of jumping it.

dun First attested in 953, perhaps of Celtic origin: *dun* is not a
colour recorded on racecards, but it does occur in *thoroughbreds*,
being principally a dull grey or dull yellow, but more generally
describing a dull version of any of the basic colours. Often dun
horses have a black stripe down the back and other black *points¹*.

dwell *Dwell* originally had two horse-connected senses: 'to be
slow in raising the feet from the ground in stepping' (1737) and
'to pause before taking a fence' (1885). Now it is chiefly used in
a development of the first of these, to describe a horse which does
not get off to a level start with the rest of the field: such a horse
is said to *dwell at the start*. Both senses are closer to the negative
origins of the word – the first meanings of Old English *dwellan*
were 'to lead astray, hinder, delay' – than other modern uses. The
OED traces the word's origins back to a Sanskrit root, *dhwr*, 'to
mislead, deceive'. 'Diamond Blue: dwelt, went fifth straight...'
(*Racing Post* 29 May 1990).

Each-way   Describes a bet, half of which goes on the horse to win, the other half for it to be *placed*: first attestation 1869, 'one pound on Blue Gown each way'. The term has slipped easily into the general language, as in the OED's example from *The Times* in 1963: 'Why should Britain back the 625 line horse to win when we can place an each-way bet on the dual standard:' A *good each-way bet* describes a horse which will start at a decent *price* and which seems certain to finish in the first three. Such horses invariably finish fourth.

Each-way betting becomes complicated when doubles and other *multiple bets* are concerned, for there are two distinct ways of settling such bets: *each-way all each-way*, traditional in the North of England and in Scotland, and *win-to-win place-to-place*, traditional in the South. In each-way all each-way doubles, all of the *returns* from the first selection are equally divided for an each-way bet on the second; in win-to-win place-to-place doubles, win returns and place returns are kept separate throughout the bet. So, if one backs two 10/1 shots in a £1 each-way double, and they both win, then the winnings from the each-way all each-way will be £91 (£14 equally divided from the first horse, meaning that £7 each-way goes on the second), and from win-to-win place-to-place the returns are £130 (from the first horse, £11 to win and £3 a place on the second). If one wins and the other is only placed, the returns are, respectively, £21 (£7 each-way going on to the second) and £9 (£3 for a place going on to the second). If both are only placed, the returns are £4.50 (£1.50 each-way going on to the second) and £9 (£3 for a place going on to the second).

ear stripping   See *strip*.

ease¹, easy¹   A horse is *eased* when a jockey stops riding hard: *won easing up* describes a finish where the winner is so far ahead that it is allowed to slow up as it approaches the line. Such a horse is said to win *easily*.

ease²   In betting, a horse *eases* when its odds *lengthen* slightly: e.g. from 2/1 to 9/4. 'We haven't seen a penny for Creator, so we have eased him to 6/4 favourite from 5/4' (*Sporting Life* 4 July 1990).

easy²   *Easy to back* describes a horse which the bookmakers are prepared to *lay¹* to large amounts, for whatever reason – they may know something about the horse which makes them think it will not run well or there may be little money for it in the *ring*: 'Cole Porter, although favourite, was easy to back, and drifted from 6/4 to 9/4.'

eat up   When horses *eat up* after a hard race the signs are that they have not suffered any ill effects: 'If I wanted to know before finishing a selection whether a horse had eaten up and was in good heart, it was the exception for Steve to be unable to discover the answer' (O'Sullevan, 79).

edge   Trainers talk about putting an *edge* on a horse; that is, getting it absolutely race ready. The OED records as an obsolete sense of 'edge' the meaning, from the seventeenth century, 'stimulate, incite', for the phrases 'give an edge to', 'set an edge upon'.

enclosure   A British racecourse consists of a number of *enclosures*, so organised that those in the most expensive enclosure may go to and from the cheaper ones, but those in the cheaper ones may not go into the dearer ones – as modelled on the class-system. The most expensive is the *members'* or *club* enclosure, followed by *Tattersalls*, the *silver ring*, and the *course*. The OED's first attestation of the word to describe an enclosed space on a racecourse is from 1867, although here it seems to describe a place for the horses to be saddled. As a place for spectators, the first example is from 1910, contrasting French racing with British: 'There are none of the clubs and special enclosures such as at Sandown, Kempton...though portions of the stand are set apart for privileged persons.' The first British course to be entirely enclosed, and separated into distinct enclosures, was Sandown Park.

enough   To *do enough* is to win without excessive expenditure of energy. Some horses are characterised by their habit of winning narrowly by just doing enough:

> Quest for Fame is a lazy horse without having to be hard ridden. He only ever does enough and you certainly would never think you had seen a Derby winner if you'd seen him work at home. (*Racing Post* 6 July 1990)

enquiry   Short for *stewards' enquiry*. An enquiry normally takes place immediately after a race, either because of an *objection* or, more often, because the *stewards* have seen something in the running of a race which has caused them to be concerned that the rules of racing might have been transgressed: possible *interference*, misuse of the whip, a horse showing unprecedentedly good *form*, a horse not running up to its form, etc. Any enquiry which might affect the placing of the horses – essentially, one concerned with interference – will be announced, ensuring that no bets are settled until the result of the enquiry is known. The key word to listen

out for when an enquiry is being held is 'remain': if the places
remain unaltered, the result stands. On greater issues, or those
which arise some time after the race is over (e.g. a positive *dope*
test) a *Jockey Club* enquiry will be held.

Stewards' enquiries are invariably held *in camera*, the results
being announced and posted on the racecourse; but Steve
Donoghue tells of at least one occasion when the stewards held
their enquiry in public. This was when he was beaten on the
apparently invincible Diadem in the 1919 King George Stakes at
Goodwood:

> Next, the stewards questioned me, and I was told there must
> be an enquiry. A few minutes afterwards I was called, and was
> making my way to the stewards' room, the proper (and custom-
> ary) place for an enquiry to be held, when I was astounded to
> learn that this one was to take place on the *open verandah
> outside*, in full view of the public!
>
> "Why is this?" I asked myself. "For the special edification
> of my cut-throat friends?"
>
> I could think of no other reason, but heart-broken as I was
> at the disaster to my little favourite, I was able to endure this
> ordeal with stony indifference, and for twenty-five happy howl-
> ing minutes the roughest "toughs" in the crowd thoroughly
> enjoyed themselves! No one concerned in the enquiry could
> hear a word that was being said about the accident, but we
> carried on amidst what seemed to be a perfect bear-garden,
> and my special well-wisher, the Australian crook, raved,
> stormed, yelled and swore to his heart's content!
>
> I should *not* think that the experiment was considered to
> have been so successful as to warrant its being established as
> a precedent for any more open-air enquiries!
>
> Of course, I was eventually exonerated from any blame, and
> the incident was officially closed. (Donoghue, 177)

enter   The first stage in nominating a horse to run in a race is to
pay a fee to *enter* it: 'Richard Marsh Handicap. £6,000 added to
stakes; for three-year-olds and up . . . £60 to enter.' A horse which
is *entered up* is one which has been entered for a number of races
in the near future, or, in the case of a good horse, which has been
entered for the season's major races. 'Thakib is well entered up
on the Continent, but could also run in the States' (*Sporting Life*
8 September 1990).

entire   An *entire* is a male horse which has not been gelded. The
OED notes that this word is used in this sense in all Romanic
languages.

equitrack   One of the two *all-weather* surfaces (at Lingfield); also,

the surface of the widely-praised Al Bahatri gallop at Newmarket.
It is composed of graded sand particles encapsulated in a polymer/
oil mix to five-inch depth. *Equitrack* is used as a racing surface
in America, at Remington Park, Oklahoma, and in Hong Kong's
two racecourses. The name probably derives from a play on
'equal' and 'equine'.

even-money, evens *Even-money*, more commonly *evens*,
describes *odds* of one to one: a development of 'even' in the sense
'equal in magnitude, number, quantity, etc.' It is difficult to trace
this back to its earliest usage since the first forms of betting on
horses are likely to have been at even money, the owner of one
horse betting another a level sum of money that his horse is
superior. Only when other, graded odds were introduced would
it be necessary to have a word for evens too. In *Hyde Park* (1632)
James Shirley has one of his characters at the races deliberately
play with the word, relating the wager he is laying to his prospects
with a lady he is courting:

Lord Bonville:	I am o' thy side Frank.
Frank Trier:	I think so,
	For all the Park's against me; but six to four
	Is odds enough.
Julietta:	Is it so much against you?
Frank Trier:	Lady, I think 'tis two to one.
Lord Bonville:	We were on even terms till you came hither –
	I find her yielding – And when do they run?

This makes the OED's first attestation for 'even money' seem rather
late, coming as it does from Nat Gould's *Double Event* (1891):
'The book-makers were roaring themselves hoarse, "Even money
Perfection, 3 to 1 Captain Cook."' A common term for evens is
levels.

excuses Short for 'excuses for defeat', these are the common
currency of the racecourse. Jockeys and trainers offer excuses to
owners, to explain why a horse which was beaten should, or
might, have won, and therefore should be persevered with, and
backers find excuses for horses with losing form to justify themselves why they should back the horse another time. In a sixteen-
runner race there will be one winner and fifteen excuses.

exes From 'exis', back-slang for six: *exes to fere* is odds of 6/4.

expected Short for 'expected to win': a common racecourse
whisper is that such and such a horse is *expected* in the last. The
implication is that the *stable*, not the betting public, has the expec-
tation – which is not to say that the public will not share it too
when they see the money going on and the *price* shortening.
'Tarikhana was fully "expected" on her reappearance at Lingfield

and duly obliged' (*Sporting Life* 16 June 1990).

exposed   The opposite of a *dark horse*: an *exposed* horse is one whose *form* is well-known and which holds no surprises. 'Fascination Waltz, who is still relatively unexposed, can show he is still a step ahead of the handicapper' (*Sporting Life* 5 September 1990); 'Airedale, a progressive three-year-old, is fancied to account for his more-exposed senior rivals' (*Sporting Life* 30 May 1990).

extended[1]   In descriptions of races, *not extended* means that the horse in question had much more to give if necessary. Such a victory is easier than a 'comfortable' one and, perhaps, not quite as total as an 'unchallenged' one.

extended[2]   In race *distances[1]*, *extended* means that the actual distance is slightly longer than the conventional one; e.g. 'Maximilian . . . ran Defensive Play to a neck over the extended ten furlongs at Haydock' (*Sporting Life* 6 September 1990) – Haydock's ten furlongs is actually ten furlongs plus 130 yards.

extra   In descriptions of races *no extra*, or *found no extra*, means that the horse was unable to go faster in the closing stages of the race. To give an example, in a mile and three-quarters race at Newmarket, the winner (by ½ length) 'quickened to lead inside final furlong'; the second had 'every chance 1 furlong out, stayed on well close home'; the third, a further ½ length behind, 'led over 2 furlongs out, headed and no extra inside final furlong'; and the fourth, ¾ length behind the third, was 'ridden and every chance 1 furlong out, no extra close home.'

F **ace**   A *face* is a backer who is well-known in the betting *ring*: usually one who is 'in the know' and prepared to bet heavily – but not always, as this analysis of one way of finding *value* shows:

> The size of the bet is no criterion in 'betting to faces.' There are certain backers whose fiver is more significant than the monkeys of others... One trainer who very rarely backed his horse would occasionally go up to a Boardsman and have a fiver on one of his runners. This bookie was indeed fortunate provided he 'knew the face' – the horse was virtually past the post as he struck the bet. The layer could obtain value from such a situation by extending the prices of the other runners or by hedging the trainer's runner. (Sidney, 120)

This sense is not recognised by the OED.

fake   An early word for *dope*, used in the second half of the nineteenth century. The original meaning of the verb *fake* was, in thieves' or vagrants' language, 'To perform any operation upon; to "do", "do for" ... to tamper with, for the purposes of deception': first attested in 1812. Partridge defines the noun as 'a mixture for making a horse safe' (1870).

fall   In most horse-related sports a *fall* occurs when, to quote Summerhay's *Encyclopedia*, 'a horse collapses at a fence ... to such an extent that he must recover his legs before proceeding.' In *chasing* and *hurdling*, however, a fall occurs only when the jockey is unseated: if a horse *blunders* at a fence, loses its footing, and while it recovers the jockey stays seated, then no fall has taken place. See *unseat*.

false pace   A race run at a *false pace* is one which is run very slowly – not, for instance, a long-distance race run unusually fast.

false start   Because of starting *stalls false starts* are now rare, but racing has a long tradition of them. In the 1827 St. Leger there were more than thirty false starts because the *starter* was in league with a gang who had laid heavily against the favourite – the aim was to start the race when the horse was unprepared. The OED's earliest example is from the *Racing Calendar* of 1812: 'Industry ... was distressed by having been pulled up soon after starting, in consequence of a repeated cry of "False start".'

fancy   A shortened form of *fantasy*: ultimately from the Greek *phantasia*, 'a making visible'. The word's special use in racing is

75

recognised by the OED's definition of one of its senses as 'to view
a horse favourably as a likely winner of a race'; but its first attestations, from James Joyce's *Ulysses* and P.G. Wodehouse's *The
Inimitable Jeeves* (1922 and 1923) are certainly antedated by the
music-hall song which went:

Always back your fancy
When you really fancy it,
If you're fond of what you like;
I rather think you should.
Never mind the price
If what you fancy's really nice:
Back it if you fancy it,
It's bound to do you good.

farm If a *stable*, or a horse, regularly wins a certain race, or type
of race, it is said to *farm* it. 'Farm' is ultimately derived from the
Latin *firma*, 'a fixed payment', so that the idea behind the verb
in this context is partly one of cultivation and partly of having
ownership by paying rent. Compare the cricketing sense, first
recorded in 1955, of a batsman 'farming the bowling' when he
contrives to receive most of the balls bowled. 'Luca Cumani
farmed the race in the 80s. All bookmakers were extremely wary
of his horses' (*Racing Post* 31 July 1990). Cp. *standing dish*.

farrier From Old French *ferrier*, ultimately derived from Latin
ferrum, 'iron': a *farrier* is a shoer of horses (1562). A different
word, from the same ultimate origin, was *ferrer*, or *ferrour*, 'a
worker in iron, a smith', current from the mid-fourteenth century.
This exists as a separate form into the eighteenth century, but
the two words gradually merged, 'farrier' becoming a general
term for the man in a smith's forge who prepares the horse's feet,
and makes and nails on the shoes. On the racecourse the farrier's
skill is most apparent when a horse has to be replated at the start:
to shoe a highly-strung thoroughbred when it is all wound up for
a race, with other horses around, takes a cool nerve and steady
hand.

favour A horse *favours* a leg when it goes slightly lame, avoiding
placing its full weight on the leg which is affected. 'Favour' in
this sense – 'to avoid overtasking' – is first attested in 1526, and
was soon in general use. The first horse related example is from
1617: 'When a horse doth stand but firme upon...three feete...
favouring the other.'

favourite Not the best-looking horse in the race, nor the most
popular, nor the one with the best *form*, but simply the one upon
which most money has been wagered and which, accordingly,
offers the most cramped *odds* in the betting. The OED's first

attestation is from boxing, in 1813: 'By the third round Carter became the favourite (as it is termed)' – the parenthetical explanation indicates that it had scarcely entered respectable language. The first racing example is from 1857: 'all the favourites were out of the race early' – which shows that little has altered in the intervening 150 years. *Favouritism*, that is, leading the betting market, is first attested in 1880. *Beaten favourite* is a bookmaker's favourite phrase. When two or more horse share favouritism they are *joint* or *co-favourites*. *Second favourites* are horses which are second in the betting market.

feather   *Feather-weight*, meaning the lightest weight which a horse can carry in a *handicap*, is not attested until 1812, but even this is some seventy or more years before its first recorded boxing usage. However, the shorter form *feather*, to describe the weight and, by extension, the lightweight jockeys who could *do*[2] the weight, is found in 1760: 'Mr Turner's bay ... 5 years old, carrying a feather.' In 1850 the feather-weight was four stone, rising to five and a half stone in 1876. Today the lightest weight a jockey might do is 6st 7lbs – a handicap bottom weight of seven stone minus a seven pounds *claimer*'s allowance. 'He can follow up off a feather weight in the Royal Hunt Cup' (*Sporting Life* 20 June 1990).

feature   *Feature races*, until the end of the 1989-90 season, were the second best type of jump races, designed to prepare horses for *championship* races. Formerly known as Grade Two races, from 1990-91 the Grade Two designation was restored, but with more races elevated to this standing.

feeler   A *trial* race: first attestation 1883, 'Osborne journeyed from Manchester ... with the express purpose of having a "feeler" on Mr Adrian's colt.' The idea is that the trial 'feels out' how fit or good a horse is: 'They run thus till nearing the Bushes, when the leader who ... has "had his feeler" drops back' (Badminton, 86).

fence   A shortened form of *defence*. The larger obstacles jumped in *steeplechasing*, are called *fences*, as opposed to the easier obstacles jumped in *hurdling*; the horses which race over them are *fencers* (1852), and the verb itself is sometimes used as a synonym for 'jump', as in the OED's first attestation, from 1884: 'What he lacks in speed is ... compensated for by the cleverness with which he fences.' For different types of fences, see *drop fence, open ditch, water jump*.

fetlock   The joint at the lower extremity of the cannon bone, just above the pastern, with a tuft of hair, also known as the *fetlock*, just behind the joint. The Middle English form was *fetlak*, or *fytlok*, corresponding to Middle High German *viszlach*, perhaps connected to the German *fessel*, 'pastern'. The modern English spelling has emerged via the erroneous assumption that the word is a compound of 'foot' and 'lock' (of hair).

fibresand   One of the two *all-weather* surfaces (at Southwell): composed of silica sand and synthetic rot-proof fibres treated with a polymer binding.

fiddle   A horse *fiddles* a fence when it gets too close to it at take-off but still manages to get over it without *blundering*: probably a development on the lines of 'fiddling through', although the ideas of dexterity and cheating, two distinct senses of 'fiddle', seem inherent within the racing usage. Far from being a fault, the ability to fiddle is the sign of a *clever* jumper.

field[1]   The *field* is all of the horses in a race, as in 'There is a small field for the Derby this year.' The OED offers no explanation or link between the senses of 'field' meaning open country and 'field' meaning competitors in an outdoor contest: but one of the open country senses is 'that part of the open country which is hunted over' (1732), and it records, from 1806, the hunting sense of 'field', meaning 'those who take part in the sport'. This sense is first recorded in the hunting phrase *to lead the field*, meaning 'to be first in the chase'. This is common racing usage now. Partridge records *crop the field* as slang (1870) for winning easily: a double pun.

field[2]   In betting, *field* commonly describes all of the horses except for the *favourite* (1771), as in '6/4 Strongboy, 5/1 the field'. If a bookmaker calls simply '6/4 the field' he is offering a price on the favourite. He *fields* a horse when he offers a *price* on it: hence the use of *fieldsman* as an early term for a bookmaker.

The OED's definition of 'field' used in this verbal sense is worth glossing because it explains something of the early evolution of betting. The definition is 'to bet on the field against the favourite', the first attestations being from the *Daily News*, one in 1886, 'A marked disposition to "field" on the Grand Prix of Paris', the other in 1890, 'The professionals fielded staunchly.' Since betting emerged from *match* betting, one horse against another, so for much of the nineteenth century it still took this form, even when fields for races were made up of many more than two runners. One horse was found for which there was support and the bookmaker would bet 'between one and the field'; i.e. one price was offered for this one horse, and another for the rest of the field *en masse*. This practice was giving way to the idea of pricing all of the runners some time before the OED's examples, so its definition is probably wrong in these cases, but it does explain how 'field', as a verb, came to be an important bookmaking term.

To 'play the field' came into English as an American colloquialism, and probably has a racing origin, since *play* is a common American term for 'bet', the phrase therefore meaning that
one spreads one's bets over all the runners.

field book   The book in which the bookmaker's clerk keeps a
record of the bets he has struck on a race. The *field book* has
several columns, so that the clerk can use it to keep not only a
record of which ticket goes with which bet, but of the running
field money for each horse and the running total of the *take-out* of
each horse.

field money   The total stake money of the backers as recorded in
the bookmaker's *field book*. To give a simple example: if, in the
early stages of the betting, two backers each put £5 on horse A
at 3/1, two put £5 on horse B priced at 4/1, and one puts £10 on
horse C at 6/1, the running field money total is £30 (four bets at
£5 and one at £10), to be set against *take-outs* of £40 if horse A
wins, £40 if horse B wins, and £70 if horse C wins.

fieldsman   See *book*, *field*[2].

fifth leg   A horse finds a *fifth leg* when it recovers cleverly from
what seems a certain fall at a fence.

fig   To *fig up* or *fig out* a horse is to make it 'trot out in a lively
condition': a development of *feague*, from the Germanic *fegen*, 'to
polish, furbish, sweep'. Jon Bee defines *fig*, *figged* as: 'Ginger;
little lumps whereof are thrust into the rectum of horses to give
them a short-lived vigour; they are then said to be *figged*, and
carry better while the stimulus lasts.' From this practice came
the verb *ginger*, used first of horses and then, with *up*, broadened
into general use. The OED's first horse attestation is from 1823,
'Whether he's ginger'd, spavin'd, gall'd, or injur'd'; its first general usage comes from Disraeli, writing to his sister in 1849:
'Whether they were gingered up by the articles in the "Times"
or not I can't say.'

filly   A female horse under the age of five, although some authorities say under the age of four. From Old Norse *fylja* – not the
French *fille* – it is first attested in 1400. In most *stakes* races there
is a fillies' *allowance*, a weight concession for fillies running against
colts and *geldings*.

find[1]   *Find*, on its own, refers to a horse's chances on its known
form: 'Truelove has a bit to find on his last running against Mr
Valentine.'

find[2]   A horse which *finds more* is one which keeps running on
and will not be passed. Conversely, one which *finds little* or *finds
nothing* is one which goes no faster when it comes under pressure.

find[3]   In betting *find* is commonly used as a synonym for selecting a winner. 'He bets to big money and don't often find 'em' says a happy bookmaker in *A Pink 'Un and a Pelican* (209). 'Are you finding them?' is a common greeting on the racecourse.

find out   Horses are *found out* when a fast-run race or adverse *going* or a stiff course exposes their lack of stamina, want of gameness, or simple inferiority. 'My Ruby Ring may have been found out by the soft ground at Leicester' (*Sporting Life* 14 June 1990).

finif   From the Yiddish *finnef* (German *funf*), *finif* is a £5 note, *double finif* a £10 note, *ready finif* is ready money: 'in 20th C. often heard in low racing slang' (Partridge).

finish   Jockeys are prized according to their ability to *ride a finish*; that is, to get the maximum out of their horse in the closing stages of a race. Since the grandstand is by the final furlong, this part of the jockey's job is the most obvious to the crowd and a jockey who gets a reputation for not being able to ride a finish, no matter how well he handles the horse in the earlier stages of a race, is liable to lose rides. Much of the prejudice against women riders comes from the opinion that they cannot ride a finish.

fire   A horse which has been *fired* has had its leg, or legs, cauterized to strengthen the tissues: the word is recorded in this sense as far back as the seventeenth century – e.g. from 1677, 'a Hunting Gelding . . . fired for the spaven on the near leg behind'. *Line-firing* involves the burning of lines with a red-hot iron; *pin-firing* involves the burning of small holes. 'Mandarin won the King George VI for a second time but shortly afterwards succumbed to tendon trouble, had to be fired and missed the remainder of the season' (*Sporting Life* 16 May 1990).

first   *First past the post* is a solecism: the winning horse is the first *to* it, not the first by it – hence the idea of winning on the *nod*.

first run   Describes the tactic by which a jockey goes for home before his rivals can get going: the common idiom is to *get first run on* the others:

> "I saw Buckle," old John used to say, when telling the story in after days, "preparing to go; and it seemed as if something told me that if I went first I should beat him. And I did – I got the first run and I beat him." (Thormanby, *Famous*, 31)

'Billy Newnes took a deserved slice of the limelight when stealing first run on Eradicate in the Zetland Gold Cup at Redcar' (*Racing Post* 29 May 1990). See *run*[2].

flag-man   There are several *flag-men* on the racecourse. One is positioned down the course in the middle of the track, with the job of standing his ground and waving a flag to signal a *false start*: this takes some courage when the race is a five-furlong sprint. Another flag-man, positioned by the start, signals to the jockeys

when they have come under *starter's orders*. He was placed there
originally by Lord Bentinck, in the 1830s, with the express purpose of curing the problem of false starts which was ruining racing:
   Hitherto, the functionary who had performed the office of starter, after doing his best, or rather his worst, to put the horses
   in line, simply ordered the jockeys to 'go!' as frequently having
   to recall them by a distant signal, after they had galloped over
   three parts of the distance, by reason of some obstinate brute
   – man or horse – refusing to obey the order and remaining
   fresh for the next essay. Lord George rectified this very
   inefficient plan by an equestrian trigger of his own invention,
   viz, the posting a man with a flag directly in view of all the
   jocks – on whom they were to fix their undivided attention
   and to 'go!' without fail, on pain of a pecuniary fine, on seeing
   the colour dropped in front. (Thormanby, *Famous*, 70)

flags *Between the flags* describes *point to point* racing, where
obstacles are marked with flags.

flag start A *flag start* is employed where it is impossible to use
stalls or a starting tape. As the name implies, the race is started
by the lowering of a flag.

flank From French *flanc*, the *flank* is the part of a horse's body
between the ribs and the hip, above the belly (first attested 1100).
Whipping a horse on the flank is frowned on by the *stewards*,
who may well interpret it as a contravention of their *guidelines*.

flapping *Flapping* is racing which is not licensed by the *Jockey
Club*. A course where such racing occurs is a *flapping track* (first
attestation, 1911). Partridge suggests that the word came to be
so used because of its associations with senses involving a 'lack
of dignity': 'flap', from the seventeenth century, was slang for 'a
female of little repute' (as in 'flapper'). In his book *The Pitmen's
Derby*, Mike Kirkup records that Blaydon Races, well known
from the song, was a flapping meeting which raced until 1916,
when a crowd of 4,000 rioted because a horse called Anxious
Moment 'was involved in a disputed decision, resulting in furious
backers tearing up their tickets, the weighing room and everything
which moved, before dispatching the lot into the River Tyne.'
Anyone found participating in, or even attending, flapping races
is liable to be *warned off*. Even the annual race for nuns at Trim
in Ireland 'is officially regarded as a flapper meeting and any form
of involvement can prove disastrous for racing's professionals'
(*Sporting Life* 14 June 1990).

flash A bookmaker's banner (Partridge, 20th C.): an abbreviation
of the *flash part*. 'Flash', as something of 'superficial brilliancy;
ostentation, display' dates back to the seventeenth century; and

there may well be some recollection of the other 'flash' racing association – in the nineteenth century 'flash' described anything or anyone 'belonging to, connected with or resembling the class of sporting men, especially the patrons of the "ring".' In 1809 the *Sporting Magazine* referred to a horse called Crib, 'who was backed by what is termed the flash side'. Soon such characters were known as 'flash men': according to the same magazine, in 1812, the racecourse presented a 'display of the flash-men, from the Peer on the coach-box, to the most gentlemanly-looking pickpocket.'

Flat   *Flat racing* is the opposite of *steeplechasing* and *hurdling*: that is, racing over level ground with no obstacles to jump – although most British racecourses are anything but flat. Hence comes the *Flat season* – from March to November – *Flat horses*, and, as a general term, *the Flat*, which is not attested in the OED until the middle of the nineteenth century; but Jon Bee writes of *A.F.* as slang for 'Across the Flat; a very pretty course for two-year-olds, of one mile and a quarter, at Newmarket.' In jump racing *flat* describes the ground between the obstacles, so that a horse which falls 'on the flat' is one which *slips up*.

flea-bitten   Not at all the derogatory term which it seems to have become, but a technical description of a patterning of 'bay or sorrel spots or streaks upon a lighter ground'. First attested in 1570, and still usable in *The Times* in 1863: 'A tall and very powerful flea-bitten gray'. Today, however, anything flea-bitten is considered to be poor and shabby, matching the flea's decline from a familiar nuisance to an unwelcome pest.

flick   As a noun, *flick*, meaning 'a light blow', is recorded from the fifteenth century; but the sense of 'any sudden movement, a jerk' is not found until the nineteenth, and nor is the verb in any of its senses. In *chasing*, a horse *flicks* over its fences when it jumps them fast and low: 'Cockbird felt strong under me and he flicked over the first fence with a level and unbroken stride' (Sassoon, *Memoirs of a Fox-Hunting Man*). The word is echoic – the OED compares the French *flicflac*, 'the cracking of a whip' – and its use probably derives from the sound of the horse's hooves brushing through the gorse with which the fence is made.

flier   A fast start, as in 'catch a flier': less common since the introduction of starting *stalls*.

flighty   Used generally to mean 'given to flights of imagination, humour, caprice, etc.' (first attestation 1768, 'The flighty gambols of chance'); the OED records its use with reference to horses, meaning 'skittish', from early in the nineteenth century. Today it commonly describes a *filly* or *mare*. 'Chance All, a flighty individual at home, could now go for a nursery' (*Sporting Life* 20 September 1990).

floor A horse *floors the odds* when it wins at a big price: Partridge quotes, from the *Daily Telegraph* in 1882, 'The odds were... floored from an unexpected quarter.' The image is from boxing, the favourite being knocked out by an outsider.

floorman Principally a bookmaker's runner, although he might also do a variety of other jobs: 'Apart from clerk and tic-tacs, the Boardsman would also need a "floor-man" who would look after the hod, count money, pay out and generally run about' (Sidney, 114). The only sense the OED gives to this compound is 'one who helps to attract customers to a mock auction'.

flutter First recorded in the betting sense in an 1874 Dictionary of Slang, *having a flutter* being defined as having 'a good try' for something: possibly an extension of *flutter* in the sense of 'an agitated condition, a state of tremulous excitement' (1748), from the verb's sense 'to be excited with hope, apprehension, or pleasure' (1668). A flutter is a small bet, made more for the excitement than as any kind of investment.

flying handicap A form of race in which the horses pass the starting post at full speed: such races no longer occur. The OED's first attestation shows that these were often known as 'the flying...', followed by whatever was the distance of the race: from 1893, 'Windle has done the "flying" mile in 1min. 56 4-5secs.'

flying machine Very fast horses are known as *flying machines*: not a modern phrase, but one which goes back to the eighteenth century, when it originally described a form of stagecoach. The OED's first attestation is from the *Ipswich Journal* in 1764: 'A new Flying Machine, to accommodate Passengers by...the nearest way for London, will set out...on Mondays, Wednesdays, and Fridays.' 'Machine' originally meant, from its introduction in the sixteenth century, 'a structure of any kind, material or immaterial'. It took on the specialised sense of 'a vehicle of any kind', in common use in the eighteenth and nineteenth centuries, but was also applied 'to the human and animal frame as a combination of several parts', as in this example from 1722: 'the laws of Circulation in an Animal Machine'. So, this racing usage carries memories of the word's original senses as well as the flying stagecoaches of nineteenth-century roads.

fly-jump A sudden, unexpected jump by a horse. If delivered in the *stalls* at the start of a race a *fly-jump* can be fatal to its chances (and dangerous for the jockey). Possibly derived from the idea of a sudden movement as if stung by a horse fly. Not in OED.

foal From Old English *fōla*, first attested in the tenth century.

Foal describes any horse – colt, filly, or gelding – up to the age of twelve months.

follow¹   When one horse tracks another in a race. A jockey will try to *follow* a good horse in a race, not one which will suddenly fall back and get in his way towards the race's end.

follow²   To *follow the market*, or *follow the money*, is to bet on a horse which is being generally heavily backed, whose odds are accordingly shortening: 'Followers of the money were also on the mark when Silver Owl (5/4 favourite from 6/4) squeezed through …to win' (*Sporting Life* 24 May 1990).

follow³   To *follow* a horse – or a jockey, stable, etc. – is to keep backing it in race after race. Form guides are often issued under titles like 'ten to follow'; i.e. they identify ten horses to keep backing through the season. 'Both horses are reported to have done well during the close season and are certainly worthy of note in what is currently the season of finding horses to follow' (*Sporting Life* 21 September 1990).

foot   *Foot* means, simply, speed, the most valuable asset in racing. The OED gives the sense 'power of walking or running', but describes it as obsolete, its last example being from 1737: 'Horses may alter as to their Speed or Foot (as 'tis called).' Far from being obsolete, 'foot' is in common use on the racecourse. A horse may have *plenty of foot*, *no foot*, or, most commonly, a *turn of foot*: 'Mellottie…staked his claims to greater glory when producing an impressive turn of foot to take the Capolini Wines Handicap at York yesterday' (*Sporting Life* 6 September 1990). The usage, to *have the foot of*, long established in the language (17th C.), now survives mainly in racing; and the OED records another expression, now obsolete, 'to run a good foot', as in, from 1737, 'A large, nimble, strong well-moving Horse, that would run a pretty good Foot.'

forecast   A type of bet in which the first two horses in a race have to be successfully selected: a *straight forecast*, offered in betting shops, involves naming them in their correct order – the successful backer wins a computerised dividend based on *S.P.*s, so this bet is officially known as the *computer straight forecast* (or C.S.F.); a *dual forecast*, offered by the *Tote*, is a *pool* bet in which the two horses can be named in either order. A combination of 'fore' (meaning beforehand) and 'cast' (meaning reckon, calculate), the word first meant 'to contrive or scheme beforehand' (14th C.); and then 'to estimate, conjecture, or imagine beforehand' (15th C.). The OED recognises no special betting sense. On the analogy of 'hamburger' being falsely etymologised to lead to 'beefburger', so 'forecast' has led to *tricast*, a bet in which one nominates the first, second, and third in a race in their correct order.

forfeit   The terms of a race may include one or more *forfeit* stages: e.g. '£50 to enter, £100 extra if forfeit not declared by August 1st', meaning that it will cost the owner £150 to keep the horse in the race if he does not *declare* it a non-runner by 1 August. If he does so declare it, he forfeits the £50 entry fee. The word's derivation is from Latin *foris facere*, 'to transgress' (literally, 'to do outside'), via Old English *forfet*. The original English sense was a 'misdeed, crime, offence, transgression', leading to the idea of 'something to which the right is lost by commission of a crime or fault; hence a penal fine' (15th C.). This was eventually diluted to 'a trivial mulct or fine imposed' (17th C.), which is really the main racing one, the owner being 'fined' for not running his horse in a race for which he had entered it. Something of the word's earlier senses survives, however, in the *Forfeit List*, a record of arrears published under the sanction of the Turf authorities. Anyone who owes money to trainers, bookmakers, etc. and appears on the list is liable to be *warned off*.

forge   The OED's first attestation is from 1831: 'a singular species of over-reaching, termed Forging or Clicking'. What is described here is:

> The striking of the inside of the fore-shoe with the outside of the hind shoe – an irritating habit sometimes so persistent as to give the impression that the horse is doing it on purpose and is deriving some pleasure from the sound. (Goldschmidt, 127)

The OED suggests a derivation from 'forge' in the sense of shaping 'by heating in a forge and hammering', with reference to the sound.

form   As in: the horse has *good form*, *no form*, is *in form*, is *out of form*, has *shown form*, is *coming into form*. The last phrase looks back to the original racing usage of the word, in the senses 'condition in regard to health and training' and 'fitness for racing', senses which relate principally to the horse's appearance and physical development. This usage is still common enough – 'Gulmarg was in terrific form this morning, though I was worried earlier in the week' (*Racing Post* 6 October 1990) – but most followers of racing now use *form* to describe a horse's race record, normally the record of its recent races. So, a horse which had won all three of its races as a two-year-old, but which has run three times unplaced as a three-year-old, could be described as one which has shown good form in the past but which is out of form now. If it finishes third and second in its next two races, then it is running into form. Accordingly, the word may well be used in absolute contradiction of its dictionary senses: e.g. 'While Sleeping Beauty looked out of condition for her first race, she showed good form in finishing second'; or, more commonly, 'Sleeping Beauty looked trained to the hilt, but showed no form at all.'

Form is a matter of interpretation. Sleeping Beauty beats Ugly Sister by two *lengths* at level weights over a mile on a *galloping* track on soft *going*. Two weeks later they are due to meet each other over a mile and a quarter, with Ugly Sister now carrying seven pounds less than her rival, on good going over a tighter circuit. The weight difference should be enough to *turn the form around*, but which of the two will be better suited by the extra *distance¹*, the changed going, and the different track? Some answers may lie in the *form-book*, horse-racing's equivalent to the Bible. The OED's first attestation of this compound is from Wodehouse, in 1923: 'The race went by the form-book all right.' As with the Bible, the form-book can be found in a multitude of competing versions, all offering the vital information in a language which requires some interpretative skill. Just as not believing the Bible is a certain road to perdition, so ignoring the form-book is one of the two certain ways of losing money when backing horses. The other certain way is to follow it.

The close relationship between the racecourse and the prison has probably led to the extension of 'form' to describe a criminal record. 'Bad form', from *c*.1860, is, according to J. Redding Ware, 'derived from the racing stable' (*Passing English of the Victorian Era*). For *run to form*, see *run¹*.

forward   The opposite of *backward*. When a horse is *forward* it is in good condition and soon ready to race: 'Thurlestone also made a couple of mistakes when failing to cope with a more forward Pinemartin at Stratford' (*Sporting Life* 11 October 1990). The OED definition which fits its racing usage is 'that is in an advanced state or condition'.

fox   See *kid*.

frame   To finish *in the frame*, or *make the frame*, is to be in the first four in a race: from the number frame on the course in which the numbers of the first four home in a race are displayed. 'Barry Hills's colt has made the frame in both the Epsom and Curragh Derbys' (*Racing Post* 31 July 1990).

free   Recorded as long ago as the fifteenth century to describe a horse which is 'ready to go, willing': 'It shall never neede to prykk nor threte a free horse.' An early sense of *free* was 'generous'. In racing, however, the word has negative as well as positive associations: a *free mover* is a horse which stretches out well on the prevailing *going*, but a *free runner* is one which will not take easily to the jockey's control and may, therefore, have little or nothing left to give at the end of a race. 'Alnaab...had the advantage of two previous runs behind him here and his free-running style was always likely to test this largely inexperienced field' (*Sporting Life* 4 August 1990).

freeze   Like *tighten* or *shorten*, a word used to describe the contracting of a horse's *price* in the betting exchanges:

If the backer goes up and enquires the price...and is quoted 3/1 before any betting is general, then, if he takes the offered price it is fair enough – even if the animal later drifts to 20/1. It could have frozen to Evens! (Sidney, 117).

French   *To speak French*: 'of a horse, to be an excellent steeplechaser' (Partridge, 1923).

fresh¹   Describes a horse which has not had a recent run. Horses which show their best *form* on their first or second runs are said to go better when *fresh*.

fresh²   Describes a horse which behaves in too exuberant a way, by doing 'any of the following or combinations of them: shying, bucking, refusing, rearing, kicking, pulling, napping, and biting.' Goldschmidt, who wrote this description, blames such behaviour on overfeeding, which leads to a state 'akin to mild intoxication' (Goldschmidt, 128). If true, this relates the word's usage to one of its nineteenth-century senses, 'exhilarated by drink; partially intoxicated'.

friendless   When a horse is *friendless* in the market it is an *outsider*, not being backed at all. 'Balwa had been friendless in the betting on her debut at Windsor (8/1 from 2/1)' (*Sporting Life* 16 May 1990).

full¹   *Full brothers* or *sisters* are horses which have two common parents: *half brothers* and *sisters* are those which share the same *dam*. This sense of 'full', 'answering in every respect to a description: possessed of all the qualifications', is one of the earliest meanings of the word (from 1036: 'He wæs-þæh full cyng ofer eall Engla land').

full²   A *full* horse is one which has not been gelded: not recognised by the OED as a special sense, so presumably included in its definition 'complete, entire, perfect'. Such horses were known as *store-horses* (17th – 19th C.). See also *entire*.

full³   In betting, bookmakers use *full* to describe their 'having already sufficient money laid against a particular horse' (Partridge, 1860). From this sense developed the use of the phrase 'full against', meaning 'very inimical to' (Partridge). Similarly, when a bookmaker is *full on* a horse he stands to lose a lot of money on it.

full of running   See *running*.

furlong   Two hundred and twenty yards, still the basic measure
of distance in racing. The word is derived from 'furrow' plus
'long', i.e. the length of a furrow. The numbered posts on British
racecourses are *furlong markers*, counting back from the winning
post. On occasions the word may be omitted, and should be
understood: e.g. 'There was some interference two out.'

furnish   Originally an East Anglian dialect variation of *burnish*, a
word which meant 'of the human frame: to grow plump or stout,
to spread out'. The derivation is unknown, there being no apparent connection with the more common 'burnish', meaning 'to
make metal shine by friction'. The first attestation of 'burnish'
with reference to the human frame is from 1338: 'This age is calde
adolescencie, for it is full age to get children, and able to barnisch.'
The word is still recorded in use in a Sussex Dialect Dictionary
in 1875: 'You burnish nicely, meaning, You look well.' *Furnish*
was stable slang to begin with, describing the filling out and gaining in strength of a horse, first attested in 1862: 'The horse had
furnished so since then.' Now the word is a respectable, almost
technical term, especially in the form *unfurnished*, to describe a
horse which is not well grown. 'Fighting Son has had plenty of
time to furnish in the meanwhile' (*Sporting Life* 9 June 1990).

G **aff** One of the lesser racecourses, especially on the *chasing* circuit. *Gaff* was originally used as a slang term for a fair, then for 'any public place of amusement'. A verb 'to gaff', meant 'to gamble', hence the word 'gaffer'. 'Baluchi... has now won... more than £50,000 in win and place money – no mean feat considering he has been pounding round the gaffs for much of his career' (*Sporting Life* 24 May 1990).

gallop[1] A horse's fastest *pace*. The OED defines it as 'the most rapid movement of a horse... in which in the course of each stride the animal is entirely off the ground, with the legs flexed under the body.' This definition was written before Muyrbridge's photographic demonstration of how a horse actually places its legs when galloping. George Gaylord Simpson offers a more precise description:

> A three beat cadence with broken rhythm... as follows: beat, pause, beat, quick double-beat, beat, pause, etc. The corresponding sequence of footfalls (for the left lead) is: near-fore, off-hind, near-hind and off-fore almost together but the hind foot slightly earlier, near-fore, etc. The pause in the cadence represents a short time when all four feet are off the ground, which occurs only once in each stride as opposed to twice in the trot or pace. The off-hind foot is lifted almost immediately as the near-hind foot comes down, and before the off-fore hits, so that there is not normally any time when three feet are on the ground. (*Horses*, 1951, 57)

The word's derivation is from the Old French *galop*, first attested in the sixteenth century. But the Old Northern French form *walop* had been adopted in Middle English, and *wallop* is used in this sense in English from the fourteenth to the sixteenth centuries. In its earliest uses the noun only was used, preceded by another verb, as in its first attestation, in 1523, 'rode a great Galoppe'. The verb is first attested in 1533: 'The horse would neither trot nor galop.' *Full gallop*, meaning 'the extreme pace of which a horse is capable', is first attested in 1569; *to gallop to a standstill*, meaning 'to tire out', in 1892: 'Silvercrown... having galloped eighteen horses to a standstill in the Crawford Plate.' *False gallop*, meaning a *canter*, is first attested in 1533, when Lord Berners translated 'les petis galops' as 'they returnyd a fause galop'. The quotation the OED offers from 1587 is fully explanatory of the term: 'that your horse know thorowly from his trot, to rise to his false gallope, from his false gallope yet to a swifter, and then from his swifter to descend to his false gallope, and trot againe, by turnes.' This sense of the term dies out as canter takes over.

gallop[2] According to the OED it is only since the mid-nineteenth century that *a gallop* or *the gallops* have been used to describe the horses' training grounds. Its first attestation is from Trollope, in 1848: 'They've proper gallops there, which we haven't.' However, Queen Anne is reported to have founded Ascot by looking in pleasure at the heath for the first time, clapping her hands, and exclaiming 'See, Gentlemen, a Gallop for my two-year-olds.' An overtrained horse may be described, even before the race, as having left its race behind on the gallops.

galloper, galloping *Galloper* is usually a term of praise, prefixed by an epithet like 'resolute'. Such a horse is one with a good long stride, capable of keeping up a strong racing *pace* for the whole of a race. A possible negative implication of the word is that such a horse does not have a turn of *foot*: it wins its races by galloping others into the ground. This type of horse is suited by a *galloping track*, that is, a course with long *straights*[2] and bends (the opposite of a tight or *sharp*[2] track). A galloper who can *quicken up* at the end of a race is the ideal racehorse. The OED's first attestation in this sense is from 1650: 'he loved her above all the Horse in his Stables, she being an excellent galloper.'

gammon To *gammon* was originally thieves' slang for the trick of distracting a person while someone else steals from him. The OED quotes, from 1821, 'Going out of the door, Bagrie called the woman of the house, kept her in gammon in the backroom, while I returned and brought off the till.' In racing it came to describe a jockey's trick of seeming to be doing more than he actually is. This is Pierce Egan's account of the great nineteenth-century jockey Frank Buckle: 'There was one feature in Buckle's riding which deserved notice; and that was a knack of *gammoning* (as it is termed), in a race, by appearing to be at work, when, in reality, he was waiting' (Egan, 186).

gammy See *gummy*.

gee-gee The *gee-gees* is a slang term for horses, and, by extension, the races; as in, 'He lost all his money on the gee-gees.' The probable source is the command *gee!* which instructs a horse to turn to the right: Partridge traces this back to 1628. The OED describes 'gee-gee' as originally a child's word for a horse, its first attestation coming from *Lorna Doone* (1869), 'The "great Gee-Gee" – as all the small ones entitled me.'

gelding The verb *geld*, from Old Norse *gelda*, is first attested in

1300; the noun *gelding*, in the sense of a castrated horse, in this splendid sentence from a 1380 will: 'Et qe Lawrence eit sie demure en vie un hakney bay gelding et xl. s. (i.e. 40s 0d).' Geldings are common in *steeplechasing* but second-class citizens on the *Flat*. Because the aim of racing is to 'improve the breed', since 1902 geldings have been prohibited from running in the *classics* – two geldings ran in the 1900 Derby. Tom Jones promises that if he catches his enemy 'he would qualify him to run for the geldings' plate'. This reference is to a race specially for geldings. One notorious, and probably fictional, anecdote related to such a race concerns Tregonwell Frampton, the Keeper of the Running Horses for William III, Queen Anne, George I, and George II, who is supposed to have 'cut his favourite horse, Dragon, on a racecourse in order to qualify him for a race only open to geldings' (Hugh McCausland, *Old Sporting Characters*).

gentleman Describes a good-natured, well-behaved horse: first attestation 1889, describing a carthorse 'who in pacing, prancing and stepping to music proved himself every inch a gentleman.' Racehorses, just as much as carthorses, may be described as *gentlemen* – the approval implied in the word is not as strong as that implied in *christian*. The verb 'gentle', in the sense 'to tame, break in, render tractable', is first attested in 1735 in reference to horses; and 'gentle' as an epithet applied to an animal, meaning 'of excellent breed or spirit', goes back to the fourteenth century, a direct link to the word's source in the Old French *gentil*, 'high-born, noble'.

genuine The best term of approbation for a racehorse, often in the phrase *game and genuine*: it describes a horse which will always give its *running*. Its opposite, *ungenuine*, is probably more common, given the nature of the beasts: 'Thompson confirmed those instructions and said he was completely baffled as to how to win a race with such an ungenuine gelding' (*Sporting Life* 5 September 1990). This racing sense is probably a development of one of the late meanings of the word, describing persons as being 'free from affectation or hypocrisy'; but an earlier meaning of *genuine*, from 1728, was 'pertaining to the original stock, pure-bred', and some sense of this may underlie this racing usage, such a horse reproducing the ideal consistency of the true *thoroughbred*.

get[1] A horse *gets* a certain *distance* – or fails to; the OED's first example, from 1898, puts the word in quotation marks, showing that it was still thought slightly slangy: 'There are not a few horses that can not fairly "get" even five furlongs.' In this sense 'get' means 'to hold out for, to stay (a specified distance).' Much speculation centres on a horse's pedigree as it approaches the *classics*, to see, for instance, whether it is likely to get the Derby's mile and a half. A slight extension of the idea is *get home*, as in the *excuse* often offered for a horse's being passed and beaten in the closing stages of a race: 'He just didn't get home.'

get² Describes a horse's progeny: 'to beget, procreate (said of the male parent); now only of animals, esp. horses.' 'Unanimous is a son of Fairy King, who gets precocious performers, and he can beat these' (*Sporting Life* 3 July 1990).

get³ *Get* has several betting senses – see *get on* and *get out* – but by itself it simply means that a backer has put money on a horse at a certain *price*:

> The purchase was made on the first day of the Ascot meeting, with the condition that the bargain should not be made known for four-and-twenty hours, in order that Gully might get 10,000 to 1,000 about him for the St. Leger. (Thormanby, *Famous*, 76).

Gossip in the stands before a race, among those who have been backing in the *ring*, often runs along the lines, 'I got 2/1 . . . I could only get 7/4 . . . He told me he got 5/2, but I didn't see that anywhere.'

get at To interfere with a horse, usually by drugging it: 'Zoedone . . . fell heavily, and suspicions that the mare had been "got at", that is to say drugged, were noised abroad' (Badminton, 370). The OED identifies this usage as part of the more general sense, 'to tamper with; to influence by underhand means, to corrupt, bribe; to practice dishonest tricks on (a horse, etc.) in order to prevent (it) from winning': its first attestation, from 1865, is a political one, electors being "got at by money"; its second, from *The Spectator* in 1870, talks of how profitable it is for scoundrels to 'get at' horses.

get in Horses *get in* a race on a particular handicap *mark*. The phrase usually describes the allocation of a low weight and, in particular, one which just falls within the stipulated weight range for the race. 'Mellottie's main problem now will be to get in the big Newmarket handicap as he only has 7st 2lbs and badly needs to pick up a 5lbs penalty which he would get with another success' (*Sporting Life* 6 September 1990).

get off A jockey *gets off* a horse when he decides to ride another one in a race when he has regularly ridden the first horse, or has been firmly booked to ride it.

get on In betting, to *get on* is to succeed in making a bet on a horse, usually at a decent price – as in, 'I got on Bubblebath at 10/1.' This usage is first attested in 1869. Getting on becomes a problem when the investment is large, particularly if the bookmakers suspect that the bet is based on good inside information, hence the idea of *commissions*. To *get on after time* is every backer's dream, but strictly illegal. It means that by some kind of fraud one has placed a bet on a race whose result is already known (not the same thing as betting in *running*). However, so eccentric – and trusting – are the relationships between bookmakers and their clients that even this practice is not unknown. The *Sporting Life* of 13 October 1990 related the amazing story of a wealthy Lincolnshire potato farmer, a racehorse owner himself, who liked to bet but was too busy to do so. In those days – the 1940s and '50s – racing results were not broadcast nor so easily obtainable as they are today, and the farmer came to an agreement with his bookmaker that he would telephone the bookmaker's office at the end of his day's work, when the racing was long over, and go through the *card* placing his bets on each race, the bookmaker's clerk telling him whether each horse had won or lost. The bets were large – in hundreds and even thousands of pounds – but the arrangement was never compromised. On one occasion the clerk waited in some trepidation to hear how much the farmer had decided to bet on his own horse which had run that day, and had won at the rewarding odds of 100/8. When he came to the race in question he announced that he could not bet on it because his damn fool trainer had already sent him a congratulatory telegram.

get out To *get out* – less often, *get round* – originally meant to *hedge one's bets*. The OED quotes, from 1884, 'Johnson . . . had taken more than one opportunity of what is termed "getting out", that is backing the horse against which he had previously laid.' Now, however, the common use of *get out* relates to the idea of recovering money which one has lost, usually with one winning bet; hence the description of the last race on the *card* as the *getting out stakes*: 'And if the battle with the bookies is going against you by the time of the last race, then Chirkpar is recommended for the getting-out stakes' (*Racing Post* 31 July 1990). This race used to be known as the *getting-home race*, the idea being that one hoped to make enough money from it to pay the fare home.

get up[1] To *get up* is to achieve a close victory with a late run: 'Christie Kinane . . . waited until close home where he got Gentle Lad up to score by half a length from Lucky Bride' (*Sporting Life* 6 July 1990).

get up[2] Used to describe a bookmaker's readiness to take bets on the course: 'Aspirants would get up (one "gets up" to bet) with all their worldly possessions in an endeavour to establish themselves' (Sidney, 38). The expression is quite literal, a strong wooden box or two often supplying the platform from which the bookmaker looks down on his customers. See *betting boots*.

ginger See *fig*.

girth From Old Norse *gjorð*, 'girdle', the *girth* is the belt or band around the horse's body, drawn tight so as to secure the saddle. This is the original meaning of the word in English, its first attestation, in the fourteenth century, being 'Brydyl and petryl al to-burst Hys gerth, and hys stiropes alsoo.' The word's more general sense of a 'measurement around the circumference of an object' is not attested until 1664. In racing, jockeys will talk of getting their horse 'up to the girths' of another, i.e. nearly *upsides*, their horse's head being alongside the girth of the other. The OED records the phrase 'run head and girth', meaning 'to keep pace with in racing', from 1809: 'The mare ran him head and girth nearly the first half mile.'

give¹ Slight softness in the ground. The noun *give*, in the sense 'a yielding, giving way', is not attested until 1887 ('the give of the rod'), and the OED does not record an example close to the racing usage until 1970: 'If the weather stays fine we should have a fair surface with some give in it.' None the less, the word is in very common use on the racecourse, most horses liking some give in the *going*.

give² A horse *gives* weight to another when it carries more weight: 'Desert Orchid... gave two stone and an eight length beating to Delius' (*Sporting Life* 5 June 1990). A racing maxim is that 'you can give weight, but not distance'; i.e. it is easier for a horse to concede another pounds rather than yards.

give³ In betting, *give* is used to describe a *tip*. You are given a horse for a race when tipped that it is going to win – even if you have to pay for the tip.

give and take *Give and take plates* were races run in the eighteenth and nineteenth centuries where horses were weighted according to their height:

> The usual conditions were that a horse of 14 hands carried 9 stone, and for every eighth of an inch more or less of height, he was penalised, or received fourteen ounces, or 2 stone to a hand. (Prior, 98)

The OED's first attestation is from 1769: 'Will be run for on Huish Downs... A Free Plate of £50 Give and Take, by any Horse, Mare, or Gelding.' This specific racing sense developed into a more general meaning, 'implying the alternation of favourable and unfavourable conditions', and then developed the wider senses of 'the practice of mutual yielding' and 'exchange of talk, esp. of repartee, jest or raillery'.

gloves To *go for the gloves* is to bet recklessly: 'hardly worth mentioning are the backers who are in for a hit-or-miss dash at the ring – "to go for the gloves", as it is called' (Badminton, 255). Partridge says that the phrase originates in 'women's tendency to bet in pairs of gloves on the "heads I win, tails you lose" principle.' From the evidence of this exchange from James Shirley's *Hyde Park*, the tradition was well established early in the seventeenth century:

Julietta	Shall we venture nothing o' the horses?
	What odds against my lord!
Carol	Silk stockings.
Julietta	To a pair of perfumed gloves? I take it.
Carol	Done!
Bonavent	And I as much.
Julietta	Done, with you both!
Carol	I'll have 'em Spanish scent.
Julietta	The stockings shall be scarlet; if you choose
	Your scent, I'll choose my colour.
Carol	'Tis done; if Venture
	Knew but my lay, it would half break his neck now.
	A shout within, and cry of A Jockey!
Julietta	Ha! is the wind in the coast? Hark! the noise
	Is jockey now.
Carol	'Tis but a pair of gloves...

go[1]   One of the more specific senses of the word *go* was to describe the way a horse moved, in such expressions as *go wide* and *go narrow*, as in these examples from the OED: 'If he...goeth wide, his pace will be the surer' (1577), and 'Stolen or strayed...a young Black Gelding...goes narrow behind' (1681). While such compounds may still be used, *go* is more commonly found on its own to indicate a horse's running to the best of its abilities. The earliest example I have found is from Steve Donoghue:

> Many horses go much better for some jockeys than others, and trainers should realise this more, and understand that if a horse goes less kindly for one jockey than another, it is because the animal has his peculiarities and is at least equally at fault. (Donoghue, 74)

Today it is most often used in the phrase *never going*; i.e. always looking and acting as if it has no chance in a race: 'Safawan, the 7/4 favourite, was never going on the wide outside, but Distant Relative...was going ominously well under the stands rails' (*Sporting Life* 20 June 1990).

go[2]   Used as a synonym for 'offer' in relation to bookmakers' *prices*: 'Hills and Ladbrokes go 6/1...about Barry Hills's colt, while Corals offer 13/2' (*Sporting Life* 19 September 1990).

go away   The phrase 'won going away' means that the winning horse had begun to draw clear of the field: 'Baxter managed to keep him fairly straight from the distance and the colt quickened up nicely in the end to win going away' (*Racing Post* 29 May 1990).

go close   A horse *goes close* when it finishes second or third, beaten only a short distance: 'should go close' describes a confident, but not too confident, assessment of a horse's chance in a race. 'Madagans Grey, who spreadeagled his field in an auction event at Newmarket last month, should go close in the... Woodcote Stakes' (*Racing Post* 6 June 1990).

go down   The runners *go down* before the start of a race; i.e. they canter from the paddock to the start. Good advice is to watch a horse going down to see how it *acts* on the prevailing *going*.

go in   To win: used particularly of favourites. 'Palace Yard is not the sort that goes in first time up' (*Sporting Life* 14 September 1990).

going   Describes the condition of the ground on which horses race, ranging from *hard* to *heavy*, through *firm*, *good to firm*, *good*, *good to soft*, *soft*. The origin of this sense seems to have been American, the OED's first attestation coming from an 1859 American Dictionary. *Going* is of some importance in estimating *form*, some horses running a stone or better according to the state of the ground. A liking for a particular type of going is often passed on through the generations, so that even an unraced two-year-old's chances may be estimated when one knows its pedigree. Racecourses must issue a going report six days, two days, and one day before a meeting: 'Epsom was hit by a heavy shower yesterday afternoon, but it was not enough to change the official description of the Derby going, which remains good' (*Racing Post* 6 June 1990). See *penetrometer*.

goliath   See *multiple bet*.

gone   Succinctly describes a horse which has had enough racing and whose career – or, at least, whose season – is over:

Following more than fourteen months' absence he returned, a 20/1 forgotten horse, in Newbury's L'Oreal Handicap Hurdle to run a very respectable third, beaten only a short head for second prize. In July that year I asked Lester Piggott if he'd ride him at Lingfield. "Why?" he reacted sharply. "Has he 'gone'?"

I hoped not, I said, asking what prompted the question.

"You only want me when they've 'gone'," he grinned, recalling his previous appearance in my colours nine years and nine weeks earlier on Be Friendly, when the old horse was seemingly over the top. (O'Sullevan, 316)

good   Describes the best type of *going*, when a horse's hooves just print in.

good thing   Originally a *good thing* was 'a successful act of speculation'; the OED's first racing example is from 1883: 'Now and again... Jack Clinker managed to pull off some "good thing" on the turf.' This sense may not have died out, but the phrase is now more often used to describe a certainty for a race: i.e. the sense has transferred from the retrospective to the prospective, as in 'Boomerang looks a good thing in the first.' The OED's later examples gradually trace this change in reference: from 1913, 'Master at Arms is not a big horse, and with 12st 7lbs in the saddle he hardly looked like a good thing for the Sunbury Steeplechase.' The good thing is the holy grail of the racecourse, everyone there, in their own ways, searching for it; but, just as in the wider world all good things come to an end, so, in racing, good things usually come second. 'Something good' meant a reliable racing tip (Partridge, 1890), and gradually broadened into the general language – 'I'm onto something good.'

go on   To take the lead in a race: 'Precentor, always going easily under bottom weight, went on approaching the final furlong' (*Sporting Life* 5 September 1990).

go out   In betting, when a horse's odds *lengthen*[2], it is said to *go out* in the market: 'Despite visiting 9/2 in places from 11/2, he went out to 6/1 – 13/2 in places – despite a bet of £18,000 to £3,000' (*Sporting Life* 7 June 1990).

graduation   A *graduation race* is one designed to develop inexperienced horses. Coincidentally, *graduate* was nineteenth-century slang for 'a horse that has proved itself good' (Partridge, 1870).

grandstand   See *stands*.

green   Inexperienced. A two-year-old is said to *run green* when it does such things as look around in a race, move off a straight line, or refuse to go by another horse. The sense 'unripe, immature, undeveloped' is an early one – from the fourteenth century – but its first attestation with reference to an animal is as late as 1894: 'Actea ran very green, and had a small boy on her back.' The OED defines this sense as 'untrained', but this is only relatively so: even a well-trained horse may run green simply because of lack of actual racing experience. 'Criminal Law is still very green and was peeping at every thing when he was in front today' (*Sporting Life* 16 May 1990).

grey   In horses *grey* is not strictly a colour but the failure of pigment to produce colour. Greys are usually born dark brown or black, their greyness becoming more pronounced with age: a grey two-year-old may appear very dark, a grey seven-year-old may

well be white. In discussing the persistence of certain markings
through generations of horses, Prior notes how a 'bunch of grey
hairs at the root of the tail has been observed in particular lines
of blood for approaching two hundred years', and cites the maxim
that 'one seldom sees a bad horse with a grey tail' (Prior, 55).
Greys are becoming fewer because the colour cannot be inherited
unless one or other of the parents is a grey.

grief   From the mid-nineteenth century 'come to grief' described
a fall when hunting or steeplechasing – soon spreading into the
wider language. *Grief* itself is first attested in this sense in the
1890s: e.g. from 1898, 'A pace sufficient to test the condition of
horses and their riders and to bring about a considerable amount
of grief.' This usage looks back to older and nearly obsolete senses
of the word, namely 'damage inflicted or suffered' (14th – 16th
C.) and 'bodily injury or ailment' (15th – 18th C.).

grind   Nineteenth-century university slang for riding in a steeplechase: a *grind* was a steeplechase.

groom   See *jockey*.

ground   The space occupied in a race by a horse: to *take* another
horse's *ground* is to move across and into its path, a form of *interference* which may lead to disqualification: 'An objection by Nick
Smith, who finished second on Smoke, for taking his ground
from the second last [fence]' (*Sporting Life* 17 May 1990). To *lie
out of* one's *ground* is to adopt slightly exaggerated *waiting* tactics:
'As a rule, though it is frequently a good thing for a rider to wait,
it is rarely a good thing for him to lay out of his ground' (Badminton, 326).

group race   See *pattern*.

guard   'To see that horses...from one stable are separated in a
race' (Partridge). The OED quotes, from 1893, 'the list of disasters
caused by starting Siffleuse and putting T. Loates up, without
guarding the favourite.'

guidelines   Until the twentieth century *guideline* had only technical senses – originally, it seems, it meant a line by which to guide
a saw cut. The idea of a guideline as a rule which governs
behaviour does not appear until after 1945; and its prominence
in racing derives from its use by the *Jockey Club* to describe its
instructions on the use of the whip. In response to public concern
over possible cruelty, but not wishing to lay down a strict law on
the whip's use, the Jockey Club issued guidelines on the number
of times a horse might be struck in the closing stages of a race.
However, because guidelines lack the specificity of laws, their
variable interpretation by local *stewards* has led to much discon-
tent among jockeys. 'A renewed call for a change of attitude says

the guidelines should focus on correct use of the whip, not the frequency with which it can be used' (*Racing Post* 6 October 1990).

Guineas The *Guineas* is either of the two *classics*, the One Thousand Guineas and the Two Thousand Guineas, for fillies and colts respectively.

gummy *Gummy* or *gammy* legs occur when the horse's legs, below the hocks, are puffy, to the extent that the line of the tendons is obscured. Gummy legs generally result from a horse's having been worked too hard. The OED defines the sense as 'said esp. of the ankles and legs: as if charged with lumps of gum; puffy, swollen', and gives examples, from the eighteenth century onwards, of the word's use in relation to human legs as well. But the first attestation, in 1737, is from a work on farriery: 'The great sinew behind shall be large and a good way from the Bone... otherwise he is what we call gummy in this particular Part.'

guy To *guy in* is to win easily: from a nineteenth-century slang expression, 'to do a guy' or 'give the guy to', meaning to run away from. The OED quotes, from the *Daily News* in 1898: '"He's done a guy"... The Coroner – "Done a what?" Witness – "Done a guy, bunked".' The source is, evidently, the Guy Fawkes effigy – although the association between it and this sense is hard to understand. As a verb, *guy* is found in the sense 'to go off, run away', from 1879.

H **ack** *Hackney* comes from Old French *haquenee*, 'an ambling horse or mare, especially for ladies to ride on', and is first found in English in the fourteenth century. *Hack* is a short form which appeared in the eighteenth century to describe any horse used for ordinary riding, rather than for racing, hunting, or military purposes. Hence comes the expression *to hack up*, meaning to win easily; i.e. at the pace of a hack *canter* rather than at full racing pace because the horse is so far ahead of its rivals. This sense is not found in the OED, although 'hack', meaning 'to ride on horseback at ordinary pace', is first attested in 1857. 'Accolade... made up for a disappointing debut at Headquarters when hacking up at Nottingham next time' (*Sporting Life* 28 May 1990).

hackamore From Spanish *jaquima*, 'halter, head-stall of a horse', a *hackamore* is a single-rein bitless bridle: it employs two long, curved metal cheeks attached around the nose by leather pieces. Hackamores are occasionally used in racing, essentially on horses with poor mouths. The word is first attested in 1889 in a Dictionary of Americanisms. 'She was a well-bred filly but for some reason she had a tendency to hang to the left. Initially she reacted well to being ridden in a hackamore, but the cure did not work beyond a couple of days' (*Racing Post* 31 July 1990).

half-brother See *full¹*.

hand¹ Horses are measured in four-inch units called *hands*. When used more generally, a hand was three inches, as the OED's first example (1562) demonstrates: 'Foure graines of barlye make a fynger: four fingers a hande: foure handes a foote.' In the sixteenth and seventeenth centuries a common alternative was 'handful', first attested in 1535: 'Two mares... of the altitude or height of xiii handefulles at the least.' An early meaning of 'handful' was 'a lineal measurement of four inches'; so it seems likely that the modern 'hand' measurement is actually a shortened form of 'handful'.

hand² When a horse *comes to hand* it is ready to run well: 'Bluefield Boy showed he was coming to hand when finishing a close fifth to Causley in a handicap at Haydock' (*Sporting Life* 14 September 1990). The closest the OED comes to this sense is one of its definitions for 'to hand', as 'into subjection, under control', citing, from 1607, 'Alexander... at last wan the horse to hand.' Coming

100

to hand is partly a result of the trainer's skill, but as the phrase implies, wisely, much of this skill lies in patiently waiting for the horse to grow into itself. Cp. *handler*.

hand³ In betting slang *hand* means five; i.e. odds of 5/1. Cp. *handful²*.

handful¹ In the phrase a *double handful*: a horse which comes to the front with, or wins with, a double handful, is one whose jockey still has him on a tight rein. Similarly, a jockey has his *hands full* when his horse is going easily on a tight rein: 'Dettori cruised up on the outside with his hands full on Madagans Grey' (*Sporting Life* 1 September 1990).

handful² On the racecourse *handful* means five: to win by two handfuls is to win by ten lengths. The OED records its use, since 1930, to mean 'a five years' prison sentence', so cp. *carpet*.

handicap, handicapper *Handicap* is a word whose present widespread currency, as noun and verb, probably originates in its racing usage. *Handicap matches* seem to have begun in the seventeenth century, the word being derived from 'hand in the cap'. This was an old bartering game in which an umpire fixed the difference in value between the two articles to be exchanged, and open or closed hands in a cap signified the participants' acceptance or refusal of the deal; if both accepted, the umpire won a sum of money which all three had contributed. In a handicap match the umpire decided which of the horses was the better and how much more weight it should carry, the owners showing their acceptance of his judgment in the traditional hand in the cap way. Pond's Laws of Racing, in 1751, gave these directions for framing a handicap:

> A handicap match is A, B, and C to put an equal sum each into a hat; C, who is the handicapper, makes a match for A and B, who, when they have perused it, put their hands into their pockets, and draw them out closed. Then they open them together, and if both have money in their hands, the match is confirmed; if neither have money, it is no match. In both cases the handicapper draws all the money out of the hat; but if one has money in his hand, and the other none, then it is no match; and he that has money in his hand is entitled to the deposit in the hat. (Prior, 176)

This rule held until 1851, when the allusion to the hat was dropped.

From this practice emerged the modern handicap, the most common type of horse race, in which each horse is allotted a weight to carry – usually between seven and ten stone – depending upon the handicapper's assessment of its ability. This assessment is known as its *handicap mark*. Horses qualify for such a mark after a win, or after three runs, normally in *maiden* races. If they are entered in a handicap before they have qualified for a mark, they are given automatic top weight. The handicapper's aim is to have all the horses finish in a straight line. This never happens because horses are not machines, but are as human as the rest of us; and, anyway, trainers are in a constant battle of wits with the handicapper to ensure that their horses' abilities are not fully known. So, a jockey who wins a race by six lengths when he might have won it *cleverly* by only one is unlikely to be asked to ride again by that horse's trainer. A horse which is *laid out* for a handicap is one whose preparation has been aimed at a particular handicap race for several months. This might well include provision for his not running up to the best of his abilities in earlier races, although such a practice would, if detected, be a serious offence against the rules of racing. 'Although recent winners have tended to be more lightly-raced than Masnun, he appears to have been laid out for the race' (*Racing Post* 31 July 1990).

The *long handicap* is the list of weights for a race, extending beyond the stipulated minimum. Thus, while the minimum handicap weight may be 7st 7lbs, no horse being allowed to carry less than this (except for riding *allowances*), horses at the bottom of the handicap may be on a mark which would put them in the race, hypothetically, with a lower weight, say 7st 5lbs or 6st 10lbs. Such horses would be described as two pounds and eleven pounds *out of the handicap*. So good are certain horses – Arkle and Desert Orchid, for instance – that in any handicap they would carry the stipulated top weight and all of the other runners would be out of the handicap. Long handicap weights are normally given at the foot of each list of runners.

In earlier days other forms of handicapping were occasionally practised. In a match at Newmarket in 1753 one horse was started a *distance*[3] behind the other; and at York in 1778 Colonel Thornton gave his rival a distance start over a four-mile course. See *flying handicap*.

Handicapper has two meanings. One is the title of the official responsible for allotting weights, the successor of the old hand-in-the-cap umpire. His fate is to be regarded with extreme suspicion by most trainers, each of whom suspects him of bearing a personal grudge, and of giving his horses excessive weights to carry – for an example, see the quotation under *mark*[1]. If a horse is *ahead of the handicapper* then it is improving at a faster rate than the handicapper may have allowed for: 'A filly in tremendous form and certain to get the mile, she may still be ahead of the handicapper

and a hat-trick is possible' (*Sporting Life* 20 September 1990).
The other meaning of *handicapper* is to describe the kind of horse
which runs in handicaps. If not prefixed by some such epithet as
'good' or 'bad', then it refers to the ordinary, common or garden
racehorse, not good enough to get near *pattern race* company but
better than a *selling plater*. 'Jubilee Trail comes from a family
whose progeny are often better than handicappers' (*Sporting Life*
3 October 1990).

Handicaps are the most risky races to bet on. Occasionally one
encounters a *handicap snip*[2], or *handicap good thing* – a horse which
all experts agree is well *in*[1] at the weights and which will certainly
win the race and embarrass the handicapper who has framed the
weights for the race. These horses always finish second.

handler   A horse's *handler* is its trainer: a usage which goes back
to the original – and still current – sense of *handle*, 'to touch or
feel with the hands, to pass the hands over, stroke with the hand'.
To 'handle' a horse meant 'to get him accustomed to the hand':
the OED quotes, from 1698, 'The hardness of the winter forces
the breeders there to house and handle their colts six months
every year.'

hands   The best thing that can be said about a jockey is that he
has *good hands* or, even more simply, that he has *hands*: 'How
well or badly you use the reins depends upon whether you have
good or bad hands (skill or lack of skill in handling the reins)'
(Hislop, 30). The OED's early examples, from the fourteenth to
the nineteenth centuries, use *hand* in the singular – as in this
eighteenth-century citation: 'A horseman is said to have *no hand*,
when he only makes use of the bridle unseasonably.' By the
nineteenth century, however, the plural had become the common
form. Having hands is not merely a matter of dexterity, but
involves firmness and gentleness too, and, above all, the rider's
ability to transmit what he is thinking to his horse by way of his
hands and, equally, to feel what the horse is thinking. Squire
Osbaldeston describes a *match* between Clinker and Radical in
1826, both ridden by poor jockeys, which began like this:

> When they reached the gate both made for the gap, but having
> no hands, their horses got so jammed together that neither
> could pass through; and, Radical stopping, Douglas tumbled
> over his head over the gate. (Osbaldeston, 54)

See also the quotation under *collect*[1].

hands and heels   When a jockey rides a *finish hands and heels* he
does not use the whip at all: 'Quip battled back ahead approaching
the final furlong under his rider's hands-and-heels urgings'
(*Racing Post* 6 June 1990).

hands down   A racing phrase which has entered common speech: to win *hands down* is to win so easily that the jockey drops his hands on the reins, not *asking* the horse for any further effort. The OED quotes, from 1867, 'There were good horses in those days, as he can well recall, / But Barker upon Eleppo, hands down, shot by them all.'

hands full   See *handful¹*.

handy¹   Used in racing to mean close to the leader, up with the *pace*. To *keep* a horse *handy*, or to *lie up handy*, means that one is always within close touch of the leader. 'After beginning well she was handy to the lead throughout before going on inside the final furlong' (*Racing Post* 31 July 1990). The closest definition the OED offers is the general one, 'ready to hand, near at hand, conveniently accessible or ready for use'.

handy², handiness   Describes a horse's ability and readiness to turn quickly and efficiently:

> I was again forced to the conclusion that he did not stay, but remembering the handiness of him over the Epsom course the previous year, and his wonderful speed... I quite shared Mr Joel's opinion that despite his failure in the Guineas, he would take a lot of beating in the Derby. (Donoghue, 195)

hang   Horses *hang* when they veer to one side in a race instead of keeping a straight *line¹*. Probably this verb is used because when a horse does this it tends to hang its head to one side. Surprisingly, the OED's first attestation is as late as 1951. A horse will often *hang away* from the whip: if the jockey uses the whip in his right hand the horse will begin to run across the course to the left. Certain courses, most notoriously Epsom, have a camber which causes horses to hang towards the rails. 'John Dunlop's colt was a winner on merit at Goodwood, but hung left in the final furlong and was placed last by the stewards' (*Sporting Life* 31 August 1990). See *swerve*.

harden   A horse's *price hardens* when the odds become shorter: e.g. from 2/1 to 6/4. The OED records a commercial sense of the verb, 'of prices: to become higher, to rise', first attested in 1674.

head¹   Since races are won by getting to the line first, not getting past it, winning distances begin to be measured by how far one horse's nose is in front of another's. Whereas *nose* is used as a unit of measurement in other countries, in Britain the minimum winning distance is a *short head*: this means any measurable distance shorter than the horse's head. Then follows a *head*, a neck, ¼ length, ½ length... See *distance²*.

head²   To *give* a horse *its head*, or *let* him *have his head*, is let the

horse go freely. The OED's first attestation, from 1579, shows that
such phrases were already in wider, figurative use: 'You are no
sooner entred, but libertie looseth the reynes, and geves you
head.' The literal sense is still in common use, as when a jockey
lets a horse have its head because it is *pulling*[1] and would expend
too much energy if it were *held up* any longer.

Headquarters   Newmarket. The racing extension of this military
term is probably one of the earliest, the OED dating its general
use as 'a centre of operations' from 1851. Newmarket was 'discovered' by James I in 1605 as an ideal location for hunting hares.
Charles I continued the royal patronage, and Charles II, who first
visited it in 1666, established it as the racing centre of the country.
He rode in a *match* there in 1684.

heads   Those in the know (cp. *face*) or, more properly, those who
try to be in the know, as this anecdote by Steve Donoghue indicates. He is describing his reception after winning the Gordon
Stakes on Prince Palatine in 1911:

> On returning to the paddock the trainer met me, overjoyed at
> the great performance just put up by the horse; indeed, Prince
> Palatine had won in the style of a champion.
>
> In great excitement he asked me: "How did he win, Stephen?"
>
> Crowds of the "heads" were gathering round, listening with
> all their ears, so I did not say much then, but afterwards in
> the weighing-room I told the trainer quietly, "The horse won
> very easily. I think he is sure to win the Leger for you."
>
> "Do you really?" he replied. "That's fine! Don't say a word
> to anybody, and I'll back him to win a nice stake, and you
> must ride him." (Donoghue, 127)

head to head   Describes, literally, a close finish, with one horse's
head beside another's. The OED's definition of this phrase as 'face
to face; in private conversation' misses most of the confrontational
implications of its present-day usage. The phrase's origins might
lie in boxing, but the OED's second example, from 1799, points
to a racing origin: 'The contest here commenced ... and horses
never being more than a length asunder ... and generally head to
head.'

heat   In its early days horse-racing was largely structured around
heats: often horses ran three heats, the winner of two being the
overall winner of the race. This meaning of *heat*, which has now
entered the general language, was a development of the word's
earlier sense of 'a run given to a race-horse by way of exercise in
preparation for a race', a usage which goes back at least as far as
the sixteenth century. The OED's first example, from 1577,
demonstrates how the development from 'heating' to 'heat'

occurred: 'They walk him to chafe him, and put him in a heate.'
The title-page of a 1683 book reads: 'Methods for the Training
of Horses up for Racing, with their Heats and Courses'. 'Heat'
developed its modern sense of 'a single course in a race or other
contest' in the second half of the seventeenth century. The OED
quotes, from Falkland's *Marriage Night* (1663), 'and will ride his
heats as cleanly as a dieted Gelding.' That both senses – exercising
a horse and racing it – were current in the nineteenth century is
borne out by Jon Bee's definition of the word:

> A race or run for a prize. One heat a day while the horse is
> training is good to bring him in order for running. *The heat* is
> the first of a series, with short time intervals, the horse which
> comes in being declared the winner of the heat. *Heats* are
> repetitions of the same, and are called the first, second, and
> third as the case may be.

See *dead-heat*.

hedge   To *hedge* a bet is 'to secure one self against loss . . . by making transactions on the other side so as to compensate more or
less for possible loss on the first' – first OED attestation in the late
seventeenth century. However, an earlier racing usage occurs in
Shirley's play *Hyde Park* (1632), in a dialogue between two young
blades Rider and Venture. Venture is about to ride in a race and
is disconcerted at the sound of a cuckoo (4:3):

Venture: The bird speaks to you.
Rider: No, 'tis to you.
Venture: Now do I suspect I shall lose the race.
Rider: Despair for a cuckoo!
Venture: A cuckoo will not flatter.
             His word will go before a gentleman's
             In the city; 'tis an understanding bird,
             And seldom fails; a cuckoo! I'll hedge in
             My money presently.
Rider: For shame, be confident.

The origin of this sense seems to be the practice of 'hedging in'
a debt, that is securing it by including it within a larger one for
which better security is obtained. In racing it is common to hedge
a bet on a short-priced favourite with a smaller bet on an outsider.
More accurately, a true *hedger* takes a bet at good odds on a horse
– say £1,600 to £100, taking odds of 16/1 early in the *ante-post*
market – and then *lays off* the horse at a shorter price with someone
else – say £1,200 to £150, laying odds of 8/1. So, if the horse
wins, he wins £400; if it loses, he wins £50. Jon Bee describes
this practice under the heading *edge-off*. In *A Pink 'Un and a
Pelican*, Arthur Binstead describes one bookmaker, Joe Capp,

whose men were 'so woefully short of brass' that,

> instead of being able to stick to their work with the clear mind that a tenner in the inside pocket assures, [they] had to go hedging and ditching about the ring and the paddock in search of winners, in order to square the hotel bill. (*A Pink'Un*, 25)

Throughout the history of betting on horses, hedging has always been the strategy which separates the serious backer from the rest. Here is Squire Osbaldeston, writing in the 1850s about a lifetime of betting:

> I can only say that I have a clear conscience; I have never made any money by betting against my own horses, and only hedged my bets when I doubted their chance of winning. "A bet is not a good one until it is hedged", they say.
>
> On a fair calculation I have lost nearly £200,000 by betting and keeping racehorses during a period of 45 years; and £100,000 through the misdeeds of agents, etc. I blame my own folly and extravagance. I am an example of the adage that "A fool and his money are soon parted." (Osbaldeston, 2)

And this is Peter O'Sullevan looking back on his betting practices:

> I say this in the sure knowledge that if I had never hedged any one of around ten thousand (yes, ten thousand) vouchers accumulated over the years, I would, *on paper*, be better off. But paper profits may be furlongs short of reality. Betting is an emotional as well as a cerebral activity, in which a punter's pride operates to the bookmaker's advantage quite as potently as any horse bearing the *Timeform* symbol for unreliability. Hedging may limit the profit potential, but it reduces frustration – the element which breeds temptation to chase losses. (O'Sullevan, 35)

Hedging is an idea which can be applied to all kinds of situations. One of Osbaldeston's acquaintances lived as wild a life as the squire for a long time, then 'retired from the hunting field and also from the Turf. He has lived a most retired life ever since, and is what his sporting friends call "hedging for the next world".' (Osbaldeston, 53)

heinz   See *multiple bet*.

help   To *help one self* is racecourse slang for betting on a certainty, particularly when one is in the know about the horse's chances:

> After it was over, Lord Wilton, Lord G. Bentinck and many others would not speak to me when I went into the weighing room. William Scott said to me: "Squire, you have done us this time!" I answered: "Yes, Will. You know, I am just twelve miles further north than you are...and it is high time we should give you a rap on the knuckles to prove to you and the

handicappers that we have seen through them for a long time, and on this occasion we have helped ourselves." (Osbaldeston, 144)

hobday A *hobdayed* horse has had an operation to cut away paralysed muscle in the larynx, enabling it to breathe properly in a race: named after Sir Frederick Hobday (1869-1939), the veterinary surgeon who pioneered the operation. Hobdaying will sometimes improve a horse's *form* dramatically. 'The trainer came to the conclusion that his Hobdayed four-year-old performs better when his races are a month apart' (*Sporting Life* 21 September 1990).

hock The joint in the horse's leg between the knee and the *fetlock*, corresponding to the human ankle. The original form was *hough* – pronounced *hoch*, like 'loch' – first found in the fourteenth century, and referring to a number of animals, including man (meaning the hollow part behind the knee-joint). *Well-let-down hocks* are hocks which are close to the ground, a sign of power and strength in a horse. *Hock-deep* describes, in exaggerated fashion, very heavy *going*.

hocus Slang for drugging horses, from early in the nineteenth century: a shortened form of *hocus-pocus*, itself an early seventeenth-century name for a juggler. This exchange comes from Richard *Tattersall*'s evidence before a Parliamentary Special Committee on the Gaming Laws in 1844:

What is the term "robbery" applied to upon the turf? *They think it is robbery when they lose their money.*

What do they mean? *They mean that the horse has been done something with, but those are fellows that lose by the race.*

Did you ever hear of horses being hocussed? *No, I did not; I believe this, that horses are fit to run today and not tomorrow, just as a man is often fit to do any exertion today and not the next.* (Orchard, 293)

hod A bookmaker's money-bag. 'The "tools"...consist of a tripod which supports the board on which the prices are displayed, the board itself, the all-important "hod" (the large leather satchel no longer worn around the neck) and the even more important large umbrella' (Sidney, 111). 'Hod' is first attested, as a bricklayer's receptacle, in 1573.

hog's back See *roach*.

hold A horse *takes a hold* when it *pulls[1]* hard, especially in the early stages of a race: 'Abigail's Dream...put up an even better effort when fourth to Daisy Girl...fading in the finish after taking a strong hold' (*Racing Post* 15 September 1990). When it wins *hand held* it wins very easily: the reference is to the jockey's short rein: 'Rainbow Quest... was allowed to linger alongside eventual runner-up Old County before Pat Eddery asked him to saunter home hard held' (*Sporting Life* 12 June 1990).

hold together   On the Flat, to *hold* a horse *together* is to keep it balanced and running straight when it is very tired or at the extremes of its stamina; 'Mark felt her go wrong passing the Bushes in the Rockfel Stakes and held her together after that' (*Sporting Life* 7 September 1990). In *chasing*, a jockey holds a horse together when he keeps it on a firm rein and steadies it for the jump.

hold up   To *hold up* a horse is to keep it towards the rear of the field. Not in OED, but it does record 'hold up!' as a command to a horse not to fall. Some horses will only win if held up until very late in the race: 'Sally Rous... is a filly who has to be held up for a late run' (*Sporting Life* 21 June 1990).

holding   Describes *going* which is soft enough for horses to have trouble running through it: often the consequence of heavy going drying out. Not one of the official descriptions of going, but one which is frequently used.

hollow   A *hollow victory* occurs when a horse wins very easily. The phrase is not confined to racing and derives from the use of 'hollow' in the sense 'complete, thorough, out-and-out'; but this is a development of its adverbial use to mean 'thoroughly, completely, out-and-out', and the OED describes this as a usage whose origin is 'obscure, and has excited conjecture from its first appearance in literature.' It quotes, from Chesterfield's *Letters* (1764), 'He set up for the County of Middlesex, and carried it hollow, as the jockeys say.' It may be worth making a connection with *hollo*, a hunting call, common from medieval times.

hollow back   See *dipped back*.

holy ghost   Rhyming slang for winning-post (Partridge, 1932).

home   The winning-post. When the *going* is heavy horses are said to find it difficult *getting home* in the ground: 'He said: "Calvanne Miss did not get home against Green Dollar over six furlongs at Brighton last week, so we switched her back to the minimum trip"' (*Sporting Life* 4 July 1990). As well as meaning to win, *get home* means, in betting, to recover losses and leave the racecourse having come out quits.

home and hosed   Describes an easy victory. A horse which comes clear of its field may be so described, the idea being that it is so far ahead that it has time to be unsaddled and hosed down before the others finish. 'When Stephen Craine kicked for home on Missing You, Tommy Stack's filly looked home and hosed. However, Gilson brought Dshanilja with a lovely run to take it up in the final furlong' (*Sporting Life* 6 September 1990).

hood   The *hoods* sometimes refers to *blinkers*; otherwise a *hood* is a more extreme form of head covering for the horse, covering head and ears. The OED records the word's use, in 1884, to mean 'a covering for the head of a horse', but the example it gives is not of something meant to be raced in: 'that part of a horse blanket which covers the horse's head and neck'. This hood, also known as the 'head-cap' or 'head lap', is to protect travelling horses in cold weather. The racing hood, an adaptation of this, is to protect very nervous horses from the sounds – and sights, if blinkers are attached – of a race.

horse   One popular etymology of *horse* is to take it back, via a supposed Teutonic form *kurso*, to the Latin *currere*, 'to run'. Originally, in English, the word was neuter, applying to male and female alike; now, while still the general term, it also has the specific sense of the male of the species. *Hors* is first attested in 825. The singular form could also be used with a plural meaning for a long time, but *horses* is also found from the beginning of the thirteenth century.

   Horse-race is first attested in 1581, in Philip Sidney's *Apologie for Poetrie*: 'Philip of Macedon reckoned a horse-race wonne at Olimpus among hys three fearefull felicities.' *Horse-racing's* first attestation is in 1654, 'Each taking his horse . . . and so go to horse-racing.' Alternative eighteenth-century forms were *horse-course* and *horse-coursing*, and *horse-running* occurs in the seventeenth century.

   Horse sense is what prevents horses from betting on people. 'Straight from the horse's mouth' is first used by P.G. Wodehouse, in 1928.

hot   First attested to describe a very well backed *favourite* in the *Daily News* in 1894: '. . . one of the hottest favourites on record'. Perhaps derived from the use of *hot* to mean 'fervent, ardent, passionate, enthusiastic, eager, keen, zealous', as in 'hot pursuit' – the favourite being the horse in the race which most backers are keen on.

hotpot   Perhaps an extension of *hot* to describe a favourite: *hotpot* came into racing as a term for a horse which had been heavily backed (first attestation, 1922). Now, however, it equally well describes a star performer: '. . . the eclipse of another Michael Stoute hotpot in the Coronation Stakes cost some high rollers dear' (*Sporting Life*, 21 June 1990).

HT   *aitch-tee*; betting slang for eight, i.e. odds of 8/1.

hunt   A horse which races several lengths behind the others is said to *hunt up* the field: the image seems to be a double one, of keeping one's position in a chasing pack and of being prepared to pounce. 'Gymcrack Lovebird has the right calibre of form, having hunted up Zarna at Doncaster' (*Sporting Life* 14 June 1990). In *chasing*, a horse which takes its own time to get round the course at the back of the field is said to *hunt round*: here the image is of slow, careful jumping. Neither of these expressions is in the OED.

hunter *Hunter* is first attested in the sense of 'a horse used, or adapted for use in hunting' in 1687: 'A milk white Mare above 14 hands...a very good Hunter.' Such horses were the original *steeplechasers*: in a Sporting Dictionary of 1810 steeplechasing is defined simply as 'a race over the country for hunters' (Eliot, 11). If nothing else reminds us of this, the chasing *season* is essentially the fox-hunting season, beginning in August, at cubbing, and ending soon after the last meet in April. A more obvious reminder is the *hunter chase*, a form of race restricted to horse which have been hunting with hounds, ridden by amateur jockeys. That the riders should be amateurs is one of the last echoes of a continued debate through the nineteenth century, and into the early twentieth, to distinguish between the gentleman rider and the professional. If chasing began as a series of *matches* between gentlemen to see which one's hunter was the better, as the stakes rose so did the employment of proxy riders; then *handicapping* meant that many horse were set to carry weights lower than their gentleman owners could *do*[2]. The hunter chase, where weights are kept high and horses have to have experienced the hunting field, guarantees some element of sport for sport's sake in chasing. That the spirit of amateurism lives on is demonstrated by the things which happened before, during, and after a hunter chase held at Cartmel in May 1990. To quote the *Sporting Life*'s account:

> The race was jinxed from the start. Pauline Robson, due to ride her father's Windmill Cottage, slipped and fell, injuring her back, as she was carrying her saddle from the weighing room.
>
> A call went out for any available amateur and, from the holiday throng, Peter Lewis just pipped John Edwards's daughter Sophie for the privilege of the ride. Lucky for her!
>
> Lewis got no further than the second fence before his saddle slipped, decanting him on the floor, while Windmill Cottage proceeded to do a bucking-bronco act as the misplaced equipment wrapped itself indelicately underneath his hindlegs.

The race continued for another ten fences when, as the field entered the straight to finish the second of the race's three circuits, one of the jockeys, riding a completely unfancied horse, Dr

Cornelius, under the illusion that this was the end of the race, began to ride a *finish*, cheered on by the other jockeys:

For the first time in his life Dr Cornelius experienced the euphoria of being in front on the run-in, but the tape he breasted was not the winning one.

Instead it was the "not this time, lads" barrier held across the course by Cartmel's enthusiastic band of toilers who were almost yanked off their feet as Dr Cornelius charged through it.

All too late Robertson realised he had been duped. He unwisely compounded his error by doing a U-turn halfway up the run-in to rejoin the race at the tail-end.

At the inevitable stewards' enquiry the hatless rider... fainted under interrogation and had to be revived with a glass of water.

The stewards fined him £250.

hurdle, hurdler National Hunt racing takes place over *fences* or *hurdles*: the latter are lighter, lower obstacles, more suited to ex-Flat horses or to future *chasers* in their first season. A hurdle is 'a portable rectangular frame ... used chiefly to form temporary fences', a usage which can be traced back to the eighth century. The OED takes its etymology back, by way of the Latin *cratis*, to the Sanskrit root *crt*, 'to fasten together'. The use of 'hurdles' to describe obstacles in a horse-race is first attested in 1833. The practice goes back only a little earlier if this account is true:

Hurdle racing had its origin some years ago, when, in the absence of better sport, a royal hunting-party on the Downs near Brighton, when George IV was king, amused themselves by racing over some flights of sheep-hurdles. The fun was thought to be so good that regular races over hurdles were organised. (Badminton, 334)

Squire Osbaldeston describes an experience in his youth – it must have happened some time around 1805:

One day while on our way home after hunting we came across some hurdles put up to pen sheep, and proceeded to jump them. The shepherd became very abusive, swearing that if we attempted to do it he would stick us with his pitchfork, and he stood by the hurdles ready to put the threat into execution. The captain and I held a council of war, and agreed to charge him simultaneously, the captain in front, myself in the rear; this manouevre so confused the enemy that he did not know which of us to try and stick. Mad Bridges was riding a highly *menaged* horse which could gallop round a shilling, and when the shepherd attacked him Bridges twisted his mount round, thus avoiding the thrust, while I, passing behind the man, caught the pitchfork out of his hands. We carried it for a couple of miles and threw it into a pond. (Osbaldeston, 7)

The first recorded hurdle race was at Warwick in 1831: two miles, over six flights of hurdles – very close to today's minimum *trip*, two miles over eight obstacles. Originally hurdle races were included in Flat-racing programmes as well as jump meetings. In 1867, however, the *Jockey Club* resoved that 'in future HURDLE RACES shall not be considered as coming within the established Rules of Racing and shall not be reported in the Calendar with flat races' (Eliot, 84). In effect, then, hurdle races had been handed over to the Grand National Hunt Steeplechase Committee which, in the same year, established the rules for hurdle races.

The verb *to hurdle* is first attested in the racing sense in 1897. A *hurdler* is a horse which specialises in hurdle races.

I **dle**   Many horses have a tendency to *idle in front*: that is, once they get to the head of the field they slow down, thinking they have done enough. There are two good reasons for this. Horses are pack animals and do not naturally enjoy detaching themselves from the herd; and recognition of the winning-post is not part of a horse's training. This use of *idle* as a verb is uncommon before the twentieth century, and it may well be that the motoring sense – 'of an engine: to run while disconnected from a load or out of gear' – has influenced the racing usage. 'He would have won more easily except for his tendency to idle in front' (*Sporting Life* 5 September 1990).

if cash   See *any to come.*

illegitimate   In the second half of the nineteenth century *illegitimate* was a frequent term of description for National Hunt racing, which was not yet subject to an official set of rules. The OED quotes, from 1888, the description of a horse as 'a much smarter performer at the illegitimate game than she was at the Flat.' Just how illegitimate steeplechasing became in the nineteenth century – in the worst senses of the word – is borne out by such descriptions of it as this one by Tom Colman:

> Though I established Steeplechases, I never ran but one horse, Shylock, formerly the property of the Duke of Rutland, a very vicious beast, who had killed a boy. I should have shot him had I not been stopped; and ran him to punish him not with an idea of winning. I was disgusted to see horses ridden to death in them as they were by people knowing nothing about it. (Eliot, 61)

impost   An *impost* was originally 'a tax, duty, imposition, tribute': since the nineteenth century it has been racing slang for 'the weight which a horse has to carry in a handicap race'.

in¹   Commonly used to refer to a horse's chance at the weights. A horse which is twelve pounds *better in* than another is one which is twelve pounds better off at the weights than, say, in a previous run, or in comparison with a future *handicap*. A low-weighted horse may be described as *very well in.* 'She's 7lb better in than she'll ever be in a handicap again' (*Racing Post* 31 July 1990); 'Nataharya...might well have been let in lightly for her first run in handicap company' (*Racing Post* 20 September 1990).

in²   Short for 'in before the stewards': to be *had in* is to be sum-

moned to see them. 'I'll have you all in' is a typical *starter*'s threat
to jockeys who are reluctant to make a proper line at the start.

in and out   Describes a horse's inconsistent running, something
which arouses the wrath of the public and the attention of the
stewards. In the 1890s such inconsistency had become so common-
place that it brought racing into bad odour, hence the OED's
quotation from the *Times* in June 1897, 'Have you heard of what
is called in-and-out running?' The phenomenon goes back much
further, of course:

> Sam, however, retorts with effect on Sir Charles by quoting
> the in-and-out running of some of the baronet's own horses,
> as, for example, Bellario, at Newmarket, in 1770, when he
> was beaten easily one day, and beat better horses the next.
> (Thormanby, *Famous*, 23)

The general sense of the phrase – erratic, variable – seem to come
from this racing usage.

inside   Betting *inside* occurs when bookmakers *lay*[1] off bets with
each other. The reference is to 'inside the ring', that is, within
the *Tattersalls* enclosure. Charles Sidney explains the origin of
this usage, tracing it back to the original Tattersalls, in which
The Room became the focus of betting in London:

> Until about 1790 the betting in The Room was mostly confined
> to the Members but as the fame of The Ring became more
> widespread greater and greater crowds gathered about The
> Room. They came not so much to have a bet but to learn the
> current information and latest prices . . . Inevitably, among this
> crowd were to be found "the lesser legs" offering odds to those
> who had no access to The Room and this crowd crammed
> itself, if not outside the railings, at least outside The Room.
> These loungers, Legs, backers and regular frequenters were
> collectively called "Outside". (Sidney, 34)

inspect, inspection   When racing is in doubt because of bad
weather, *stewards inspect* the course. A *stewards' inspection* may
take place at any time before racing, or after racing has begun if
there are grounds for concern about possible danger to jockeys
and horses.

interfere, interference   *Interference* is a general term for any
offence by which one horse impedes another in the course of a
race. Significantly, the verb *interfere* originally referred only to
horses, meaning 'to strike the inside of the fetlock with the shoe
or hoof of the opposite foot': from the Old French *s'entreferir*, 'to
strike each other', first attestation 1530, 'My horse entreyreth all
redy, I feare me the jade will fayle me.' The extension of meaning
to describe a collision between any objects is not found until some

eighty years later; and while the word has gradually lost its strong physical sense of things actually touching, this is largely retained in the racing usage – although interference can occur without any actual contact between horses.

irons   The stirrups: not recognised by the OED as a special sense, but probably to be understood under the general heading 'an instrument, appliance, tool, material, or particular part of one, made of the metal', with the added note that the defining word is often prefixed. So, *stirrup irons* first occurs in 1474. 'Motcombe: jumped badly in last, rider lost irons second, soon tailed off' (*Sporting Life* 7 September 1990).

J **acket** Although blouses are now worn, *jacket* is still commonly used to refer to a jockey's *silks*. The first attestation in this sense is from 1856, in a description of Sam Chifney in 'the magnificent "purple jacket with scarlet sleeves, and gold-braid buttons" of the Prince.' Phrases like 'retain his jacket' and 'send in his jacket' were used to describe a stable's employment or sacking of a jockey. 'Jacket' goes back to the Old French *jaque*, 'thought by some to be identical with the proper name *Jacques*, perhaps as originally worn by the peasantry'; and since *jockey* has connections with Jock and Jack, it seems that the two words were made for each other.

jackpot See *pot*.

jade Of unknown origin, *jade* is first found in Chaucer (1386), and while it has broadened into the general language as a noun, to describe women of Fortune (somewhat archaic now), and as a verb to mean 'tired or worn out', it still keeps its original sense of 'a contemptuous name for a horse'. While it generally describes an inferior kind of horse, and cannot therefore be accurately used in reference to *thoroughbreds*, its use in racing is to describe a race-horse which does not behave as a thoroughbred should – a non-trier. See the quotation under *squiggle*.

jam Racecourse slang for 'clear profit, an advantage, or a certainty of winning' (Partridge, late 19th C.). The OED quotes, from an 1874 Dictionary of Slang, its definition as 'a sporting phrase, meaning anything exceptionally good' – a formulation very close in time to Lewis Carroll's rule 'jam to-morrow and jam yesterday – but never jam to-day' (1871).

jar The verb *jar*, not found until the sixteenth century, is probably derived from an imitation of the sound of an echo – especially if the 'r' is trilled. *Jarring*, in the sense of vibrating or shaking from an impact, is first attested in 1735. In racing jarring occurs when a horse's legs are damaged by running on firm *going*: such a horse is described as being *jarred up*. 'He would really love a bit of cut in the ground. He got jarred up as a two-year-old and I don't think he's forgotten it' (*Sporting Life* 19 June 1990).

jib Derivation uncertain, although the OED points to the similarity with the French *giber*, 'to kick, sometimes said of horses'. *Jib* is used when a horse stops and refuses to move: the first attestation is in a letter of Jane Austen's, 'the horses actually gibbed on this

117

side of Hyde Park Gate' (1811).

job¹   From the original sense of the verb *job*, 'to pierce to a small depth with a forcible but abruptly arrested action', a *job* is a rider's sudden jerking of the bit in the horse's mouth: first attested in 1611.

job²   In betting, a *job* is, first, 'a commission to back a racehorse' (1889), and then 'a horse on which such bets are placed': such a horse may well be described as a big 'starting-price job'. To *have got the job* is to 'have a commission to bet on a horse' (Partridge, 1875). A further development of 'job' in this sense is *job-jockey*, describing a rider who can be relied upon to win on such horses.

jock-off   See *jockey*.

jockey   The word developed like this: originally a Scottish and Northern English pet form of the name John or Jock, it then became applicable to any man of the common people (16th C.). In the seventeenth century it was applied to strolling minstrels or beggars and to horse-owners and horse-dealers. Since horse-dealers were then regarded as used-car salesmen are today, it came to mean 'a crafty or fraudulent bargainer; a cheat', as well as 'one who drives a horse' and, eventually, 'a professional rider in horse races' – perhaps helped by connection with *jack-boy*, 'a stable-boy, groom, or postillion' (from 1573). In the seventeenth and eighteenth centuries *riding groom* was as common a designation as *jockey* for the men who rode the horses, and 'jockey' itself might well describe the man who owned the horse and employed the groom to ride for him – see *Jockey Club*. In the play *Hyde Park* (1632) one character is a jockey, and is referred to by the other characters as Jocky, as if the word were still as much a name as a designation. During the race which occupies one of the play's scenes, the crowd's shout is 'A Jockey!' – see the quotation under *gloves*.

In a report of the York races in 1709 we read that 'nothing but jockeying and fowl play was offer'd; excepting one man that rid fair' (Prior, 90). As a verb, *jockey* still keeps some of these negative connotations, jockeying for position being a general term for rough tactics on the racecourse or in life itself. *Jock* remains a familiar form of the word: Partridge dates this abbreviation from 1825. There is also a verb to *jock off*, describing the increasingly common practice, in these days of free-lance riders and fickle owners, when a top jockey is given the ride on a good horse from a *stable* whose jockey is not so highly rated: the stable jockey is, accordingly, jocked off – 'It is nice to see Fitzgerald's young jockey keep the ride on a good horse as he has been jocked off the likes of Gipsy Fiddler and Sapience in favour of Pat Eddery' (*Sporting Life* 6 September 1990).

When women began to ride professionally the word *jockette* was introduced. It soon dropped out of favour, and *woman-* or *lady-jockey* is generally preferred.

Jockey Club   The *Jockey Club*, which runs racing, has no jockeys among its members. The name comes from the days when jockey meant horse-owner. Its title first occurs in 1752, in the *conditions* of a race to be run at Newmarket:

> A Contribution Free Plate, by Horses at the Property of the Noblemen and Gentlemen belonging to the JOCKEY CLUB at the *Star and Garter* in *Pall Mall*, one Heat over the Round Course, weight eight stone, seven Pound. (Prior, 131)

The Club's first order, signalling its government of racing, appeared in 1758:

> Every Person who shall Ride at Newmarket, for Plate, Sweepstakes or Match, shall be obliged to Weigh when he comes in, allowing Two Pounds above the Weight, and no more. That every Rider who shall neglect to obey this Resolution is guilty of Contempt of the Order of this CLUB, and shall be disqualified from Riding hereafter at Newmarket, unless any Gentleman, or his Rider, shall declare before starting that the Rider is above the Weight allowed of by the aforesaid Resolution. (Prior, 141)

By owning Newmarket, and having the right to *warn off* those who disobeyed its authority, the Club evolved as the government and law-maker for British racing. See *calendar*; *headquarters*.

joint   A bookmaker's stand on the racecourse: a development of *joint* in the sense of a fairground stand (1896).

> His personal requisites were a good pair of lungs, the heart of a lion and a little cash. Endowed with these attributes it was only necessary to set up 'The Joint' (as a pitch occupied by 'tools' is called), mark up a few prices and he was in business. (Sidney, 111)

jolly   Short for the *jolly favourite*: perhaps influenced by the use of *jolly* to mean 'a cheer', this being the crowd's response to a winning *favourite*. 'Supporters had a few anxious moments when the "jolly" lost a few lengths at the start' (*Sporting Life* 6 July 1990).

jostle   From *joust*: the original meaning of *jostle* was 'to come into collision in the tournament'. In racing, *jostling* meant pushing against a rival to impede him, and was a common, accepted tactic well into the nineteenth century. The OED's first example, from 1723, gives the rule: 'Jostling allowed on by the two foremost Horses for these Plates and no other Horse.' Later in the eighteenth century, John Pond's Rules of Racing included: 'Jostling allowed in Matches if no agreement to the contrary.' Finally, in 1792, the *Jockey Club* decreed 'that when any Match is made in which Crossing and Jostling are not mentioned, they shall be understood to be barred.' The 1913 Derby, famous for the death of the suffragette who threw herself in front of the king's horse, was also marked by the disqualification of the winner Craganour on the grounds that he had jostled the second horse, Aboyeur, who was awarded the race.

judge The official – formerly known as the *trier* – who decides the placings of horses at the finish of a race; hence the phrase 'waiting on', or 'waiting for' the *judge*, when the finish is a close one. In earlier days there was often more than one judge, a situation which could easily lead to problems and bad feeling. In 1733 a race at Durham had so close a finish that three of the six triers called one horse the winner, the other three called the other horse. The stakes were divided 'to avoid the consequence of law' (Prior, 109). When a single judge was appointed the position was not entirely free of suspicion, of either his honesty or his competence, as the following anecdote makes clear:

> On one occasion at Kelso he won the principal hurdle race by at least a length and a half on Nimble Girl. On the strength of what was an obvious win the owner...went to have a bottle of wine with Johnny Marr, of Glasgow. When they came out of the little bar they were astounded to find that Nimble Girl had been placed second to a horse called Didn't Know. The rider of this latter animal told the judge (Mr 'Piggy' Finlay) that *he* had not won, and that Nimble Girl had beaten him in a canter, and there were many expostulations from others, but Mr Finlay, who was suffering from bad sight, would not alter his decision...I often noticed him holding a race card close up to his eyes to read it, and it was the general opinion that he should have retired from a position requiring perfect sight, coolness, and accuracy. (McGuigan, 58)

Even today, when the *photo-finish* may be thought to have ruled out such travesties, there are occasional examples of the judge misinterpreting the photo and giving the wrong horse as the winner. As well as determining the placings, the judge also decides on the *distances*[2] between the placed horses.

Trier, the early name for a judge, was a common term for any kind of sports umpire. The OED's first attestation, from 1607, relates to horse racing: Gervase Markham defining triers as 'certaine indifferent Gentlemen, chosen by both the parties that make the match, who are to see that there be faire play, and that the Articles be fully performed on both parties.'

To *trouble the judge* is to finish in the first four in a race: 'Ron

Boss's youngster had never troubled the judge since scoring at Newmarket in May' (*Sporting Life* 1 September 1990).

jump, jumper, jumping   *Jumping* is a general term for *hurdle* racing and *steeplechasing*. *Jumpers* are horses engaged in either or both; *jump-jockeys* are riders of hurdlers and chasers.

jumper's bump   A name given to the protuberance at the top of a horse's *croup*: so called because it is supposed, by its size, to indicate a horse's jumping ability.

jump off   Horses *jump off* when they start a race, whether from the *stalls*, the tape, or by flag. 'Grand Blush was tried in blinkers for the first time on the training ground, but she almost ruined the work when failing to jump off' (*Sporting Life* 15 June 1990).

jump up   To *jump up* a jockey is to give him a leg up on a horse:

"Walk straight up to near me and stand by the bushes in the middle. I'll lead him up to you. I'll jump you up."

"Jump me up?"

"Jump you. I gotta take yer knee an' jump you. Like the horse was too high for you to get on."

(Enid Bagnold, *National Velvet*)

Keen The Old English *cene* had two distinct senses: 'wise, learned, clever' and 'brave, bold, valiant, daring'. In racing *keen* leans more towards the second of these. It may be used positively, as with people, to describe horses which are eager to race – and to be described as *not keen* is a definite slur on a horse's reputation. But often 'keen' is used slightly detrimentally, to describe a headstrong, hard-pulling horse which needs special care in riding. 'He is still a bit fresh and went down to the start a bit keenly, but he has run a good race' (*Sporting Life* 24 May 1990).

keep on A horse which continues its effort is said to *keep on*. 'Qui Danzig's connections also appeared disappointed by their colt's run. But to my mind he kept on encouragingly on his reappearance' (*Racing Post* 19 May 1990).

keep up When a horse *idles* it needs to be *kept up* to its work; that is, ridden a little more vigorously, or given a tap with the whip, to remind it that it still needs to make an effort even though it is in the lead. 'He took the lead...two out and was kept up to his work by Ray Cochrane to win by two lengths' (*Sporting Life* 5 September 1990).

kickback New in British racing language – imported from America – *kickback* describes a consequence of racing on *all-weather* surfaces, particularly *equitrack*, when the loose surface is kicked back into the faces of the following horses. 'All-weather kickback causes many of the runners to cough...Head lad David Jefferies said "Wizzard Magic came from the rear to win his race, and so would have got plenty of kickback"' (*Sporting Life* 1 November 1990). Not only the horses, but jockeys too are affected by kickback and have taken to wearing masks to protect themselves against it.

kick on To *kick on* is to take a horse into the lead, and often to go for *home*. The phrase refers to the jockey's action: 'Michael Roberts kicked on fully three furlongs out at Doncaster' (*Sporting Life* 3 October 1990).

kid Perhaps adapted from the noun, the verb *kid*, meaning 'to hoax', may convey the idea that in doing so one makes the victim seem like a child. Its original use was to describe the diverting of someone's attention when he was being robbed (cp. *gammon*). One racing sense is to deceive a horse so that it does not realise it is in a race, an achievement of the best jockeys when riding difficult horses: 'The jockey rode a good race to kid on Saryan' (*Sporting Life* 14 September 1990). Another – also known as *foxing* – is to deceive other riders into thinking that one's horse has nothing more to give: George Fordham was so good at doing this that 'Fordham's kid' became a popular Turf phrase in the nineteenth century.

killing To *make a killing* is a phrase in general use, on the racecourse as well as the stock exchange: but Partridge identifies it as originally Australian racecourse slang, meaning 'to win substantially from the bookmakers' (1919).

kink Often used to describe an odd twist in character which a horse possesses. The word originally meant, as is still one of its common uses, 'a short twist or curl in a rope, thread, hair, wire' (1678), and began to gain its psychological senses in the nineteenth century, intensifying from fairly gentle aberrations to the serious, often sexual, peculiarities which some of its twentieth-century usages convey. Its horse sense is much closer to the latter than the former, *kink* often referring to really vicious behaviour on a horse's part. The OED quotes from T.S. Eliot, in *The Cocktail Party* (1950), significantly putting the word in quotation marks – 'And so you suppose you have what you call a "kink"?' – while, in the same year, Cyril Luckman described Diamond Jubilee as the 'colt with a kink' (Bland, 102).

knacker A word of unknown origin: *knacker* first meant a 'harness-maker' or 'saddler'. Not until 1812 is it attested in the sense of 'one whose trade it is to buy worn out, diseased or useless horses, and slaughter them for their hides and hoofs, and for making dog's meat, etc.' On the racecourse the knacker's van (formerly cart) is a constant reminder of the risks horses undergo, particularly over the jumps.

knock Bookmakers *knock out* a horse when they *lengthen*[2] its odds, usually quite dramatically – say, from 5/1 to 10/1. See *knock-out*. They *knock back* a punter when they refuse to lay the odds they *offer* to the amount he wishes to bet: 'knock back', meaning 'to refuse, rebuff', came into English via Australian and New Zealand slang in the 1930s. To *take a knock* is racing slang from the 1890s, meaning to lose more than one can afford: 'When a bookmaker takes the knock he must either leave off or take to welshing' (*Pitcher in P.*, 58). This idiom has broadened into the general language from racing, either as 'take the knock' or 'take knocks'. A bookmaker is *knocked off the joint* when he has taken a series of heavy bets on a particular horse at too long a price – a danger of *going up* early.

knock about   A horse is *knocked about* in a race either if it meets heavy *interference* or, more commonly, if it gets harsh treatment from the jockey's whip. 'No Finesse, not knocked about when eighth in the well-contested claiming race won by Princess Tiara ... should make her presence felt' (*Sporting Life* 3 July 1990). The implication here is that the horse was given an easy race.

knock-out   The *knock-out* is a maneouvre by which a bookmaker or a group of bookmakers, force a horse's *price* to *lengthen*[2] artificially – i.e. beyond that which market demand would require – by *commissioning* bets thinly spread across the country to be paid out at *S.P.*, while he himself offers the horse at a long price on the course, no matter how heavily it is backed there. Because he continues to *stand*[2] the horse at a long price, other bookmakers will be forced to lengthen its price as well:

> The rest of The Ring would eventually follow the bookmaker 'at the knock-out' and the S.P. returned for the horse would be far in excess of its true price. A 6/4 chance might be returned at 5/1 or 6/1 or even bigger. The tactic worked not because The Ring was unaware of the knock-out but because The Ring and its clientele could not be sure whether the lengthening of price was indeed a reflection of a non-trier. The layer knocking out a horse would be a knowledgeable man and it could be assumed that he would know whether or not a horse was fit.
>
> The knock-out Bookmaker operated only with horses about which he had reliable information, so the operation amounted to backing winners and naming your own prices. (Sidney, 128)

Advanced communications between betting shops and racecourses have made the knock-out more difficult to operate, but it still occurs.

knuckle   Not only the bones at one's finger-joints, but the end of any bone at a joint 'which forms a more or less rounded protuberance when the joint is bent' is a *knuckle*; and on quadrupeds it is 'the projection of the carpal or tarsal joint'. As a verb, *knuckle over* describes a condition in horses brought about by overwork, when the fetlock joints protrude. Another name for this condition is *grogginess*, but this is hardly a problem in *thoroughbred* horses. Instead, *knuckle* and *knuckle over* describe a kind of fall in *chasing*, when the horse jumps the fence but cannot keep its feet on landing and goes down on its knuckles.

ad, lass A *lad* is, to quote the OED, 'a stable groom of any age; also a female one' – but *lass* is still in common use. In this sense *lad* is first attested in 1848. One of the lad's jobs at the racecourse is to lead a horse around the parade ring, so that the OED's speculation that the word is derived from a form of the verb *lead* makes its racing usage coincidentally apposite. The *head lad* will certainly not be a youngster: he or she is responsible for the general efficient running of the stable. 'I started as a stable lad and then went from travelling lad to head lad to trainer' (*Sporting Life* 21 September 1990).

lady *Lady jockey* or *woman rider*? The phenomenon seems new enough for no one to be sure what to call it; but in 1805 Mrs Thornton, on Louisa, beat the great Frank Buckle by half a neck in a two-mile race at York, getting four stone: 'she rode side saddle, in purple jacket and cap, nankeen skirt, purple shoes and embroidered stockings' (Prior, 180).

land From *land* in the sense 'to bring into a specified place', there developed the racing phrase of *landing a winner*. The OED's first example is from 1853: 'St Agatha...after one of the finest races on record, is landed a winner by a neck.' Later the phrase was shortened to *land* on its own, as in the *Licensed Victualler's Gazette*, in 1891: 'Had the French filly landed what a shout would have arisen from the ring!' The word is also used in betting as a development of its angling sense: to *land a bet* is to make a fair sum from a wager. For *land the odds* see **odds**.

lark *Lark*, as in the phrase 'lark around', seems to be derived from *lake*, 'to play, sport'. The OED suggests that it might be 'lake' as heard 'by sporting men from Yorkshire, jockeys or grooms'. Its original senses were 'to play tricks, frolic; to ride in a frolicsome manner' (1813), with later senses including 'to ride a horse across country' and 'to clear a fence with a flying leap' (1834).

lasix A trade name for furosemide. Like *bute*, *lasix* is a prohibited drug in Europe and some American states, but in other states is used to prevent the breaking of blood vessels. This is a supposed side-effect of the drug, whose main purpose is to act as a diuretic.

lass See *lad*.

lather See *soaping*.

lay¹, layer Bookmakers *lay a bet*, hence are often called *layers*.

That *lay* should now be used in this sense draws attention to the fact that a bookmaker is engaged in wagering as much as is the punter who backs with him, for *lay* had long meant simply 'to wager, bet'. So common was this sense that it could be used on its own in this meaning: the first printed English Bible, by Miles Coverdale (1535), has Isaiah saying 'Yet dare I lay that thou shalt be brought downe to the depe of hell.' In the Rules and Orders for Cockfighting (1743) *lay* is used as a noun: 'If any Man have made a *Lay or Bett*, and cannot tell, or call to mind, with whom he betted such a *lay*...' The origin of this sense probably lies in the idea of laying one's money down to make the bet: a *lay down* (or *laydown*) is a certainty: one only has to lay the money down to *collect*[2].

The distinction between a *layer* and a *backer*, given that both are betting on the race, is that the layer bets that the horse will not win, the backer that it will. If there are twenty horses in the race, the layer will be right nineteen times and wrong once: the backer who backs only one horse may be completely right, but has nineteen chances of being wrong.

To *lay off* a bet describes the bookmaker's practice – in existence for many years before the OED's first attestation in 1951 – of insuring against a large loss by placing a bet on the horse in question with another bookmaker.

lay[2] For phrases such as *lay up with*, *lay off*, *lay out of*, describing a horse's position during the running of a race, see *lie*.

lay out See *handicap*.

lead (adj. and noun) Lead weights, inserted in a *weight-cloth* under the saddle, are used to bring the total weight of jockey, saddle, and equipment, up to the amount the horse is supposed to carry in a race. Since this is a dead weight, it is not wise to back a horse which is high in the handicap and ridden by a lightweight jockey because it is carrying *too much lead*. 'I didn't want Creeager to be ridden by a lightweight apprentice carrying a lot of lead' (*Sporting Life* 7 June 1990).

lead (verb) A horse *leads* with whichever leg hits out forward while the other three legs are in support. When it changes its *leading leg*, then it *changes* legs.

lead in, lead up Stable lads *lead up* a horse when they take it into and around the *paddock* before a race; and *lead in* a horse when it has won or been placed.

lead-in A rail which directs a horse towards a fence.

lean *Leaning* is a form of interference in which one horse presses against another, forcing him out of his *ground*. In 1729 the articles for a race in County Durham included a warning of disqualification 'if any Rider shall lean, or rest, on any other Horse, etc., so as to force him, or her, out of the way' (Prior, 104). 'The Brighton camber came into play and Thin Red Line leaned over on to the weakening First Avenue, who in turn shifted Macconachie to tighten up Rathvinden House' (*Sporting Life* 3 October 1990).

leather Specifically the stirrup leather: a *broken leather* is a common cause of *unseating* a rider.

leavings What is left of a horse's *price* after it has been heavily backed. *S.P.* backers are invariably forced to take the *leavings*: e.g. 2/1 about a horse which has been backed down from 5/1.

left A horse which does not start with the field is *left at the start*, frequently shortened to *left*. Another use of the word is to describe the improvement in a horse's position when another runner falls or otherwise exits from a race: if the second horse falls, then the one behind it is 'left second'; if two horses are vying for the lead, well ahead of the rest of the field, then the survivor is 'left clear': 'Miss Club Royal: made all, left well clear two out' (*Racing Post* 29 May 1990).

left-hand On a *left-hand* course horses run in an anti-clockwise direction; e.g. Epsom, Cheltenham.

leg¹ The weakest part of a racehorse is its leg, hence phrases like *have a leg*, or *get a leg*, to describe an injury which prevents it from racing: 'Only last autumn his career again hung in the balance when he developed a touch of a leg' (*Sporting Life* 6 July 1990). A horse which is *on the leg* is one which is too long in the leg, otherwise known as 'showing too much daylight'. To *own a leg* in a horse means that one has part ownership of it: Partridge traces this expression back to 1865.

leg² In the nineteenth century *leg* was a frequently shortened form of *blackleg*: 'That's the beauty of the turf. The lord and the leg are reduced to an equality' (Surtees, 90). This example of its usage comes from Richard *Tattersall*'s evidence before a Parliamentary Special Committee on the Gaming Laws in 1844:

Richard T. These men go to a race and bet large sums of money against a horse, as if he was dead, perhaps £10,000 through their agents and themselves, and they cannot pay a hundredth part of it, and if the horse wins they bolt, and if he loses they receive the money; there are instances of men coming to our house and receiving money they have won, and the moment any one comes in that they owe anything to they bolt.

Mr Escott Are those men in the station of gentlemen?

Richard T. No; legs. (Orchard, 291)

Charles Sidney's account of the rise and practice of modern bookmaking is titled *The Art of Legging*. He traces the rise of the *leg* and his development towards what we would recognise as a book-maker, beginning early in the nineteenth century:

> All those who wanted a bet would ride or draw their carriages up to... the 'Betting Post'. The Legs were always there ready and waiting for the owners, noblemen and any who fancied a bet and all joined in the screaming melee. Even though the gentry bet among themselves they still came to the Post for that extra something that racecourse betting offered. The Legs were countenanced, even those whose settlement was doubtful, because, sometimes, their prices were too good to be missed ... As certain Legs came with regularity to the Post so did they acquire a reputation for honest dealings, or at least settlement if not quite dealings. (Sidney, 24)

legitimate   Flat racing, as opposed to *steeplechasing* (Partridge, 1888): so called because, in contrast to jumping, Flat races came under *Jockey Club* rules. Cp. *illegitimate*.

length   The basic unit of measurement by which *distances*[2] between horses are calculated: first attested in Butler's *Hudibras* (1664), in which the gallant knight 'left danger, fears and foes behind, / And beat, at least three lengths, the wind.'

lengthen[1]   The sign of a good horse is that it *lengthens its stride* when asked for an effort. 'Do not try and hit the horse at each beat of his gallop, or you will find him shortening his stride instead of lengthening it, which will make him slow up instead of go faster' (Hislop, 129).

lengthen[2]   In betting, a horse's odds *lengthen* when the *price* goes out: e.g. from 2/1 to 3/1.

let down, let out   A jockey *lets down* his horse in the final stages of a race when *asking* it for its final effort. The expression can be used reflexively, too, to describe the horse's willingness to stride out: 'The ground is perfect. That is what Moniga wants. She won't let herself down otherwise' (*Sporting Life* 16 June 1990). This sense is not in the OED, but it does record two others: 'to be broken down' – 1737, 'When a Horse... is quite let down (as the Jockeys call it) the Tendon is quite broken'; and 'to be "deep" in the girth' – 1737, 'He was a Round barrell'd Horse, and did not look much let down in the Girth.' *Let out*, meaning 'to give a horse his head', is first attested in 1885.

level   Another term for *Flat* racing, often used in contrast to jumping: 'Smoggy Spray is a smart performer on the level... but lacks an outing over hurdles' (*Sporting Life* 20 September 1990).

levels   *Even-money*: 'levels you devils', as it is affectionately known.

leviathan   'A heavy backer of horses' (Partridge). The word's origin is Biblical, from the Hebrew word for a sea-monster (described in Job 40). It first appears in English in the Wyclif Bible (1382), and is used to mean 'a man of vast and formidable power, or enormous wealth' from 1607. Under this definition the OED includes this example, from *Punch* in 1884: 'Punters, plungers, leviathans, little men'. But the word's use in a racing sense goes back at least another forty years, probably originating with 'Mr William Davies...soon to be known as 'Leviathan Davies' – the undisputed leader of the Ring from 1844 onwards' (Sidney, 48). Just how monstrous this leviathan was may be measured by the famous account of his having laid Lord Enfield '£12,000 to £1,000 against The Cur for the Cesarewich...Next morning he walked into the Ring and handed his lucky lordship twelve crisp "long-uns" before he had taken a penny himself' (Sidney, 50).

lick   Meaning speed, in such phrases as *at full lick*, *a great lick*: it originates in the racing sense of the word, 'a spurt; a short, brisk spin'. The OED's first attestation is from 1837, first found in American and Australian slang.

lie   Used with various prepositions to describe a horse's position in a race. It may *lie up* with the leaders, or the *pace* – meaning that it keeps within a length or two of the leading horse; it may *lie off* the pace – meaning that it keeps further back in the field; or it may *lie out of its ground* – see **ground**. In all such cases it is common to find *lay* used instead of *lie*. *Lie off*, on its own, means to ride a *waiting* race (first attested in 1898). A horse *lies on* another when it *interferes* with it in a race, a lesser form of *bumping and boring*.

life-boat, life-saver   See *neck-strap*.

lifter   Stable slang for a horse which kicks.

light[1]   A horse which is *light in the mouth* is fairly sensitive to the bit. The OED quotes a comparable usage, from 1727, '*Light upon the hand* is said of a horse that has a good tractable mouth and does not rest too heavy upon the bit.'

light[2]   When a horse *runs up light* it has no spare flesh, not necessarily a good sign:

> The condition of Lord Derby's Canezou, when she ran second, after a desperate race...for the St Leger of 1848, left nothing to be desired on the score of bigness. The fact is that, trained light, Canezou could not beat a hack. (Badminton, 208)

limit   Each bookmaker has his own set of rules, including the *limit* he will pay out on each bet. Such limits are not related to stakes: e.g. a limit of £100,000 will apply whether the bet in question was £5,000 on a horse which started at 25/1 – the backer only getting, in effect odds of 20/1 – or £1 on a six-horse *accumulator*.

There may be special limits imposed on across the *card* bets because the bookmaker will not have time to *lay off* the bet.

line¹ Horses *come off a line* when they fail to keep straight in a race: 'Peter Easterby's luckless five-year-old, who appeared to be carried off a true line by the winner' (*Sporting Life* 5 September 1990). The original use of *line* in this sense was in hunting: the OED quotes, from 1836, 'Nothing is so unsportsmanlike or so dangerous as to cross a man at a leap; every one should keep his own line, and if a man when he gets close to it fears the fence before him, he should pull up.' Squire Osbaldeston, describing the preparations for a match which took place in 1826, remembers Mr Holyoake, the owner of one of the horses, training his jockey Captain Ross:

> He had a great deal of money on his favourite, and for fear the captain might miss the line he made him ride over it three or four times a week for five or six weeks before the match came off. (Osbaldeston, 54)

line² At the start of a jump race, or a Flat race in which *stalls* are not used, horses are required to *form a line* or *line up*.

line³ The *line* is the line of bookmakers on a racecourse: 'I have been up and down the line, and not seen a better price than 6/4.'

line⁴ A *form line*, usually shortened to *line*, is a way of comparing one horse's *form* with another's. If Supersub beats Cucumber by two lengths at level weights, and Cucumber beats Lilypond by a length at level weights in another race, then the form line suggests that Supersub is three lengths better than Lilypond, commonly expressed like this: 'On a line through Cucumber, Supersub should beat Lilypond.'

list The list of runners on a bookmaker's board looks innocuous enough, but it has a chequered history. In the nineteenth century *lists*, written or printed documents with the names of horses engaged in particular races, and appropriate odds against each name, were open to view in hotels, inns, and other public places: an estimated thousand in London alone. *List betting* was held to be a principal cause of the nation's moral decline. The OED quotes, from 1902: 'Most of the "list-houses" (in Long Acre and elsewhere), whose name was legion, had their shutters up on the morning after Lord Zetland's horse had defeated Pitsford.'

Leviathan Davies probably began the posting of lists:

> He extended the idea of paid-on bets to off-course Betting for, as well as his appearances at the Races and at The Corner, Mr Davies had lists posted in at least two establishments. He would lay the odds from half a sovereign to half a plum (50p to £50,000) and tickets were issued on receipt of ready money

from the punter; payment to winners being made on the day following the race... Tickets were only issued for bets of £1 upwards and such was the confidence of the public in this bookie that his list department took upwards of £300,000 a year from small punters who invested between half a sovereign and five pounds. (Sidney, 49)

List sellers act for the list printers: they walk along the *line*[3] before the races begin, selling their lists to the bookmakers. It was competition between them which supposedly led to the race gang-wars which Graham Greene featured in *Brighton Rock*.

listed   On the Flat, a *listed race* is the second best type of race, inferior only to a group race (see *pattern*): usually a *conditions* race, not a *handicap*. In *chasing*, a listed race was, until 1990, the third best type of race, after *championship* and *feature* races: many of these are handicaps.

live   A *live* horse is one which the stable expects to win – the opposite of *dead meat*: 'As for laying "live" horses, that has been, and continues to be, the perennial whinge of bookies down the ages who believe they somehow have a divine right to win' (*Racing Post* 9 December 1989).

livery   In a sense, nearly all horses in training are *at livery*: 'kept for the owner, and fed and groomed at a fixed charge' (first attested, 1440). The origin is Anglo-French *liveree*, connected with *deliver*.

long   Jockeys ride *long* when they ride with long stirrup leathers.

long shot   See *shot*.

Long Tom   A long hunting whip, used to encourage reluctant horses to start on the *gallops*, or, sometimes, the racecourse. The *starter* is not allowed to touch the horse with this whip. The OED records five distinct meanings for *Long Tom*, but not this one.

long 'un   £1,000, particularly a £1,000 note: see the quotation under *leviathan*.

look about, look around   A horse which goes to the front in a race and then loses concentration, *looking about*, is running *green*. *Looking around*, similarly, is often a sign of greenness in jockeys.

look after   Some *ungenuine* horses are said to *look after* themselves in races, meaning either that they avoid undue exertion or that they keep out of the way of other horses.

loose   *Running loose* is stable slang for a horse which has no confidence behind it and which the stable has not backed. *Turned loose* was nineteenth-century slang for a horse which had been very leniently *handicapped*.

loose box   *Loose* was used to describe a stable in which animals were kept free of restraint: the OED records, from 1813, the term *loose stable*. *Loose box*, to describe a large walled area within a stable, giving the horse more freedom than a *stall*, is first attested in Thackeray's *Pendennis* (1849). One great advantage of a loose box is that there is very little chance of the horse's getting *cast* in it.

loose-schooling   See *school*.

lot   Horses go out to the *gallops²* from their stables each morning in *lots*: *first lot* goes out often at the crack of dawn, *second lot* at something approaching a civilised hour. 'I ride out two lots a day, some times three – and I ride a lot of work' (*Sporting Life* 24 May 1990). Not in the OED.

lumber   'Superfluous fat in horses': perhaps derived from the verb *lumber*, 'to move in a clumsy or blundering manner'. The OED quotes, from 1891, 'Sir Tatton seldom praised a horse without adding "there is no lumber about him."'

lump   In common use on the racecourse, to *lump* money on a horse is to bet a large amount on it. The OED gives a sense for the verb, 'to lay the whole (of a particular sum of money) on a single object', with its first attestation, from 1864: 'He lumped it all upon an outsider, and backed him to win the Chester Cup.'

Machine   The *machine* is slang for the *Tote*. The OED identifies this as originally a New Zealand expression, its first attestation, from 1889, being 'What a lot [of money] you left behind in the "machine".' Its popularity today probably derives from the impression it gives of the Tote's impersonality, in contrast with the all too obvious personalities of the bookmakers in the *ring*.

maiden   A horse which has never won a race: probably from the idea that such a horse is a virgin, not having consummated its racing career by winning a race. Its first attestation is in 1760, in the conditions of a race: 'All Maiden Horses favoured 2lbs.' *Maiden races*, usually shortened to *maidens*, are designed to give such horses a winning opportunity and are, normally, the first step in a good horse's career: 'That was a good run by Toller's colt and he duly won a maiden at Newbury next time' (*Sporting Life* 16 June 1990). The word's use in cricket (a maiden over) is not recorded until the middle of the nineteenth century.

major-stevens   Rhyming slang for *evens* (Partridge, 20th C.).

make   Short for *make the running*: if a horse *makes all*, it leads the whole way. 'Choice Challenge: made all, quickened four out, comfortably' (*Sporting Life* 18 October 1990).

make up   Describes a horse's development: 'Dazzle did little at two but has the scope to make up into a good three-year-old.' The OED records a sense of *make up* which anticipates this modern usage, that is 'to get (a horse, etc.) into good condition', quoting, from 1794, 'He thoroughly understands (what is termed by dealers) *making up a horse*.'

manage   When we talk of the way a jockey *manages* his horse in a race we are in contact with the earliest uses of this word in English: it meant originally 'to handle, train, or direct a horse in his paces' (1561), with a common noun, the *manage* – now usually spelt *manège* – meaning 'the training, handling and directing' of a horse: 'Speak terms of manage to thy bounding steed' (*1 Henry IV*, 2:3:52). The source is the Italian *maneggiare*, 'to handle or train horses'. The word ultimately goes back to the Latin *manus*, 'hand', so cp. *handle*.

mark¹   Each horse has a *handicap mark*, expressed now as a figure from 0-140, constantly updated according to its *form*. A horse with a mark of 100 will have to give ten pounds to one with a mark of 90 in a handicap race. 'Owner Peter Savill is to sell off most of his team of forty horses in a gesture of protest over their handicap marks' (*Racing Post* 20 September 1990).

mark[2]   To *mark* someone's *card*, now in general use, comes from the practice, common on racecourses, of giving tips: the card is the racecard. Partridge dates the usage from 1945, as barrow boys' slang.

market   A general term to describe the betting on a race. A *weak market* is one in which little money is being wagered, a *strong market* one in which there is a lot of money, with several horses being heavily backed. The OED's first attestation of the word's use in this sense is from 1886. For the history of the connection between commodity markets and the betting market, see the quotation under *ring*; the following account, too, shows how, just as in all other markets, one's perception of the strength or weakness of the betting market depends upon one's viewpoint. The scene is a racecourse well over a hundred years ago, but the bookmakers' gloomy perception of what is going on is instantly recognisable:

> On arriving at the rails which separate the private stands' enclosure from the ring, he finds the market well set. Romanus is firmly established first favourite at evens; the public fancy him, and despite his seven-pound penalty the public will not be stalled off.
>
> The watchword of the day is "Charley Wood, good business", and the mashers are plunging on him. Paul Pry is second in demand, his weight, his public and (reputed) private form, and the fact of his being Archer's mount, naturally placing him in that position. Three to one is offered against Ambrosia, hundreds to thirty, in some instances four to one, against Osmunda, five to one Amulet, and the others are at prices ranging from ten to twenty to one; quotations which the bookmakers unblushingly assert represent the worst betting-race that ever was known.
>
> "A man can't get round nohow, and there's no money in the market for the favourite neither." (Badminton, 85)

A *market leader* is the *favourite*. *Market-horse* describes 'a horse kept on the lists simply for the betting' (Partridge), a nineteenth-century practice whereby punters were induced to bet on horses which would never run in the race. The verb commonly used with *market* is 'form': when a horse is withdrawn just before a race, bookmakers will try to *form a new market*.

martingale   A strap, or arrangement of straps, connecting the noseband, bit, or reins to the girth. Its purpose is to prevent a horse from rearing or throwing back its head. It was supposed to have been invented by Evangelista, an Italian riding-master, and comes into English from French; but the word's ultimate origins are unknown. The first attestation is from 1589: 'Thou shalt be broken as Prosper broke his horse, with a muzroule, portmouth, and a martingale' – a *muzroule* is the nose-band of a bridle (better known as a *musrol*); a *portmouth* is a *port-bit*, a bridle-bit with an arch-shaped mouthpiece.

match From Old English *gemaecca*, related to *make*, 'an equal, peer, match', *match* originally meant 'one of an associated pair', e.g. a husband or wife, or 'one's equal in age, rank, station, etc.' In the fourteenth century the sense developed of 'a matching of adversaries against each other'. In racing, a *match* is a two-horse race, either because the field has been reduced to two runners by withdrawals, or, less common today, because one owner challenges another. The latter practice was the origin of modern horse-racing. In 1728 'a considerable number of matches were made at Newmarket, the invariable distance being four miles, the weights usually ranging between eight and nine stone, and the stake 200 guineas, half forfeit' (Prior, 104). The OED's first horse-racing example is from 1676, but it is possible to find earlier ones. In *Hyde Park* (1632) a character boasts:

I would lay the world upon my mare, she shall
Run with the devil for an hundred pieces,
Make the match who will. (4:2)

meant *Meant* and *not meant* mean, respectively, meant to win and not meant to win: if a horse is not meant, then no one in the stable is backing it.

meet The verb is used to describe the way a horse encounters a *fence* or *hurdle*: he *meets* it well or badly or all wrong. This usage is close to the sense of 'meet' as in one road meeting another, but this sense is confined, in the OED's words, to 'inanimate things' which 'come into contact, association, or junction with (something or someone running in a different course)'. An older use of the verb, to mean 'to come or light upon, come across, fall in with, find', now generally superseded by *meet with*, is the basis of this usage.

meeting 'A gathering or assembly of a number of people for purposes of intercourse, entertainment, discussion, legislation, and the like': in this sense the word is first attested in 1513; *race-meeting* in 1809, but *meeting* on its own in 1764: 'Westminster races... Spring meeting.'

members The *members* – or, more strictly, *members'* – is the *enclosure* reserved for members of the racecourse *club* – either those who pay an annual subscription or those who buy a daily membership. Standards of dress are often more rigorous in the members', and it is the one enclosure where bookmakers are barred from betting: see *rail*.

metallician Nineteenth-century slang for a bookmaker (Partridge, 1870): so named after their practice of using metal pencils and books. Cp. *pencil*.

miler A horse whose specialised distance is one mile on the Flat.

milk The verb developed connotations of financial exploitation in the sixteenth century, when the idea of 'milking' people of their money is first recorded. In nineteenth-century racing slang, *milk* came to mean, to quote the *Times* in 1862, 'keeping a horse a favourite at short odds for a race in which he has no chance whatever, only to lay odds against him.' The idea is that by keeping such a horse in the race, backers in the know will be able to get decent *prices* about the other runners. A *milk-horse* was 'a horse entered at a race to make money on, and always scratched before the affair comes off' (Partridge, 1865).

miss In *chasing*, a horse *misses*, or *misses out*, a fence when it gets in too close and has to *fiddle* it: 'Desert Orchid rounded off the season with another bold display of jumping apart from completely missing out the last when carrying top weight of 12 stone to a 12 length success in the...Irish Grand National' (*Sporting Life* 5 June 1990). In some respects *miss* is being used here in the sense of 'miss its stride at'. This usage is not recorded as a special sense by the OED.

mistake A chasing term. Like a *blunder*, a *mistake* is an error in jumping, but not necessarily one which causes a fall or even an unseated rider. 'Bishopric closed up two fences out and, with Timber Tool making a mistake at the last, it looked for a moment as if Bishopric was going to make a real race of it' (*Sporting Life* 22 May 1990).

moderate The most common epithet in racing, and virtually a euphemism: *moderate* means poor and slow. Most horses in training are what their trainers would call moderate animals; *all-weather* racing is specifically aimed at moderate horses. Steve Donoghue's words on such horses still ring true:

> There are many owners and trainers – especially the former – who cannot see, and do not want to be told, when their horses are moderate, or really bad. It would be imagined that they would prefer to know the truth, and to be in a position to decide to get rid of a bad horse. But no, some people would go on till an animal nearly 'broke' them rather than listen to the disinterested advice an experienced jockey would willingly give them. (Donoghue, 74)

money *The money's down* describes the stable's serious betting on a race which they expect their horse to win: 'so confident was Harrison of success that he says he was completely calm, despite the fact that the money was down in a big way' (*Sporting Life* 4 July 1990). *In the money*, first attested in 1902, means that a horse has finished in one of the prize-money places. To have a *run for one's money* is a phrase which originated in racing slang, first attested in 1874, and probably referring originally to the danger of having a horse scratched, so that those who have wagered on it lose their money without even seeing it race. Today, on the racecourse, it usually describes a horse which one has backed and which has been prominent in the race without winning it.

monkey[1] £500: first attested in 1856. Possibly derived from the Indian 500 rupee note, which had a monkey on its back. This slang sense has spread from the racecourse to the general language of wheeling and dealing. 'Terrhars landed a touch – a bet of 20 monkeys was registered' (*Sporting Life* 9 June 1990).

monkey[2] A mischievous horse: the sense is a little more playful, and much more affectionate, than *dog*.

moon *Moon-eye* (1607), a translation of the Latin *oculus lunaticus*, describes intermittent blindness in a horse, supposedly under the moon's influence: *moon-blind* (1668) describes the same affliction.

moral Short for *moral certainty*, describing a horse which a tipster or tout claims is certain to win: the OED quotes, from 1887, ' "Why Joe", I said, "it's a moral, if the horse is ridden fair".' The phrase 'moral certainty' is a term in logic, meaning, among other things, 'a degree of probability so great as to admit of no reasonable doubt'. The traditional racing associations of the word *certainty* probably encouraged the playful extension of this term to the sport.

morning A *morning horse* is one which fails to reproduce on the racecourse the *form* it shows on the morning *gallops*: sometimes known as a *morning-glory*. The OED has no entry for 'morning horse', but it defines 'morning-glory' as 'something which fails to maintain its early achievements; esp. in sporting contexts': first attested in 1904 as American slang, with this example from 1935: '*Morning glory*, race horse that works in fast time in the morning but fails to race well.'

mouth, mouthed To *mouth* a horse is to 'accustom it to the use of the bit' (1553). 'They are properly mouthed and driven in long reins... before they leave us' (*Sporting Life* 20 September 1990). Compounds like *hard-mouthed* and *soft-mouthed* describe a horse's sensitivity to the bit. As early as 1593, Gervase Markham writes of the 'gentle-mouthed' horse which, accordingly, requires a bit which exerts very little pressure on the mouth. In contrast, a hard-mouthed horse is difficult to control, whatever bit is used: 'He was on a hard-mouthed, awkward brute of a horse, that first behaved very badly at the tapes, and then all of a sudden decided to bolt with Smirke, and dashed off round the turn . . .' (Donoghue, 187).

move, mover   Horses are frequently described as good or bad *movers*: the word describes their *action*, particularly in their slow *paces*. 'Moved well' going down to the start, describes a horse not inconvenienced by the *going*: 'moved badly' indicates either that the horse's action is inconvenienced by the going or that there is something *amiss* with it. 'Henry Cecil's Chimes of Freedom moved nicely in company with Shavian and Dissonant on the Long Hill watered gallop yesterday morning' (*Sporting Life* 6 September 1990).

muck out   To *muck out* – to free the stables from muck – is one of the *lad*'s daily duties. Originally the verb *muck* alone was used: the OED quotes, from 1641, 'they fell to muckinge of the stables.'

muddler, muddling   Partridge records *muddler* as nineteenth-century racing slang for 'a clumsy horse'. More common now is the expression *muddling pace*, normally to describe a slow-run race, although it may also describe one run in *snatches*. 'It was a muddling race today. She would have preferred a stronger pace' (*Sporting Life* 5 June 1990).

mudlark   First recorded in 1796 as a description of gents who were 'accustomed to prowl about, at low water, under the quarter of West Indian ships'. Pretending to look in the mud for old ropes and iron, they were actually engaged in smuggling contraband cargo from the boats. The word broadened its sense to describe anyone or any animal which enjoyed playing in the mud and came into racing, via Australian slang, to describe a horse which prefers heavy *going* (Partridge, 20th C.). The OED records *mudder* as American slang for the same kind of horse, its first attestation coming from 1903: '"It's a mudder", he growled, "and the track today will be like lightning."'

mug   *Mug's game* is a popular description of betting on horses. One nineteenth-century sense of *mug* was a card-sharper's dupe: 'At pretty little Lingfield one sunny afternoon, Ramsbottom and partner had got a mug in tow' (*A Pink 'Un*, 191). *Mug-punter* has become a common term of mild contempt: the OED quotes, from Edgar Wallace (1922), 'The mug punter was he who dreamed of long-priced winners and refused to bet on the six to four certainty, preferring rather the hopeless proposition that started at twenty to one.' In 1990 an alternative racing magazine was titled *Mug Punter*. See *steamer*.

mulish   A horse is *mulish* when it behaves obstinately – like a mule – especially at the start if it refuses to go into the *stalls*. 'Commandante ran mulishly at Ascot after winning the Arkle and, even now, I don't know why' (*Sporting Life* 13 September 1990).

multiple bet   Describes a bet in which more than one horse is backed, in different races. *Multiple bets* take many exotic forms, each with its own name. The simplest examples are: a *double*, in which two horses are backed, the winnings (plus stake) from one all going on to the other; a *treble* does the same with three horses; an *accumulator* with four or more. A *trixie* involves three selections, in three doubles and a treble (= four bets); a *patent* is a trixie plus three single bets on the three horses named (= seven bets); a *yankee* involves four selections in eleven bets – six doubles, four trebles, and an accumulator; a *canadian* – or *super yankee* – involves five selections in twenty-six bets – ten doubles, ten trebles, five four-horse accumulators, and one five-horse accumulator; a *heinz* involves six selections in fifty-seven bets – doubles, trebles, four, five, and six-horse accumulators; a *super-heinz* involves seven selections in one hundred and twenty such bets; a *goliath* eight selections in two hundred and forty-seven bets. Of these names, *heinz* is derived from the number of bets being the same as that company's much vaunted fifty-seven varieties; a *yankee* may be derived from the idea of a 'yankee tournament', one in which everyone plays everyone else: in parallel fashion the yankee is the first of the multiple bets in which every horse is doubled, trebled and put in an accumulator with every other horse in the bet; the *canadian* probably derives its name from its being one selection more than a yankee, as Canada is just above the USA; *goliath* is obviously named after the huge size, massive optimism, and certain failure of the bet.

   All such multiple bets as doubles and trebles are based on a formula by which all of the returns from one horse are staked on the next. So, a £1 treble on three horses, starting at 2/1, 3/1, and 4/1, yields a return of £60 – £3 from the first, yielding £12 from the second: £12 at 4/1 returns £60. It was not always so: the first multiple bets offered by bookmakers were called *combination bets*, and they were worked out on a meaner basis, by a simple multiplication of the odds. The treble above would pay, in a combination bet, only £25 – 2 x 3 x 4 plus the £1 staked.

mush   A slang contraction of *mushroom*, the large umbrella with which bookmakers cover their *joints* when it is raining, thereby keeping their money dry and preventing spectators from seeing the race.

musical   See *roar*.

N **ag** Used entirely negatively on the racecourse to describe any horse which one backs and which does not win. The word's origin is obscure: its first attestation, in the sense of 'a small riding horse, or pony', is from *c*.1400.

nail *Nailed on* describes a horse which seems to be a certainty: 'She was a fast-finishing runner-up to Land Sun and looks nailed on for a plating event in the near future' (*Sporting Life* 15 July 1990). The idea behind this usage may be of the horse's number being firmly fixed to the *frame*. Whatever its origin, it recalls other racing usages: *nailer*, in the nineteenth century, an American term for a fast horse; and *nailing*, a slang term to denote excellence – Partridge quotes, from 1894, 'a nailing good horse', and the OED, from 1884, 'What a nailing good fencer to be sure.'

name Nowadays racehorses have to be named. In the past they were allowed to run without a name, known simply as their *dam*'s colt or filly. In 1913 the *Jockey Club* ruled that no horse of three years and upward could run unnamed, and extended this rule to two-year-olds in 1946. There are plenty of odd names on record: Lord Glasgow, who hated the idea of giving names to his horses, had three registered at Weatherbys as He-has-a-name, Give-him-a-name, and He-isn't-worth-a-name. Probably the oddest name of all, on paper at least, was held by a very successful horse of the 1770s. It was called Potooooooooo, supposedly from the stable lad's spelling of the name – in its later years it was known as Pot8o's (see *pot*). Under a Jockey Club ruling, no horse today can bear a name with more than eighteen letter-spaces, hence the fashion for 'one word' compounds like Thethingaboutitis. Horses may bear the same name if coming from different countries, in which case they will be distinguished by one having the country of its foaling in parentheses after its name. In Britain *thoroughbreds* can only be given the same name as another on the following basis: broodmares, fifteen years after death or after being put out of stud; stallions, twenty-five years after death or after being put out of stud; other horses, ten years after death. If no death is reported, then the gaps are thirty-five, forty-five, and twenty-five years, respectively, after their birth. The most often repeated name, according to Weatherbys, is Dunkirk.

nanny Short for *nanny-goat*, rhyming slang for the *Tote*: popular usage in the days when service at tote windows was notoriously slow and inefficient. A less common name was *canal boat*.

nap   From the card game *napoleon*, in which to 'go nap' is to succeed in winning all five tricks. First attested in a racing sense in 1884, meaning 'to stake all one can': 'Look here, you go nap – now hear that? nap! – on Royal Angus.' Today the word's use is largely restricted to newspaper tipsters, their *nap* being their best selection of the day: i.e. the one they recommend their readers to bet on most heavily. The word's survival is guaranteed by its brevity, making it ideal for headlines on the racing pages, as in 'Go Nap on Snorer'.

nappy   Describes a bad-tempered horse which refuses to obey the *aids*: possibly derived from the use of *nappy* to mean strong beer and, by transference, a state of intoxication. The OED's first example with reference to horses is as late as 1924, but Partridge, who dates it from 1860, quotes an 1880 definition of the word as describing 'a horse that refuses to answer to the hand or leg, tries to go the way home instead of the way you want, or plays other tricks... It is very common speech with all who own horses.' He derives it from the expression 'nab the rust', meaning 'to take offence', and used, from the late eighteenth century, to mean 'of a horse, to become restless'. Cp. *jib*.

narrow   *Narrow behind* describes a horse which is weak-muscled around the thighs so that it appears narrow when viewed from the rear.

National Hunt   *Hurdling* and *steeplechasing* are generally known as *National Hunt* racing. The *National Hunt Committee* is responsible for controlling all forms of horse-racing, including *point-to-point* meetings, which are not under the direct administration of the *Jockey Club*. The Committee's title is first recorded in Weatherbys Calendar for 1866.

National Stud   The *National Stud*, now at Newmarket, was established in 1916 in Co. Kildare, Ireland. Its original purpose was to help maintain the supremacy of the British *thoroughbred*; now, less ambitiously, it makes good stallions available to British breeders.

near   As with motor vehicles, a horse's *near* side is its left side. The first attestation of this usage is with reference to horses, in 1559, 'A filly... with a white nere foote behinde.' The sense comes from the idea that this is the side of the horse by which a jockey mounts. The word is used in all contexts except to describe the reins. Cp. *off[1]*.

neck   A *neck* is the third shortest winning *distance[2]*, after short-head and head. It is first attested, as slang, by Jon Bee in 1823. 'There was a desperate finish to the Hailsham Handicap with four necks separating the first five home' (*Sporting Life*, 5 September 1990). *Neck and neck* is first attested by the OED in 1837, but this is antedated by five or six years in Jorrocks's vision of Polly Hopkins and Talleyrand as they 'rush neck-and-neck along the cords and pass the judge's box' (Surtees, 88). Partridge quotes W.S. Landor writing to Robert Browning in 1860: 'You and your incomparable wife are running neck and neck, as sportsmen say.' *Neck or nothing*, meaning 'desperately', is found as early as 1675, and may be, in Partridge's words, 'either a hanging or steeplechasing phrase' – in 1860 Hotten confidently described it as a racing phrase.

neck-strap A thin leather strap around the horse's neck, not attached to any other piece of equipment or tackle. If the horse suddenly rears, the jockey can grab hold of it without pulling on the reins, hence its popular names, *life-boat* or *life-saver*.

net Betting slang for ten: back-slang. Cp. *rouf*; *cockle*.

net-muzzle A covering for the horse's mouth, made of netting. Outside racing *net-muzzles* are normally worn to stop horses from biting passers-by; their use on the racecourse is generally to help control a *free-runner*.

nettle A common enough verb now, meaning 'to annoy, irritate', but in earlier days it had a quite literal sense where horses were concerned. This is Gervase Markham's advice, from 1614, on how to put a mare in the right mood to receive a stallion: after giving her a drink of clarified honey and new milk mixed together, 'then with a brush of nettles all to-nettle her privy parts and then immediately offer her to the Horse'.

nick To *nick in*, common slang now, originates in its nineteenth-century racing usage, meaning 'to cut in', as in the OED's quotation from 1898: 'That beautiful filly... was lucky enough to nick in on the inside when the leaders ran out at the bend.' Another common, related phrase, is *nick past*, when a horse squeezes by another suddenly, specially on the inside. Possible earlier senses of *nick* which led to its use in racing are 'to trick, cheat, defraud' (1595) and 'to steal' (1869).

niggle A common dialect word, of Scandinavian origin, first recorded in English in the sixteenth century. In racing *niggle* is frequently used in its common sense, with *at*: a horse which will not keep up with the pace will have to be *niggled at* by the jockey. This is obviously related to the special riding sense of the word, meaning to move one's hands and reins to make a horse go faster. 'River's Lad: niggled along halfway, no impression from five out' (*Sporting Life* 18 May 1990).

night-eye See *chestnut*.

nip and tuck Neck and neck: the phrase seems to have been originally an Americanism, first attested around the middle of the nineteenth century. The OED's quotation, from W.T. Porter's *Quarter Races in Kentucky* (1847), indicates that there were a number of such phrases, all sounding like some kind of imitation of 'neck and neck': 'It will be like the old bitch and the rabbit, nick and tack every jump...Then we'd have it again nip and chuck.' Barker and Leland's *Dictionary of Slang* (1890) suggests that the origin is an old wrestling term.

nobble In general use now, but originally referring specifically to the tampering with horses to prevent them from winning, or even running in, a race. The OED's first attestation is from 1847. The derivation is unknown, but it may have developed from the verb *nab*, 'to catch' or 'to steal'. That *nobbling* includes other means than doping is borne out by the OED's example from 1868: 'Buccaneer was nobbled, i.e. maimed purposely, before the Two Thousand in which he was engaged.'

nod[1] *On the nod* describes a short-head victory, so close that it literally depends upon which horse has its head lowered when it reaches the line. 'The Michael Roberts ridden Rachel's Dancer snatched victory on the nod from Lassoo' (*Sporting Life* 21 September 1990). See *first*.

nod[2] See *peck*.

noise A horse which makes a *noise* is a *roarer* (Partridge, mid-19th C.).

nomination A *nomination* is the right, usually acquired for a sum of money, to send a *mare* to a particular *stallion*: first attestation 1912.

non-runner See *runner[1]*.

no pace Describes a lack of speed in a race, usually in the early stages. 'He was ready to run but needed the race which was a muddling one. They went no pace' (*Sporting Life* 24 May 1990).

nose In America, *nose* is used as a measure of winning *distance[2]*, equivalent to the British short-head. To bet *on the nose* is to back a horse to win, rather than to be *placed*: first attestation 1951.

noseband The lower band of the bridle, passing over the nose, under the cheeks and above the bit, commonly known as the *cavesson* from the sixteenth to nineteenth centuries; but *noseband* itself is first attested in 1611. A *drop noseband* is attached round the muzzle below the bit, to prevent a horse from opening its mouth and hanging out its tongue. The *Grakle noseband* is a double noseband meant for a horse which keeps throwing its head around, reaching for the bit: Grakle was the 1931 Grand National winner, who wore one. The Grakle is also known as the *cross noseband*.

notebook   Figuratively or literally, the *aide memoire* which every backer carries. 'One for the notebook' is a horse which runs well enough in a race to promise an early success in a future race. 'Quavering, Grey Owl and My Lord were others that made the notebook' (*Sporting Life* 24 May 1990).

novice   Horses in their first or second season over *hurdles* and *fences* are called *novices*: first attested in 1903. A *novice chase* is open to horses which have not won a chase at the start of the current season; a *novice hurdle* is for one which has not won a hurdle race before this season.

nowhere   The OED identifies the racing usage as slang, '*To be nowhere*, is to be badly beaten (in a race, contest, etc); to be hopelessly distanced or out of the running'; its first attestation being, from 1755, 'His powerful deep rate, by which all the horses that ran against him were no-where.' Its most famous racing formulation is the proverbial 'Eclipse first, the rest nowhere'; but the force of Eclipse's superiority can be better registered when one knows that *nowhere* was a technical term, indicating that the horse was officially *distanced*[3] and not, therefore, allowed to compete in any further heats.

> The next triumph of Eclipse was at Ascot, on May 29th in …[1770], and previous to that race O'Kelly had taken odds to an immense amount that he would name all the placed horses in their order. An hour before running this reckless plunger went even further, and betted evens and 6/4 that he would place the horses in their order, and when called upon to declare he used the memorable formula which has since passed into a proverb, "Eclipse first and the rest nowhere." This was literally the case, for in sporting phraseology, a horse that is 'distanced' is 'nowhere', and that was how Eclipse served his antagonists on this occasion." (Thormanby, *Famous*, 15)

number-board   In Flat racing horses are given two numbers, one their number in the race, the other their number in the *draw*[1]. Both are displayed on the *number-board* (the draw number on the right-hand side), where other information, about *going*, withdrawals, jockeys, etc. is posted. Its origins lie in the *scratching-board*, a nineteenth-century method of informing racegoers about which horses had been scratched from races. The phrase 'your number's up', World War One soldiers' slang for being killed, probably derives from the number-board on racecourses.

number-cloth   Each horse in a race has a *number-cloth*, a white linen saddle cloth which must be worn so that the number is clearly visible, and which is included with the jockey's other equipment in reckoning his weight. Number-cloths were introduced at Goodwood in 1840; previously, racegoers were generally ignorant of which horse was which until the jockey was up.

nurse   A jockey *nurses* a horse when he takes every care to make it expend as little energy as possible; a necessary tactic when he suspects that the *trip* is too far for the horse. Peter O'Sullevan reports Paddy Prendegast's comment on Scobie Breasley's riding of the Derby winner Santa Claus, 'if he hadn't nursed him like that he'd never have won' (O'Sullevan, 131). In this sense the usage is a development of the meaning 'to foster, tend, cherish, take care of'; but *nurse* had a nineteenth-century meaning, 'to impede a horse in a race by surrounding it with older and slower ones' (1859), itself a development of the use of the word to describe the way rival omnibuses kept close to others to prevent them from getting a fair share of passengers. Something of this is contained in the modern idea of nursing a horse in a race, which usually involves keeping it well *covered up*, among slower runners, only making use of it at the last possible moment. Revealingly, O'Sullevan's anecdote ends by describing the reaction of the father of the trainer of Santa Claus:

> He was convinced that the winning rider had done everything to get beaten; that quite simply he was 'not off'. Scobie was never invited to ride Santa Claus again or any other horse in the stable.

nursery   Originally slang – first attested in 1882 – but now an official term for a *handicap* for two-year-olds.

nut cracker   A horse which grinds its teeth.

Oaks   The *Oaks* is the fillies' *classic* equivalent to the Derby, run over a mile and a half at Epsom early in June (although fillies are allowed to run in the Derby). First run in 1779, its title came from the name of an estate near Epsom.

object, objection   An *objection* is 'lodged' by the rider of one horse against the rider of another which has been placed in front of him, on the grounds of some kind of *interference* or foul riding. Other forms of objection may also be lodged, notably by the clerk of the scales against a rider who is carrying the wrong weight or who has failed to *weigh in*. The OED's first attestation is from 1898, but the word's use probably goes much further back. Pierce Egan, for instance, gives an account of a *match* between Moonraker and Grimaldi, in 1832, which ended in a post-race 'objection to the stakes being given up'. In order to *object* today, a jockey has to lodge a sum of money with the stewards which is liable to be forfeited if the objection is found to be frivolous. An objection is signalled by the posting of a red flag on the *number-board*. The vital words which all interested parties then listen for are 'objection overruled, the placings remain unaltered', or 'objection sustained, the revised placings are . . .'

odds   First attested as a betting term in Shakespeare's *2 Henry IV* (5:5:111): 'I will lay oddes, that ere the yeere expire, / We beare our Civill Swords . . . as farre as France.' The word is apparently the plural of the adjective *odd*, taken substantively (cp. 'news'). From the sixteenth to eighteenth centuries it was normally treated as a singular noun, in spite of its plural form. The OED offers an exemplary definition of its meaning:

> Advantage conceded by one of the parties in proportion to the assumed chances in his favour; the inequality of a wager, consisting in the ratio in which the sum to be given stands to that to be received.

It is the ratio element which explains how the word came to be a betting term: 'odd' indicates a difference between one thing and others; and *odds*, in its original sense, meant 'the condition or fact of being unequal'. So, in all but an *even-money* bet, the relation of winnings to stake is an unequal one. In practice, a horse's odds is the same as its *price*. Theoretically, odds of 3/1 should mean that in four runnings of the race in question, the horse could be expected to win it once; odds of 1/2, that it should win the race

146

two out of every three runnings. But since odds are governed by supply and demand – the more money backed on a horse, the shorter its price – then one can determine *value* by relating its estimated chances against the odds which are actually on offer.

Odds-on means that the backer stands to win less than the amount he stakes (he gets his stake back as well), e.g. 4/6. This should never be described as 'four-to-six', but as 'six-to-four on'. *Odds against* means that the backer wins more than his stake, e.g. 6/4. The origin of these terms lies in the nineteenth-century practice of betting 'on' a horse, that is backing it to win, or betting 'against' it, that is, backing it to lose. If I offer you £30 to your £10 about a particular horse, then I am betting 'against' it and offering odds of 3/1; you are, in contrast, betting 'on' it and, in practice, offering me odds of 1/3 that it will be beaten. When bookmakers call out 'take odds', they are betting odds-on the horse (see *take*). In the nineteenth century an odds-on horse was often known as the *odds giver*. *Over the odds* means that the backer has managed to get a longer price than the one generally offered or one longer than the starting price: this phrase has broadened into the general language to mean 'exorbitant, outside the pale' (Partridge). To *shout the odds* is another general expression taken from racing, meaning 'to talk too much, too loudly, or boastingly' (Partridge): it originally referred to the bookmakers' calling out of prices on the racecourse.

off[1] As with vehicles, a horse's *off* side is its right-hand side; used in all contexts except to describe the *reins*. The first attestation of this sense is with reference to horses, in 1675: 'A black store horse, four years old, roweld for a lameness behind on the off-side.' The usage comes from the idea that this is the opposite side to the one by which the rider mounts the horse. Cp. *near*.

off[2] 'They're off', denoting the start of a race, is first attested in 1833; the *off*, meaning the start of a race, not until 1959, but is in common use: 'Drum-player had shortened to 2/1 by the off.'

off[3] Indicates a horse's age: 'four off' means that it is just into its fifth year. Cp. *rising*.

off-course *Off the course*, usually shortened to *off-course*, describes betting carried on away from the racecourse. The distinction between on-course and off-course betting has been given new life by the recent abolition of betting tax upon on-course wagers.

off the pace See *pace*.

offer Bookmakers *offer* a *price* for each horse in a race. Sometimes, particularly in the early betting exchanges, a horse may not be given a price, in which case *no offers* describes its situation in the *market*.

office A jockey *gives the office* when he asks his horse to go in a race; or, in *chasing*, when he urges it to take off at a fence. The OED records the phrase as nineteenth-century slang for giving 'a hint, signal, or private intimation', but recognises no horse-riding or racing sense for it.

old *Old one* or *old 'un*: slang for 'a horse more than three years old' (Partridge, 1860).

on To be *on* a horse is to have backed it: 'Ben Hanbury's third-placed Ikteshaf is the one to be on next time out' (*Racing Post* 19 May 1990). The OED's first attestation is from 1812: 'They declared themselves off, a thing unknown in sporting, after they had been on.' By transference, *on* is then used in this formulation: 'I am on £200 if Blackboy wins', i.e. £200 in profit. For *odds-on* see *odds*.

on-course Describes things which take place on the racecourse and which may also take place off it: *on-course* betting, for instance, is opposed to off-course betting for taxation purposes: see *off-course*.

one-horse A *one-horse race* is not literally so – that is a *walk-over* – but one in which a horse wins easily; likewise, a *two-horse race* is more likely to describe a race in which two horses battle out a finish, clear of the field, than a literal *match*. A *one-horse book* is a book in which only one horse has been seriously backed for a race: this is a dangerous situation for the bookmaker who will find it difficult to *lay¹* off without incurring a loss. The temptation to *stand* the horse may, however, lead to much heavier losses.

one pace When a horse is unable to *quicken* up at the end of a race it keeps on *at one pace*. The phrase can be used adjectivally: 'Fayafi, who ran over 1¼ miles as a two-year-old, was a one-paced fourth to Les Sylphides over the same trip at Yarmouth last month' (*Racing Post* 7 September 1990).

open The verb is used to describe the beginning of *on-course* betting on a race, often with reference to the horse itself: '4/5 Cautious Pete: opened 8/11, touched 5/6 in places' (*Sporting Life* 18 October 1990).

open ditch An obstacle in *steeplechasing*, the most difficult type of fence to negotiate. It was designed in 1882:

A new fence was invented, a hedge with a ditch on the taking-off side, six feet in width and four in depth. The fence was, indeed, a dangerous trap; for being cut sharply away from perfectly smooth and level turf with no growth on the edge, there was nothing to show the horse what he had to do . . . It was not the size of this fence, but its 'trappiness', to which owners, trainers and riders objected; they desired that a guard rail, which would

really make the fence bigger, might be put before the ditch,
and this has now been done. (Badminton, 311)

opener   The first race on the *card*: 'Al Sahil . . . can win an interesting opener' (*Racing Post* 6 October 1990).

oppose   A betting term. To *oppose* a horse is to bet against it –
used particularly of a *favourite* which is uneasy in the market.
'Rami cannot sensibly be opposed on his return to sprinting'
(*Racing Post* 19 May 1990).

order   In betting, *order* means a horse which is in demand among
backers, often in the phrase *a strong order*: 'Shopkeeper is a strong
order for the St Leger.'

orders¹   The trainer's *orders* are his instructions to his jockey on
how to ride the horse in a race. Many jockeys *ride to orders* inflex-
ibly, hence the sight, sometimes, of a race reduced to a dawdle
because all the riders have been instructed to 'drop him out early',
'Warren rode exactly to orders. He couldn't have done it better'
(*Racing Post* 20 September 1990).

orders²   *Starter's orders* mark the real beginning of a race. If a
horse has to be withdrawn before the race actually starts, but after
the horse have come *under orders*, then all bets staked on that
horse are lost.

out, outing   *Out* means, simply, a race: 'last time out' is the last
race a horse ran in; 'first time out' is its first race. An *outing*, too,
is a race: the OED's first attestation, from America, is as late as
1943.

out of   Signifies a horse's *mare*: 'Doodlebug, a colt by Bombshell,
out of Lady Gunner.' This is a short form of *got out of*.

outside   A bookmaker bets *outside* if he works in one of the cheaper
enclosures other than *Tattersalls*. For the origins of this term, see
the quotation under *inside*. An *outside man* is a bookmaker's runner, whose main job is to *lay¹* off bets with other bookmakers in
the *ring*.

outsider   Any horse at long odds in the betting, although what
constitutes an *outsider's* odds will differ according to the race. In
a large *handicap*, with the *favourite* starting at 8/1, outsiders will
start around 16/1. In a three-horse race the outsider may well
start at only 3/1. The OED's first attestation is from 1836. Here
is Pierce Egan, writing a little later in the nineteenth century:

> After all, the science appertaining to betting at times proves
> extremely fallacious; and after all the conglomeration of know-
> ing *nobs* upon the subject – the whispers – the significant nods
> – and the *ear-wigging* as to the qualities and the pedigree of
> the favourite – an outside horse runs away with the great stakes.

Originally, *outsider* meant someone who did not bet or who was not part of the bookmakers' ring – see *outside*. *Rank outsider*, a cliché now, is first recorded in 1871, its derivation being explained in an 1890 Dictionary of Slang as 'a racing term applied to a horse outside the rank.' This phrase, then, might help make the connection between the word's use to describe people and then to describe horses.

overbroke Generally, to *bet overbroke* describes a bookmaker's losing *book* on a race. More specifically, it describes the rare situation when the book is *under-round*: that is, when a backer who invests enough on each horse to ensure a return of £100, whichever one wins, needs to stake less than £100 in all to achieve this – see the £100 take-out method of calculation under *take*.

over-reach A horse *over-reaches* when it injures itself by striking into its fore leg with the corresponding hind shoe, most commonly when landing after jumping a fence. The word is first attested in 1523. The injury which is caused is known as an *over-reach*.

overweight When a horse carries more weight than it is supposed to do, taking into account *allowances*, *penalties*, etc., it carries *overweight*: usually announced in the formula '*x* pounds overweight'. Jockeys speak of 'putting up' overweight. 'The Ayr trainer's fourth runner Go On The Grain was toiling in rear under the inappropriately named Martin Lightbody, who was putting up 34lbs overweight' (*Sporting Life* 14 June 1990).

P **ace** From Latin *passus*, 'a step', *pace* has long been used to describe the various ways in which a horse moves along, hence the plural form of 'put him through his paces'. Touchstone, in *As You Like It*, presents Time as a horse (3:3:327): 'Time travels in divers paces, with diverse persons: Ile tell you who Time ambles withall, who Time trots withal, who Time gallops withall, and who he stands still withall.' Army pace requirements are: walk 4 m.p.h., trot 8 m.p.h., gallop 15 m.p.h. To keep a horse *up with the pace* is to keep it close to the leader; to keep it *off the pace* is to keep it a little way behind the leaders – in either case *pace* seems almost to be a short form of *pace-maker*, the 'pace' element meaning 'speed in running'. A horse which can not keep up with the leaders is said not to *go the pace*: 'Those two market leaders could never go the pace set by All Fired Up and Sharp Anne' (*Sporting Life* 1 September 1990). See also *false*; *one pace*; *muddling*; *no pace*.

pace-maker Has two slightly different senses: one is the original meaning, still the most common in racing, to describe a horse which goes out in the lead in order to make the pace for a better fancied stablemate which needs a true run race – the first examples are from the 1890s, in rowing and cycling. The other is the description of the leading runner in a race. Since the European style of racing normally means that in all but *sprints* the winning horse comes from off the *pace*, there is no great distinction between the two senses; but the extension of *pace-maker* – or *pacemaker* – into the general language, as a kind of synonym for trend-setter, as well as the increase in the American style of racing, in which the fancied horses go out in front from the start of the race, means that there is likely to be a greater gap developing between the two senses.

packet See *parcel*.

pad The verb, from a noun cognate with *path*, meaning 'to tread, walk, or tramp along' (1553), was used with reference to horses from the eighteenth century. The slang phrase *pad it*, 'to make off quickly', came into the general language via racing (Partridge, 20th C.).

paddle A horse *paddles* over a fence when it puts in an ungainly jump, sprawling and giving the impression of rowing its way over. Not in OED.

paddock Originally *parrock*, from Old English *pearroc*, to which *park* is related. It first meant 'a fence, or hurdles into which a space is enclosed' (8th C.), and then, by extension, 'an enclosed space of ground; a small enclosure or field'. Its racing sense, as a 'turf enclosure near the racecourse, where the horses and jockeys are assembled in preparation for a race' is first attested in 1862. A *paddock critic*, or *paddock judge*, is one who makes his estimate of a horse's well-being, or otherwise, from its appearance and behaviour in the paddock before the race.

paint Bookmakers *paint up prices* on their boards – with chalk. See the quotation under *take*.

parade The *parade* in front of the *stands* is an important part of major races. Instituted by Lord George Bentinck in the nineteenth century, its purpose is not only to give all the spectators who have not had access to the *paddock* the chance to see the horses, but also to test the horses' temperaments. This last factor makes it an unpopular practice among trainers and jockeys.

parcel Slang for the day's winnings (Partridge, 1898): to *drop a parcel* is to lose a lot of money – see *drop*; to *pack (up) a parcel* is to win a lot. Educated Evans complains of being arrested on the eve of the Newbury Spring Cup, 'when I did hope to pack a parcel over Solway' (Edgar Wallace, 'The Brotherhood'). Winning a *packet* is a comparable idea, and a later development (mid 1920s).

pari mutuel The *tote* in other countries than Britain, particularly France and America. For races taking place abroad, bookmakers may offer backers the choice of their own *prices* or *pari mutuel* prices. The phrase means 'mutual stake'; i.e. a *pool* bet.

park *Park courses* are those built especially for *steeplechasing*, other than Aintree. The phrase is usually applied to courses which are within easy reach of London, like Sandown Park. The use of *park* keeps up the sport's connection with hunting, for the word's original sense, from 1260, was 'an enclosed tract of land held by royal grant or prescription for keeping beasts of the chase'.

parlay From *paroli*, a term in card-playing for 'the leaving of the money staked and money won as a further stake', *parlay* is commonly used in America to describe *doubles* and other *accumulator* bets, as in the OED's example from Thomas Pynchon's *V* (1963): 'Both together were like a parlay of horses, capable of a whole arrived at by some operation more alien than simple addition of parts.' The word has no currency at all in British English.

parrot mouth A congenital malformation of the horse's upper jaw, in which the front teeth overhang the lower jaw, making it difficult, sometimes impossible, for the horse to graze. Some very good racehorses have had this defect. Tony Morris, writing about Dancing Brave – second in the Derby and winner of the Prix de l'Arc de Triomphe – and El Gran Senor – winner of the Two Thousand Guineas and second in the Derby – notes that 'in terms of their intrinsic merit, there was probably very little between the parrot-mouthed pair' (*Racing Post* 31 July 1990).

passport When foaled, every racehorse is registered in the *Stud Book* at Weatherbys, identified by its *pedigree* and a chart showing its physical characteristics. When *named* it is issued with a *passport* which will be checked by a vet the first time the horse runs and may, after that, be checked on a random basis. The passport gives details of the horse's breeding, sex, date of foaling, colour and markings. 'Under the Rules of Racing, trainers are required to check passports when horses come into their yard' (*Sporting Life* 7 September 1990).

pastern The part of a horse's leg, between the *fetlock* joint and the *coronet* (just above the hoof). The word's origins are connected with *pasture*, its first meaning being 'a shackle fixed on the foot of a horse... at pasture' (1343), soon extended to describe the part of the foot to which the shackle was attached: first attestation in this sense, 1530. When Samuel Johnson was chided, rightly, for a fault definition of this word in his *Dictionary*, his explanation was 'Ignorance, madam: ignorance.'

patent See *multiple bet*.

pattern A key term in the organisation of modern British racing, as in this title: *The Report of the Duke of Norfolk's Committee on the Pattern of Racing* (1965). The organisation of races, from group one races, which include the *classics*, down through group two, group three, and listed races, is known as *the pattern*: such races are often known as *pattern races*. In this racing usage the word seems to bear two of its distinct senses: its original meaning, 'an example or model of a particular excellence' (14th C.), and 'an arrangement or order of things or activity in abstract senses' (1901). 'Afwaj can bridge the gap between handicaps and Pattern races in the Group Three Duke of York Stakes' (*Sporting Life* 17 May 1990).

pay Bookmakers *pay out* after a race, but *pay on* a particular horse. *Late pay* at *Tote* windows allows collection of winnings from races earlier than the previous one.

peacock A horse 'with a showy action' (Partridge, 1869).

peck In *chasing*, a horse *pecks* when it falters or stumbles on landing over a fence: a *mistake*, but not bad enough to put it out of the race. 'Loch Raven: led to fourth, led fifth to tenth, pecked 14th, rallied three out...' (*Sporting Life* 13 September 1990). When the horse pecks, its head goes down so that its nose nearly

touches the ground, hence the apparent analogy with a bird peck-
ing for food; but the word's derivation is actually from *pick*, a
variant form of *pitch*, the action being of the horse pitching forward. The OED's first attestation is from *c*.1770, and it quotes an
1880 *Shropshire Word Book* which defines 'peck' and 'pick' as 'to
pitch forward, go head first', giving the example: 'Mind the child
dunna peck out on 'is cheer.' When a horse pecks lightly it is
said to *nod* on landing.

pedigree   Derived from the Old French *pie de grue*, 'crane's foot',
so called 'from a three-line-mark (like the broad arrow) used in
denoting succession in pedigrees'. This makes the word particularly apposite for racehorses, for all *thoroughbreds* can be traced
back to one of the three great eighteenth-century stallions,
Eclipse, Matchem, and Herod. The importance of the word in
horse-racing is borne out by Charles Darwin's observation that
'the pedigree of a racehorse is of more value in judging of its
probable success than its appearance.'

penalty   Extra weight which a horse has to carry, usually because
it has won a race since the publication of the weights for a later
race: first attestation in this sense 1885. 'Five furlong handicap:
£10,000 added to stakes...£75 to enter. Lowest weight 7st 7lbs.
Penalties, after May 26, a winner 6lbs.' Each race has a *penalty
value*; i.e. it is worth a certain sum of money which may lead to
the horse which wins it being given extra weight in future races:

> Main Reef Stakes...for 3-y-o and up...Weights: 3-y-o colts
> 8st 10lbs; fillies 8st 5lbs; 4-y-o and up, colts 9st; fillies 8st 9lbs
> Penalties: in 1990 a winner of a race value £5,000 4lbs; of two
> such races or one value £8,000 7lbs; or, at any time, a winner
> of a race value £12,000 10lbs...

and the Main Reef Stakes itself had a penalty value of £11,500.

pencil, penciller   *Penciller* was a nineteenth-century term for a
bookmaker, whose practice was to walk around with a notebook
and pencil, noting the bets which he laid:

> The last of 'The Pencillers' was seen in the 1920s. A Penciller
> wandering around with his little book and a stub of a pencil
> did not mean very much to the average race-goer, instead most
> layers elected to advertise their line of business by displaying
> prices. (Sidney, 106)

Today, if the term is used, it refers to the bookmaker's clerk.
The OED quotes, from 1887, 'when the favourite won, the accused
and his clerk, or "penciller", promptly changed their clothes and
decamped.' Partridge notes the compound *pencil-fever*, 'the laying
of odds against a horse certain to lose, especially after it has been
at short odds' (1872).

penetrometer   In Britain the official *going* is determined by the clerk of the course, usually based on how far his heel or his walking-stick goes into the ground. They order such things better in France, where they employ an instrument called a *penetrometer*, calibrated to give an official reading when it is stuck into the ground in various places around the course. The French classifications of going are, with their penetrometer readings: 1 *Sec* (bone dry); 2 *Très léger* (hard); 2·5 *léger* (firm); 3 *Assez souple* (good); 3·5 *Souple* (soft); 4 *Très Souple* (very soft); 4·5 *Collant* (holding); 5 *Lourd* (heavy). Penetrometers were originally used in road-making, to measure the depth of asphalt: first attestation 1905.

pepper   In the passive, to be *peppered*: when a bookmaker takes heavy bets on a horse (Partridge, 1870). The use of *pepper* to mean 'to inflict severe punishment or suffering upon' dates back to the sixteenth century.

permit   A *Jockey Club* licence allowing individuals to train and run only horses which they themselves own: such trainers are known as *permit holders*. Bookmakers need a *permit*, issued by the Bookmakers' Licensing Committee, to allow them to lay bets on racecourses.

photo finish   Introduced in Britain in 1947, but in operation in America in the late 1930s. In 1938 Damon Runyon has Nicely Nicely taking on 'anything on four legs, except maybe an elephant, and at that he may give the elephant a photo finish.' The OED records other forms which did not catch on, like *photo decision* in 1937. Generally speaking, the *judge* will use the *photo finish* to determine placings when the *distance*[2] between horses is half a length or less.

pick up   Describes both the jockey's and the horse's actions towards the end of a race. The horse *picks up* when it takes hold of the bit and goes faster; the jockey *picks* it *up* when he shortens the reins to make it increase its pace. 'Go down the course, two or three furlongs from home, and see how horses are picked up and balanced for the final run' (Hislop, 84). In *chasing*, a horse picks up when it jumps properly, or fails to pick up when it ploughs into a fence. In any kind of race a horse picks up another when it draws alongside and overtakes it – perhaps a development of the phrase *pick up on*, 'to draw near, begin to overtake'. 'Bill Williamson reported, "The way I was travelling I thought he'd pick up the winner as soon as I asked him, but he just couldn't use himself on the firm ground"' (O'Sullevan, 257).

pigskin   Nineteenth-century sporting slang for the saddle. Pigskin was the most desirable leather for a saddle's seat because of its durability and elasticity. In high-faluting sports reporting of the time, jockeys tended to be called things like 'knights of the pigskin':

> This particular knight of the pigskin had been riding in great form and, on paper, it was dollars to doughnuts that doubling or trebling this $1,300 was simply a question of investment. (Goodwin Bros., 53)

pinch[1]   A *pinch* is a certain winner. Partridge dates it in this meaning from the 1890s and conjectures that the usage might have come about through confusion with the American *cinch*. Alternatively, it may be a development of the verb 'to pinch', meaning 'to steal'; i.e. the horse is considered so certain a winner that backing it is equivalent to stealing money from the bookmaker.

> After seven muddy and abortive pilgrimages from where we were pulled up by the winning-post across to Tattersall's Ring to have it down on a 'moral', which each time turned out wrong, he growled as the last 'pinch' came in second. (*Pitcher in P*, 94)

pinch[2]   As a verb, *pinch*, meaning 'to urge or press a horse', is first attested in 1737: 'It is the vulgar Opinion, that a Horse has not been pinch'd, or pinn'd down, in a Heat when he does not sweat out.'

ping   A horse *pings* a fence or hurdle when it clears it low and spectacularly fast: the word probably imitates the sound of a gun shot. 'I needed to ping it to win – and I didn't' (*Sporting Life* 31 August 1990). This sense is not in the OED.

pipe opener   A gallop which clears a horse's wind or a first race to get a horse fit. The OED's first examples, in the 1870s and 80s, are from rowing and cycling.

pitch   The first bookmakers used to wander around among the betting public – see *penciller*. This practice gave way to the taking up of *pitches* in the *Tattersalls* and other *enclosures*, the best pitches being those nearest to the spectators' stands and to the *rails*. A Pitch Committee rules on the allocation of pitches (usually by seniority). 'Pitch', in the sense, 'a place at which one stations oneself or is stationed', is first attested in 1765, a development of the verb's sense 'to thrust, fix in; make fast, fasten, settle'.

place[1]   In one sense the *placed* horses in a race are those which finish in the first four in a race, even if there are only four runners. In betting, however, the success of a *place bet* depends upon the number of runners: normally the first three home are *placed*, but in fields of five, six, and seven, only the first two; and in *handicaps* of sixteen or more runners, the fourth horse is included. Place bets are normally only available on the *Tote*, but similar rulings apply to the place element of an *each-way* bet with a bookmaker.

'Placed' is also used to describe all of the horses in the *frame*, barring the winner: 'He has been placed seven times, but has never won.' In America *place* refers particularly to first and second, a place bet paying out on the first two, while a *show[4]* bet pays on the first three. The OED's first attestation of the verb's use in this sense is from 1831, in Macaulay's estimation of Boswell's superiority in the art of biography: 'He has no second. He has distanced all his competitors so decidedly, that it is not worth while to place them. Eclipse is first, and the rest nowhere.' The sense of 'place' from which the racing usage derives is that of 'position or standing in the social scale, or in any order of estimation or merit' (1325), the real sense of everyone knowing their place; i.e. where they stand in the social rankings.

place[2] *Placing* describes a trainer's skill in finding races for his horses: a horse which has been well placed to win is one which has had relatively easy winning opportunities. 'You could say this was brilliantly placed. There won't be a worse race than this before Whit Monday' (*Sporting Life* 31 August 1990).

placepot See *pot*.

plait The opposite of *dish*: when a horse bends its knee, crosses its fore feet as its trots, and looks to be in danger of striking the opposite leg. *Plaiting* takes several forms:

> If he strikes himself just below the knee or hock it is called 'speedy-cutting'. If he strikes one fetlock with the opposite hoof it is called 'brushing'. If he strikes himself between the knee and the fetlock it is called hitting. (Goldschmidt, 130)

This sense is not in the OED.

plant A horse is *planted* – or *plants* itself – when it refuses to move, with all four legs fixed firmly on the ground. The OED gives no such specific sense, but quotes, as an example of 'plant' meaning 'the way in which anyone plants himself or is planted', the example, from 1817, 'The wide area between his feet when in a standing position gave him so firm a "plant", if I may so say.' Partridge records *planter*, 'a horse apt to refuse to budge', as an Anglo-Indian colloquialism (1864).

plate[1], plater *Plate* occurs in the title of many races because a piece of silver plate, commonly a cup, was the prize. The OED's first examples are from the seventeenth century: from 1639, ' "My Lord Carlisle's white nagg", says Ralph, "hath beaten Dandy, and Sprat woone the cup, and Cricket the plate" '; and, from 1675, 'The Plate at Rowell Slade, in the County of Northampton, will be continued on the first Thursday of September, and will be worth about Forty pound.' Now *plate* is frequently used in reference to a *selling race*, so that a *plater* is a racehorse of the

lowest ability which usually runs in selling company. 'He's a good
old plater and after this win he ... will have ten stone on his back
next time' (*Sporting Life* 13 June 1990).

plate² A slang term for the saddle, not in the OED. 'He ... has to
be a threat with Peter Scudamore in the plate' (*Sporting Life* 19
September 1990).

plate³ A shoe for racehorses: first attested in 1840. A *racing plate*
weighs only 50 gramms, as opposed to the 187 gramms which an
exercise plate weighs. When a horse pulls off, or twists, a shoe it
is said to have *spread a plate*. 'Two Left Feet ... should have run
at Hamilton earlier this week, but was withdrawn after spreading
a plate' (*Sporting Life* 16 June 1990).

play To *make play* was a common eighteenth and nineteenth-
century expression for making the *pace* in a race. The OED's first
attestation is from 1799, and it quotes, from 1883, 'Fontenay
made play to the distance, where the favourite took the lead.' The
expression occurs significantly in the royal jockey Sam Chifney's
account of the instruction given to him by the Prince of Wales
before the first of two notorious races on the Prince's colt Escape:

> His Royal Highness then said, "Sam Chifney, I wish you to
> make very strong play with Escape ... I will not compel you
> to make play with Escape; providing that there should be good
> play made by any other horse, you may wait with Escape; but
> should there be no other horse make such as you think good
> play, you must take care to make good play with Escape."
> (*Genius Genuine*, c.1803).

play or pay An expression from early racing: a *play or pay match*
meant that if one party to the race failed to 'play' – i.e. engage in
the match – his backers had to pay as if he had raced and lost.
Hence evolved the *play or pay bet* – first attestation 1821 – often
abbreviated to *P.P.*, a bet which stood whether or not the horse
in question ran: this was the forerunner of *ante-post* betting.

> Ross stipulated that I should ride my own horse; I was hunting
> Northamptonshire at the time, and was rather vexed with
> myself for having agreed to this, because, hunting hounds
> myself, there was always the chance of a fall which might dis-
> able me and forbid my riding the match, in which case I should
> have to forfeit the whole £1,000, the terms being p.p.; and I
> stood all the money myself. (Osbaldeston, 57)

play up¹ When a horse behaves in an unruly manner, particularly
when it refuses to enter the starting *stalls*, it is said to *play up*.
The use of the expression to describe 'boisterous, unruly, or
troublesome behaviour', dates from the beginning of the nineteenth century, and applies mainly to horses and children.

play up² *Play* was a common synonym for 'bet', from the fifteenth century. Now it is more often used in American racing than British – the OED quotes, from Edgar Wallace (1925): 'We never say "played the races" here; we say "go racing".' The one British usage is *play up*, in the sense of playing up one's winnings, that is, staking all that one has won from one horse onto another.

plumper A slang expression, meaning 'an unusually large example of its type', it came into racing as a way of describing 'all one's money, staked on one horse' (Partridge, 1881).

plunge, plunger *Plunge*, meaning to bet heavily and recklessly, developed in racing slang in the late nineteenth century. The OED records the use of *plunger*, to mean 'one who bets, gambles, or speculates rashly or recklessly', from 1876. Thormanby, writing about Lord Derby, describes him as,

> scarcely what may be called a betting man; he certainly backed his horses for sums which he could well afford to lose, but he was no 'plunger', indeed there was nothing he more cordially detested than the making of reckless bets. (*Famous*, 39)

Whatever its origins, its use makes good sense in racing terms, where *on-course* betting often requires one to dive into the crowd around a bookmaker to get the best *price* on offer. 'Waltzer plunge continues for Ayr Gold Cup' (*Sporting Life* 20 September 1990).

poach As a development of the sense 'to trespass...in order to take or catch game', *poach* came to be used in racing to mean 'to filch (an advantage, e.g. at the start in a race) by unfair means'. The OED quotes, from the *Daily News* in 1892, 'Several...displayed a marked desire to "poach a bit" at the start.' Now that the start is a level one, all horses leaving the *stalls* at the same moment, poach is largely restricted to the idea of 'poaching a lead', when a jockey goes clear of the field at an unexpected point in the race, usually early on.

point¹ The *points* are the extremities of a horse: first attestation, from 1855, 'a particularly fast mare...bay, with black points'.

point² Often confused with *point¹*, the *points* of a horse are its physical features, especially those 'by which excellence or purity of breed is judged'. The OED quotes, from 1841, 'Much better versed in the points of a horse than in points of theology.' In this sense, a horse has some dozens of points: e.g. points on the head include lips, nose, face, forehead, eyebrows, forelock, ears, jaw, cheeks, nostrils.

point³ A betting term for a complete unit, as in *to come in a point* in the betting, e.g. from 3/1 to 2/1; or *to go out a point*, e.g. from 9/2 to 11/2. The OED's first attestation is from 1844: 'Betting reduced two points.'

point⁴   See *point-to-point*.

point-to-point   *Point* is a hunting term, defined as 'a spot to which a straight run is made', from which comes the expression 'to make one's point', meaning 'to run straight at a spot aimed at'. The OED quotes, from 1875, 'In Leicestershire especially, foxes will make their point with a stiff breeze blowing in their teeth.' The phrase *point-to-point* may be connected with this sense of 'point', being a shortened form of 'from one point to another': first attested in 1883. Point-to-point racing, for hunter chasers ridden by amateur jockeys, offers a direct link between the hunting field and *steeplechasing*. Point-to-point courses present the simplest kinds of racecourse, where jumps are marked by flags. Horse which run over them are known as *point-to-pointers*, the sport being known as *point-to-pointing*. A point-to-point meeting is often known as a *point*.

pony¹   £25. First attested in 1797, 'There is no touching her even for a pony.' Jon Bee makes a bizarre attempt to explain its, otherwise obscure, origins:

> A little horse, and also wagers of twenty-five guineas, the one being derived from the other. *Poene* is a Latin word for pain, or painfulness, and all the little horses being mal-formed, so as to give one an idea that they walk in pain...there comes pony. Dr Johnson knew no more of a pony or of a horse, than a horse knew of him.

He is probably right about Dr Johnson – see *pastern* – but the rest is unconvincing. He adds that *post the pony* means 'put down money'. Cp. *monkey*.

pony²   Seldom used in Britain, but a common American synonym for a racehorse: first attestation, from Jack London in 1907: 'I had been out to the race-track watching the ponies run.'

pool   *Pool betting* at the racecourse is conducted by the *Tote*. Not only their *jackpot* and *placepot* bets, but all Tote win, place and forecast bets operate on a pool basis, the winning dividends being estimated according to the number of such bets and the size of the 'pool' – that is, all of the money staked. *Pool* occurs in a card-playing context early in the eighteenth century, and as a betting term in the late nineteenth. In America the earliest form of betting with bookmakers was known as an *auction pool*. Each horse in the race was 'auctioned off' in the following manner:

> "How much am I bid for the first choice?"

> Whoever, in the audience, offers the most money for the privilege of having first selection, will choose Dorian, and for which he has, let it be presumed, offered $125. The purchaser we will call A.

The auctioneer then asks how much is offered for second choice.

Some one may finally bid $80, and it is knocked down to B. at that price. He selects Faro.

The total pool now is $205 ($125 and $80).

"How much am I offered for third choice?" asks the auctioneer.

Mars is the horse selected, and for which a buyer C. has perhaps given $55. (Total pool $260.)

The auctioneer will now "lump together" the balance of the remaining horses, which he offers for sale as a single one, or in turf parlance, "the field"...sold for $75 (total pool $335). D. is the buyer.

That particular pool is then closed and the auctioneer begins all over again.

From the grand total of each pool a deduction is made of 3 per cent commission, which goes to the parties having charge of the money...

If Dorian wins, A. receives all the money, which is $335, less 3 per cent, equals $325, and deducting $125, which he paid for first choice, leaves a net profit of $200; or $200 to $125, which is...8 to 5.

If Mars had been the winner, C. would have...a net profit of $270; or...5 to 1.

(Goodwin Bros., 113)

pop In *chasing*, a horse *pops* a fence when it gets a little too close to it, not having measured its stride accurately, and clears it by jumping apparently straight up and down: impetus may be lost, but the ability to do this is the sign of a clever jumper. 'Ambergate just pops his fences and stays' (*Racing Post* 6 October 1990). In *hurdling*, similarly, a horse *pops* a hurdle when it clears it at a speed less than racing pace. Not in the OED.

posi Short for *position*: jockey's slang for their position in a race. 'Coming round the bend I had a nice posi on the inside.'

post Used for the starting and finishing post, but principally for the latter, as the OED's first example, from 1642, already demonstrates: 'A Fool and a wiseman are alike both in the starting-place, their birth, and at the post, their death.' The Americanism, *post-time*, meaning the time a race is supposed to start, has not yet caught on in Britain. The finishing post is now commonly known as the *winning post*, first attested in 1820; an earlier alternative is given in a *Jockey Club* order of 1770, in which every colt or filly of two, three, or four years old, should be examined 'at the Ending post, immediately after running the first time' (Prior, 151). A *post* *match*, common in the eighteenth century, was a form of *match* racing in which one inserted only the age of the horse in the articles, 'without declaring what horse, till you come to the post to start' (from Pond's 1751 Rules).

pot   Nineteenth-century slang for the money involved in a large bet: to *put the pot on* was to stake virtually all one has. The word survives mainly in the idea of winning a *pot* on a horse. Partridge quotes, from 1870, 'Harrie...won a pot on the French horse.' From this sense developed the use of *pot* to describe the favourite for a race, i.e. the horse which has been backed to win a large sum of money. Jon Bee describes Pot8o's name as 'meaning £80,000 or guineas' (see *name*). A *jackpot*, derived from draw-poker, is a sum of money which accumulates until a player opens the bidding with a pair of jacks: in racing it describes a bet, run by the *Tote*, in which the winners of the first six races on the *card* have to be nominated. In imitation, a *place-pot* involves the nominating of a horse to be *placed* in the first six races.

p.p.   See *play or pay*.

prance   'Of a horse: To spring and bound in high mettle.' As the OED notes, the word looks as if it should have a French origin, 'but no corresponding word is recorded in French.' The word first appears in Chaucer in 1374.

prep   An abbreviated form of *prepare*, or *preparation*, but used so commonly in racing that it stands as a word in its own right. Originally American slang, a *prep race* is 'a race that is a preparation for a more important event.' The verb is first attested in a racing sense in a 1943 newspaper headline, 'Attention being prepped for New Orleans Cup.' The verb has not yet caught on in Britain, but the noun and adjective are in frequent use: 'Harwood's Ile de Chypre will be given a prep race before going for the Dubai Champion Stakes' (*Sporting Life* 19 September 1990).

present   A *present* is a sum of money paid by the owner of the horse to the winning jockey and to members of the stable staff. That the gift may not always be money is borne out by the great Fred Archer's first present: for riding the winner of a farmers' race at Yarmouth, he was given a pound of green tea. The word has always had something of the euphemism about it, often describing four (or more) figure payments to jockeys who ride in big races. 'The bonus falls outside the rule which stipulates that the jockey collects eight per cent of the prize money won by his mount. However, it seems inconceivable that the winning jockey would not be given an equivalent present' (*Sporting Life* 8 September 1990; the sum in question here is 80,000 Irish punts).

pressure   A horse comes under *pressure* in a race when the jockey *asks* it for a response.

price The *odds* at which a horse is offered by bookmakers. The OED's first attestation is as late as 1882, although it records the verb's use in this sense from 1865: 'The layers of the odds complaining that nothing but favourites were backed, notwithstanding the tempting "pricing" of the outsiders.' Earlier in the century, the practice was to *price* one horse and offer another price against the rest of the field *en masse* – see *field²*. This changed when 'Ogden, a Lancashire man ... got up at Newmarket one day, and offered prices against *all* the runners in a race simultaneously' (Sidney, 35). Ogden's act of genius was to realise 'that the laying of more than one horse in any one event is more profitable than laying one horse' (Sidney, 85). Prices can be 'short' or 'long', according to whether a horse is a *favourite* or an *outsider*. Backers are said to *take a price* 'about' a horse: 'Whitaker ... took 33/1 about Ned's Aura before he won at York' (*Sporting Life* 20 September 1990).

Starting prices, known commonly as *S.P.*'s, began to be recorded in the press in 1850 – although the OED's first attestation is not until 1891, in the *Daily News*: 'The plaintiff was a starting-price bookmaker.' This quotation is useful, because a 'starting-price bookmaker' was a phenomenon which developed in the nineteenth century, with the rise of *off-course* bookmaking. The starting price is the price which is generally on offer on the course at the start of a race. The starting-price bookmaker, instead of trading in a market where prices were constantly changing, was able to work on fixed price returns:

> Off-course bookmakers offered bets of ever-increasing degrees of complexity and issued rules for their settlement. Bookies offered to lay unnamed favourites, the horses with the shortest S.P., they offered them in doubles, trebles and any other combination that they or the backer could devise. Jockeys' mounts, trainers' selected, second favourites and numerous variations came to be the essence of Off-course betting all because the bets were to be settled at a standard rate, the S.P. (Sidney, 60)

The S.P. is a useful creation for the backer who wants to make *multiple* bets, but for the backer who bets large sums on short-priced horses, it is never preferred to the opportunity to take a price in the *ring*; for, by definition, the S.P. represents the shortest price on offer for a well-backed horse.

Pricing the first *show³* is a matter of the bookmaker's individual judgment, relying upon advice from all quarters, particularly the *tissue*; but very soon in the betting exchanges it becomes clear that the sole criterion for the fixing of a horse's price is demand.

Because of this, the betting ring represents almost the purest form
of free-market economics.

prick   An obsolete word for urging a horse on with the spurs and,
by extension, for riding fast on horseback. Today, however, *prick*
is confined to two senses: in farriery, 'to pierce the foot (of a
horse) to the quick in shoeing, causing lameness' (1591) – 'He
broke down at the first October meeting at Newmarket... when
running with the odds in his favour... but it is only fair to say
that he got pricked in shoeing three days before the race, and had
to be stopped in his work' (Thormanby, *Famous*, 33); and in the
phrase *prick* its *ears* – a horse which pricks its ears is paying
attention to what is going on and, therefore, often enjoying itself.
When it wins *with ears pricked* it definitely has something in hand
even if the winning distance is small. Partridge dates this phrase
from 1923. 'Irish Passage came sweeping through on the outside... to lead inside the final furlong and won with his ears
pricked' (*Sporting Life* 12 September 1990).

print   When a *photo-finish* is very close, the *judge* may call for a
print, a blown-up copy of the photograph, in order to determine
the places. 'After calling for a print, the judge declared a dead-heat
between Bright Sapphire and Shy Hiker' (*Sporting Life* 21 September 1990).

produce[1]   The OED says that *produce*, in the sense 'offspring, progeny', is rare, but this is not the case in racing. Jon Bee defines
the word in its narrow and broader senses:

>   The young of any given horse or mare is its produce, whether
>   colts or fillies; but in a wider sense of the word, would imply
>   any of that get, however old. Thus Haphazard's produce won
>   forty-one prizes in the season 1821.

produce[2]   The verb is used to describe a jockey's *covering up* of
a horse during a race and then bringing it with a winning chance,
normally within the last two furlongs. 'It was the four-year-old's
first attempt at two miles and he saw it out well, after being
produced to lead more than a furlong out' (*Racing Post* 8 June
1990).

produce stakes   See *stake*.

prop   If a horse suddenly stops when going at speed it *props*. The
source is Australian English, the OED's first attestation is in 1870.
When a horse props before a jump, the consequence may be that
the jockey clears the fence without the horse, to the great delight
of some of the spectators and of the horse. Steve Donoghue tells
of this incident when riding the mare Love-in-Idleness in the
Oaks, as he approached Tattenham Corner:

>   Suddenly my mare began to shorten her stride and to prick

her ears forward, first one, then the other, looking and wondering at something that disturbed her – and there, right at the turn, in the midst of all the turmoil and hubbub, I saw a gipsy's horse fast asleep, with its head peacefully nodding forward right over the rails. The mare had seen the head first, and now she "propped" herself, trying to stop. I had to do something, and that quickly, so I put out my hand and caught the horse one right across the nose. He *jumped* awake in great surprise, and I managed to get the mare past, but her stopping short so suddenly at that sharp turn had got the big field behind me into a terrible tangle, and there might have been a fearful mix-up. (Donoghue, 190)

prophet   Slang for a *tipster*: first attestation 1843, 'What's to win the Derby? What say the prophets?' *Prophet's thumbmarks* are indentations in a horse's skin.

pull¹, puller   A horse which *pulls* is one which strains against the bit (1791). A horse which does this persistently is a *puller* (1852), or, redundantly, a *hard puller*, and needs to be *covered up* in a race. If this tactic is unsuccessful, then it will *pull its way* to the front. When a horse takes hold of the bit and runs on at a point in the race where the jockey has not asked it for any effort, then it is said to *pull over* him, and to *pull over* the other horses if it goes by them in the early stages of a race. If it is going very easily it can be described as *pulling double* over the field: 'from pulling double over the others until the last furlong, he stopped all to nothing and collapsed in my hands as though shot' (Donoghue, 194). In contrast, when the jockey of a manageable animal wants to make it fall back towards the rear of the field, early in a race, he *takes a pull* on the horse. 'Carter, keeping hold of Riviera Magic's head, actually took a pull entering the final furlong to keep the winning distance down to half a length' (*Sporting Life* 12 September 1990). If, however, he *pulls* the horse, he is not letting it run properly, making it lose a race it might have won. This, of course, is a breach of the rules of racing and, if detected, would render him liable to be *warned off*. Seldom perpetrated, if the *Jockey Club* is to be believed, the *pulling* of horses is frequently suspected by angry punters. The word's origin in this sense probably lies in the idea that the horse is restrained by the reins being pulled each time the horse tries to run on. When such pulling does not work, desperate measures are called for. A jockey called Thomas Duck, riding the hot favourite for the York Plate in 1718, did his best to prevent it from winning, and when it still pulled its way to the front two hundred yards from the finish he heroically threw himself out of the saddle.

pull² A *pull* in the weights describes a horse's weight advantage with another compared to their respective weights in earlier races: 'Spectator now has an eight pound pull with New Statesman.'

pull round To *pull round* another horse is to come out from behind it on the outside in a race. Races are frequently lost because a horse gets *boxed in* and has to pull round the field to make its finishing run.

pull through A jockey *pulls through* the reins when he lengthens them or shortens them during a race, and *pulls through* the whip when he transfers it from one hand to the other:

> You must be able to get your whip quickly and easily from the carrying position to the one necessary for action...there are two ways of doing this. One is to pull the whip through the hand in which you are carrying it with the opposite hand – as if you were drawing a sword. (Hislop, 127)

pull up *Pull up*, in the sense of stopping a horse, is first attested in 1787. In racing, it describes the jockey's action after the horse has passed the post. If he tries to pull up his horse too soon, because he is winning easily, he stands in danger of being caught on the line, a mistake which could easily get him lynched and which will certainly get him fined by the stewards. On the other hand, in a five furlong sprint, it can sometimes take another five furlongs to pull a horse up. The phrase can be used reflexively to describe the horse's own action, particularly if it refuses to carry on with a race. 'Cashcard pulled up with a mile to go' means that the jockey pulled him up, probably suspecting that something was wrong with Cashcard, or because he was too far behind; 'Cashcard pulled himself up with a mile to go' means that the jockey had no say in the matter. The phrase's relationship with the verb 'stop' is interesting, for 'stop', in the sense 'to cease from onward movement, to come to a stand or position of rest', was originally used with special reference to horses: its first attestation is in 1530, 'I stoppe, as a horse...doth'; and, in a more technical sense, from 1575, 'The horse by this means learneth...first to tread the ringe, secondly to stop.' In racing today, however, 'stop' means something else (see *stop*). *Pull up*, of course, is now used to describe a motor vehicle's coming to a stop.

punt, punter From the French *ponter*, *punt* was originally a term for laying a stake in certain card games like baccarat and faro: first attestation 1706. In racing today a *punt* usually signifies a heavy bet: 'A punt from 14/1 to 9/1 narrowly went astray' (*Sporting Life* 20 September 1990). *Punter* meant one who plays against the bank, the word being extended to describe those who bet with bookmakers in the middle of the nineteenth century. The develop-

ment of the word's meaning is instructive, the OED listing its most
contemporary senses as 'a customer or client: a member of an
audience or spectator...the client of a prostitute', adding that
while in some contexts it is virtually synonymous with 'person',
its use is always depreciatory. In racing, *punter* was, and still is
to some extent, confined to small backers, those generally referred
to as *outsiders*. This may seem odd, given that *punt* often means
a heavy bet, but often the punt is actually made up out of the
accumulation of a large number of bets. See also *mug*.

purse   The winning prize money of a race. From the Latin *bursa*
and Old French *bourse*, a *purse* is 'a small pouch or bag of leather
or other flexible material, used for carrying money on the person'.
When the money subscribed for a race was collected in such a
bag, it became the *purse* for the race. The OED quotes, from 1724,
'No Horse...shall be admitted to Run for this Purse, that ever
won the value of £10.' If anything, the usage today is more common in America than Britain.

push out   To *push out* a horse is to ride it hard, in a *finish*, without
having recourse to the whip. The phrase implies a little more
vigour than riding *hands and heels*. 'Duncan Idaho: headway 7th,
led approaching last, pushed out flat' (*Racing Post* 29 May 1990).

put at, put to   In *chasing*, a horse is *put at* – or, less commonly,
put to – a fence; meaning that the jockey, properly balanced, tries
to make sure that it meets the fence correctly, at the right stride.

put away[1]   To *put away* a horse is to retire it for the season. 'Mul-
lins said that he may run Slyguff at Listowel, but added the nine-
year-old does not like soft ground so he might put him away for
next year's Galway Plate if the ground turns up like a bog' (*Sporting Life* 6 September 1990).

put away[2]   To *put* someone *away* is to give them false information;
as, for example, when *connections* tell you that their horse has no
chance today and it goes and wins easily.

put down[1]   To kill an animal humanely: originally used about
human beings – e.g., from 1589, 'Alice Stokoe...did put down
herself.'

put down[2]   Used to describe a horse's landing after having jumped
a fence. 'Llewellyn...was unperturbed by his mount's mistake
at the last. He said: "He put down again when I asked him to
take off"' (*Sporting Life* 23 May 1990).

put on   To *put* money *on* a horse is to back it: first attestation, by
Thackeray in 1849, 'Altamont put the pot on at the Derby, and
won a good bit of money.'

put up   Used in the simple sense of helping a jockey mount a
horse; but, additionally, in the more general sense of employing

a jockey to ride a horse in a race: 'Charlie Nelson and Kim Brassey, for both of whom I work, also put me up regularly' (*Sporting Life* 4 July 1990). The OED's first attestation, from the *Times* in 1888, is 'Would they put up a jockey they believed to be dishonest?'

Q **uarter marks** See *quarters*.

quarters From Latin *quartanis*, via Old French, *quarter* first appears in English in the fourteenth century, one of its earliest uses being to describe 'one of the four parts, each including a leg, into which the carcases of quadrupeds are commonly divided'. By extension, *quarters* describes the hind parts of a horse, specifically the area between the flank and the tail. Often, in races, the effort in getting one horse to go past another lies in getting to the latter's quarters – as the jockey in Shirley's *Hyde Park* (1632) boasts, 'if I get within his quarters, let him alone.' *Quarter-marks* are the brush patterns, often in the form of diamonds, left on a horse's quarters, to form an attractive design.

quicken A good horse *quickens up* in the final stages of a race; that is, it appears to run faster. Often, however, quickening up is an illusion, the winning horse actually *staying* on better than the others who are slowing up. 'In Excess has Royal Ascot's Jersey Stakes in his sights after quickening up from two out to beat Norwich and the disappointing Hasbah in the £15,000 added King Charles II Stakes at Newmarket yesterday' (*Racing Post* 19 May 1990).

Qui Tam The opening words of the ninth Act of Parliament of Queen Anne's reign: the *Qui Tam* act menaced racing for nearly 150 years because of its aim to confine betting to very small amounts of money. It laid down that any amount in excess of £10 which was won or lost by betting could be sued for and recovered, together with treble that amount, at the suit of a common informer. In 1845 a man called Russell brought thirty-four such actions, only one of which actually reached court. As a consequence, the act was repealed in that year. Such informers were known as *qui tams*.

Rabbit Early twentieth-century racing slang for a horse which shows *in and out* form (Partridge, 1882): perhaps the source for its use to describe an inferior player of any game.

race, racing While *racing* is a term which covers a variety of sports, its early uses show it to have been specially related to horse-racing; and while *race* is common to many activities, the plural form *races* now refers only to a horse-race meeting, as in Dickens's 'We're going on to the races' (*The Old Curiosity Shop*) – one still hears a sentence like 'Spectacle wins the races' to describe the winning of one race. A horse which stands no chance of winning at any point in the race is described as *never at the races*: 'Guy Harwood was less than forthcoming over the performance of Digression (11th) who was never at the races' (*Sporting Life* 7 September 1990). *Race* comes from Old Norse *rás*, 'running, race, rush (of water), course, channel, row, series'. It occurs in the sense of 'the act of riding rapidly on horseback' from 1400; and as 'the act of running, riding, sailing, etc. in competition with one or more rivals' from 1513.

Compound forms include: *race-card* – first attestation 1851, see *card*; *race-cloth*, another term for *weight-cloth*; *racecourse*, first attested in 1764, and now in competition with the American form *racetrack* – an earlier term, now obsolete, but common in the eighteenth century, was *race-ground*; *race-goer*, 'a frequenter of race meetings', first attested, as *racegoing*, in 1848; *race-reader*, which originally meant, according to the OED, 'one who forecasts the performances of horses in a given race', but the examples it gives really describe one who expertly observes the running of horses in a race – its more common sense now is that of a race commentator, at the course or on radio or television, or to describe those who contribute to *form* guides: see *read*. The most important compound is *racehorse*, first attested in Thomas Middleton's play *Women Beware Women* (1626). Its first use as a single word, rather than *race-horse* or *race horse*, occurs in the nineteenth century. The earliest references to racehorses, in the ninth century, describe them as *running horses*; and Gervase Markham's pioneering account, in 1599, is titled 'How to Choose, Ride, Traine, and Diet both Hunting-horses and Running-horses'. The Rutland Papers at Belvoir Castle record the following entry for 1549: 'Paid, the first of November, at Barwyke to Sir Fraunces Leyke, Knyght,

for iii yardes of sattyn at xs, the yard, wych my Lord lost in wager
of horse runnynge, xxxs.' *Running horse* was still in use as late as
1777.

racehorse   See *race*.

rag   A complete *outsider* in the betting. Probably an extension of
the use of *rag* to refer contemptuously to people – but the OED
records *ragge* being used in the fifteenth century to describe a
'company of colts'. Partridge notes the use of *rags*, in 1920, as 'a
bookmakers' term for the horses that ran, especially those which
"also ran".'

rail   There are two sets of *rails* at most racecourses: one which
runs round the track, the other which separates the various *enclosures*. From the first of these comes the phrase *on the rails*, to
describe the position of a horse whose jockey keeps him well to
the inside in a race, riding close to the rails around the bends.
Coming up the straight, too, a jockey will try his best to keep his
horse *on the rail*, thereby helping him to run straight and not
wander about. Horses which do this are described as running
under the rail. From the rails which separate the *club enclosure*
from *Tattersalls* comes the phrase *rails bookmakers*: these layers
line this set of rails, have no obvious *flash* or *joint*, and traditionally
strike large bets, particularly with patrons of the club enclosure.
Laying bets *on the rails* is first attested in 1931. Because they have
no *board*, rails bookmakers are said to bet 'off the card', i.e. from
a list of runners about the same size as a race-card.

rail-bird   See *tout*.

rake, raker   From Old English *racian*, 'to run, rush, skip', *rake*
has been used to describe the fast movement of animals from the
fourteenth century. In nineteenth-century racing slang a *raker*
was, first, a fast pace, and then a 'heavy bet': the OED quotes,
from 1869, 'His lordship has gone a "raker" for Lord of the Val-
ley.' A *raking* horse is a fast-going one; as in this example, from
1862: 'A well-bred, raking-looking sort of mare.' From 'raking-
looking' it seems that the word soon came to describe the appearance of a horse rather than its achievement: 'A certain big, raking
chestnut was generally thought to hold the race safe' (Thormanby,
Tales, 46).

ramp   A racecourse swindle. The verb *ramp* had the specific meaning of forcing someone to pay a pretended bet; the OED quoting,
from 1897, the case of a man charged with 'ramping' a bookmaker;
and, under *ramper*, an account in the *Daily News* of 1887 of ram-
pers as 'men who claimed to have made bets to bookmakers, and
hustled and surrounded them if they refused to pay.' Its later,
more general sense, of a swindle is borne out by the steward's

exclamation in *National Velvet*, on discovering that a woman had ridden the Grand National winner: 'By Jove, it's the biggest ramp. How'd she pull it over?' Partridge dates *ramp* from 1860. Its original slang meaning was a 'robbery with violence', a development of its sense 'to storm, rage violently... to snatch, tear'.

rangy   Or *rangey*. From the verb *range*, 'to move hither and thither over a comparatively large area', used particularly with reference to such animals as hunting dogs searching for game, *rangy* describes animals 'adapted for or capable of ranging; having a shape indicative of this'. The OED's earliest examples relate to the *conformation* of racehorses: 'The latter was a fine, rangy gelding' (1868); and 'How the dogs, like the race-horse, have grown lighter, more rangy in form, smaller, solider in bone' (1895).

rattle¹   A horse finishes *with a rattle* when it shows an unexpected burst of speed at the end of a race: coming with 'a wet sail' is another expression for this. *Rattle*, in this sense, began with racing, and is first attested in 1888. A possible source is the use of the word to describe the call made on a hunting horn at the crisis of the hunt. 'Though Distant Relative came with a late rattle, it was always going to be too late to catch Safawan' (*Racing Post* 19 May 1990) – see, also, the quotation under *cleverly*.

rattle²   A slang expression for reliable information about a horse's well-being and chances.

rattle³   Traditionally, horses' hooves rattle on a hard surface; hence the use of the word to describe firm, or good to firm *going*: a *rattle* in the ground.

read   The great art in watching a race, seeing it develop, telling which horses are trying and which are not, noting which suffer *interference* and which lose their *action*, is comprehended in the verb *read*. The verb is apposite, for a race unfolds rather like a complex narrative, and it takes a clever reader to see all the details and yet maintain a comprehensive view. For this purpose, the major *form-book* compilers employ skilled *race-readers*. The OED recognises no such special usage, but Steve Donoghue, for instance, uses the word, and its negative, quite naturally:

> A jockey is often misjudged when *winning* a race, should he sit quietly and not drive his mount out to win as far as possible. If a horse only wins a head or neck, it is frequently opined that he was 'lucky to win', or that 'the second ought to have won.' It seems very easy for people to quite misread a race. (Donoghue, 200)

ready   Used as a verb: a slang term for preparing a horse for a *handicap* by allowing it to run poorly in earlier races so that it *gets in* with a low weight. The OED quotes, from 1889, 'A handicap of £10,000 will, indeed, be worth "readying" a horse for.'

reckless *Reckless riding*, a more serious offence than *careless* riding, will lead to the horse being automatically disqualified. It is defined as riding with little or no regard to the consequences and/or risk, particularly of injury to, or *interference* with, other horses, or riders.

refuse When a horse stops before a fence it is said to *refuse*. The OED has one example of a horse refusing to jump an obstacle, from 1525, but the racing sense first occurs in the nineteenth century, used figuratively by De Quincey (1840) – he is probably thinking in hunting terms: 'We shall endeavour to bring up our reader to the fence... But as we have reason to fear that he will refuse it...'

rein From Old French *rene*, by some traced back to Latin *retinere*, 'to retain'. The noun and verb are first recorded in the fourteenth century, but the verb had a series of meanings which are now obsolete or very rare: 'to tie a horse to something', 'to fit or furnish with a rein or reins', 'to govern, control, manage or direct by means of reins'; now it is generally used with *back* or *in*, in the sense of checking and holding in a horse by means of the reins. To win *on a tight rein* is to win very easily. One oddity about reins is that they are always referred to as 'left' and 'right' rein, never *near* and *off*.

reminder A blow with a whip: i.e. something which 'reminds' the horse to *keep up* to its work.

> I knew well that if Otho could give his mount *one* reminder with the whip, the horse, though running lazily as was his nature, would gamely respond. So without touching Magpie, I kept Gay Crusader so close to him on the whip hand that Otho could not use his whip. (Donoghue, 168)

Compare the use of *persuader* to mean a spur (Partridge, 1786).

result The *result* is the final *placings* in a race: not necessarily the order in which the horses pass the post, for a stewards' *enquiry* may alter the placings. Originally 'result', from Latin *resultare*, meant 'the action of springing back again to a former position or place'. The sporting sense of a final placing is not found until the twentieth century. In racing *result* is commonly seen from the bookmakers' point of view and therefore used to indicate a win by an outsider or unfancied horse: 'The first race threw up a result, the winner starting at 25/1.'

retainer A sum paid by a trainer for the regular services of a jockey and, by extension, a jockey's connection with a stable:

> If you are paid a retainer, you will be expected to ride for the stable retaining you, whether the horse is thought likely to win

or not, even if you are offered a better ride by another trainer. (Hislop, 91)

return   In betting, a *price* is *returned* for each horse: a development of the verb's sense 'to state by way of a report or verdict', referring to the officials responsible for compiling the *S.P.*'s from those on offer in the *ring*. These prices are known as betting *returns*. A backer's *returns* are his winnings on a bet plus his stake; e.g. £10 to win on a horse at 2/1 yields a return of £30.

ribs   A horse which is *on the ribs* is one which has no chance of winning the race (Partridge, 1926).

ride, ride out   Although *ride* has its obvious general sense, in racing it has a more specific one of bringing a horse under *pressure*: 'ridden three furlongs out, no progress' would be a typical entry in a *form* guide. The OED recognises this special sense, defining it as 'to urge (a horse) to excessive speed; to "squeeze"', its first attestation being from 1863: 'When Fordham had charge of Buckstone in the St Leger, it was said that he began to "ride" his horse too soon.' To *ride work* is to exercise a horse, as is to *ride out*: part of a *retained* jockey's job may be to *ride out* for his trainer each morning. *Ride work* is not attested until 1950, while *ride out* is not recognised in this sense by the OED. 'After breaking his neck at Warwick in 1988 Mann was unable to renew his jockey's licence, though he rides out for Tim Thomson Jones at home at Lambourn every day' (*Sporting Life* 3 June 1990). *Ride out* has another sense, that of keeping a horse going all the way to the line (also not in OED): 'Fort Hall: chased leader from 5th, led 16th, made rest, ridden out' (*Racing Post* 29 May 1990). 'He was a bad third today, but his jockey did not ride him out for a place, or else I think he might have been second' (Thormanby, *Tales*, 67).

rig¹   To *rig* the prices on a race is to manipulate the betting market unfairly. There are a number of different nouns and verbs *rig*, coming from different origins: the OED traces this usage back to the noun *rig*, of obscure origin, meaning 'sport, banter, ridicule', found chiefly in the phrase 'to run one's rig upon another' – e.g. from 1753, 'You have been very fractious all night; you have run your rig upon me.' From this sense *rig* developed the meaning 'a trick, scheme, or dodge', the verb meaning 'to hoax, play tricks on, befool', and came to be used in the special sense of rigging a market: from 1855, 'We must rig the market. Go in and buy up every share that's offered.' This example relates to the stock-market, but its implications extend to the idea of rigging the betting market, for the tricky question is to rule between what constitutes unfair manipulation of the market – rigging – and the normal influence upon market changes which any heavy investment would lead to. One rule of thumb which seems to operate now is that if a backer influences the market by wagering in a certain way, he is a price rigger; if a bookmaker does so by strategically *laying off* bets, his practice is legitimate. Generally speaking, bookmakers will refuse to pay out if they suspect rigging – a policy which has led to much ill feeling and, in one case at least, the super-gluing of betting-shop door locks by frustrated syndicates whose betting *coups* had not been paid out because of suspected rigging. As well as the *S.P.* market, the *Tote* can be rigged too: Tote rigging involves the heavy backing of other horses at the Tote windows on the course, and even heavier backing of the favoured horse at outlets throughout the country which pay out at Tote odds, but whose tote bets do not get back to the totalisator pool. In the past few years, with increasingly close supervision of the betting market by the big bookmaking concerns and the Tote, rigging has virtually disappeared.

rig²   A horse one of whose testicles has not descended. Just occasionally a *gelding* turns out to be a *rig* and achieves an unexpected siring. Alternative forms are *ridgel* – its origin explained by the OED as coming apparently from *ridge*, 'the testicle being supposed to remain near the animal's back, instead of descending into the scrotum' – and *riggald*, a Northern variant form of *ridgel*. These forms are both first attested in the sixteenth century; *rig* can be traced back to 1430.

right-hand   A *right-hand* course is one on which horses race in a clockwise direction; e.g. Ascot, Sandown.

right side   To keep a horse on the *right side* is to *hedge* one's bets by backing it, whatever else one has backed in the race: the reference is usually to a horse which has shown promise and is expected to improve. 'We should keep him on the right side until he loses his unbeaten record' (*Sporting Life* 15 May 1990). The origin of the phrase may lie in the arrangement of a betting *book*, the right side of the page having the column summarising profits if a horse wins: 'No. 1 is a good horse, and must be kept on the right side of the book' (Thormanby, *Tales*, 126).

ring   The *ring* – or *Ring* – is the enclosed space where the bookmakers operate on a course, normally in the *Tattersalls* enclosure. By extension, the course bookmakers as a whole are also called the ring. The first recorded betting use is in 1859, but the practice of forming a ring goes back at least to the eighteenth century, when it was the custom of those who intended to *match* their horses to meet in the morning of the race in an informal ring for the striking of bets. In practice this was an extension, or adaptation, of the custom among dealers in commodities to 'arrive at a fair price' by gathering

at some pre-assigned place [where] offers, quotations and acceptances would pour forth. If a sufficient number of dealers were present then the quotations were held to be fairly representative and a 'Market' was said to have been formed. The quotations became the Market Prices. Now, to arrive at the number of dealers required to form a Market a circular rail was used. The dealers would stand around this rail and when the circle was closed then it was assumed that the sufficient number were present. Not surprisingly, such gatherings came to be known as 'Rings', and the Ring evolved Market Prices which were then considered to be generally acceptable as a basis for trading.

The Room at Tattersalls emulated this practice and an hexagonal table was installed... around which the Members gathered and the prices issued, offered and accepted came to be the Market Prices of the Racing Game. (Sidney, 32)

See *roar*[2].

ringer A *ringer* is a horse which is illegally substituted for another in a race. Originally American slang, first attested in 1890, and now found in the general language in such phrases as 'a dead ringer for'. The verb *ring* had eighteenth-century slang senses, 'to manipulate; change illicitly' (Partridge).

rising Used originally about horses (1760), meaning that they are approaching a certain age: *rising four* means nearly four years old. '"Rising four, Joe," said my father, "and quite unbroken." "Umph!" said Joe to me, "she's out six, if she's a day"' (Thormanby, *Tales*, 106).

roach From the shape of the fish, *roach back* is a malformation of the horse's spine making it curve upwards – also known as *hog's back*. The OED's first horse connected example is from 1688 – 'A Baye Mare... flat ribb'd, Roach back'd' – and it records the word's application to other animals than horses. 'With her parrot-mouth and slightly roached (arched) back, the filly looked better qualified for a part in Lawrence of Arabia' (*Sporting Life* 20 June 1990).

roan From French *roan*, the word describes not a colour but an effect produced by an even mixture of white hairs with other colours: first attestation 1530. The prevailing colour generally qualifies the word; e.g. 'black roan'.

roar[1]**, roarer** A *roarer* is a horse which makes a noise when it gallops because of a defect in its wind: a tracheotomy may well cure the trouble. The OED's first attestation is from 1811, and it quotes, from 1889, 'The records state that Eclipse also was a roarer, or "high blower", as the term was in his day.' Eclipse's day was 1789. The OED records, from 1900, the use of *musical* to describe such a horse; and *whistling* describes a lesser form of roaring.

roar² The *roar of the ring* may still be heard, as bookmakers and their *workmen* let out a great cheer when something comes along to beat the *favourite*: see *ring*. In earlier days the roar was a more general thing:

> The roar was no exaggeration even in those early days of the Racing game... The roar continued throughout the race for betting in running was common. Those who were not screaming from a position near the winning line, followed the runners down the course on their horses all the while shouting at the tops of their voices and waving their hats. (Sidney, 23)

rogue Occasionally used to describe a vicious or intractable horse, but most commonly a name given to one which will not try its best. *Blinkers* are sometimes known as the *rogue's badge*.

roll A horse *rolls* when it wanders off a straight line because of tiredness. Usually the sense is of rolling away from the *rails*: a combination of the senses 'wander, roam, travel or move about' and 'of a ship: to sway to and fro; to swing from side to side'.

> Mountain Call was powering along the rail to such effect, with Be Friendly in his wake, that the older horse... was by no means free-wheeling behind him. As I called the horses I was riding with Scobie's dilemma. He wasn't going well enough to come off the fence and challenge. Yet if he didn't do so he'd got no chance – unless Mountain Call got tired and edged off the rail as he did so. Scobie stayed where he was, knowing he was doing right; knowing he'd get plenty of 'stick' if the ploy failed.
>
> Well inside the final furlong Mountain Call rolled. For several strides the two chestnuts ran head for head. The judge called for a photo. (O'Sullevan, 261)

romp To *romp in*, *romp away with*, *romp home* are phrases in general use now, but their origin is in racing slang: from the verb *romp*, 'To play, sport, or frolic in a very lively, merry, or boisterous manner' (1709), itself an adaptation of *ramp*, meaning originally 'to bound, rush, or range about in a wild or excited manner' (1627), there developed the sense of a horse moving and covering the ground 'easily and rapidly' and winning 'a race or prize with the greatest ease'. The OED's first attestation of this last sense is from Thormanby's *Men of the Turf*: 'Eclipse... simply romped in, the easiest of winners.'

room The *Room* was the Subscription Room at *Tattersalls*, where betting was first organised. Any infringement of Tattersalls rules of betting, or disputes over the settling of bets, were heard at special meetings of members in the Room, hence the survival of the phrases 'going to the Rooms' or being 'taken to the Rooms' to describe the hearing of disputes between bookmakers, long after the Room had ceased to exist. See *inside*; *ring*.

rope, roper   In late nineteenth-century racing slang to *rope in* was 'to hold a horse in check so that it shall not win' (Partridge). A *roper* was 'a jockey who prevents a horse from winning by holding it in', its meaning extending to describe jockeys 'who intentionally lose any race by similar methods'. 'Walton told me afterwards that their jockey was no other than the notorious Roper Headstall – you know, he was suspended for six months last season' (Thormanby, *Tales*, 79). To *put the strings on* meant the same thing: 'to hold a horse back in a race' (Partridge, 1860).

rough   The OED records the use of *rough* as a verb meaning 'to break in a horse', from 1802. Its common use now is in the phrase to *rough off*, meaning to retire a horse for the season and put him out to pasture. 'Hallett...is another West Country trainer who has roughed off most of his jumpers because of the firm ground' (*Sporting Life* 16 May 1990).

round   To *get round* – a corruption of *bet round* – is to *hedge* one's bets successfully, covering all the horses likely to win. In the early days of racing those *legs*[2] who aimed to bet round were the antecedents of today's bookmakers: 'He worked on gradually as a layer of odds – a "bettor round", or "leg", as he was called in those days' (Thormanby, *Famous*, 75). A race in which the bookmakers bet round is one in which the backers would need to stake £100 to win £100, whichever horse wins (see *take-out*). In practice, they bet *over-round* on nearly every race, usually between 10-15%; i.e. backers need to stake £110-£115 to win back £100. In *Pitcher in Paradise*, a bookmaker who has been committed to an asylum describes his fellow inmates: 'They're all backers of 'orses in 'ere; they punts in grub, an' cigarettes, an' fruit, an' all sorts o' things, and I'm over-round on the book every race' (*Pitcher in P.*, 143). On very rare occasions an *under-round* book occurs: see *overbroke*.

roust   A jockey *rousts* a horse when he brings it under vigorous pressure, usually when asking it to make its final effort. The word is derived from the Norwegian *raust*, 'voice, cry, shout, roar', and is first attested as a verb, 'to shout, bellow, roar, make a loud noise', in 1513. Rousting may include shouting at the horse, but it largely describes whipping and kicking. 'Swinburn had to roust her to chase leader Alcamantis with three...furlongs left' (*Sporting Life* 19 May 1990).

rub   After exercise, or a race, a horse is *rubbed down*; that is, cleaned up from the sweat, dirt, and dust which covers it – first attestation 1673. In the first decade of the eighteenth century a mare called Bonny Black 'offered to run with any Horse in England four times round the Heat being Sixteen miles without Rubing' (Prior, 137). The *rubbing house* was the place appointed for the rubbing down of horses after a race; the OED's first citation shows how it became the central location from which the organisation of racing developed: 'The Horses to be shewn and entred at the Rubbing-House nine days before.' Jorrocks sees the lads gallop by on their hacks at Newmarket just before the start of a race, 'with the horses' cloths to the rubbing-house' (Surtees, 87). When horses ran successive heats, the rubbing house's efficiency was of vital importance.

rug up   To cover a horse with a rug. A horse is *rugged up* after a race to protect it from the cold after its exertions.

Rule Four   The rule most commonly cited in racecourse announcements. It covers the deduction of a proportion of winning bets when a horse is withdrawn before the start. The rules in question are *Tattersalls* rules of betting, *Rule Four* being, actually, Rule 4 (c). The amount deducted depends upon the *price* of the withdrawn horse; e.g. if an even money shot is withdrawn, bookmakers will deduct 45p in the £ from win and place returns (excluding stakes); a 10/1 shot will lead to deductions of 5p in the £.

Rules   When used on its own, *Rules* generally signifies racing under *National Hunt* rules as opposed to other forms of racing, either Flat or *point-to-point*. 'On the two occasions moderate point-to-point winner Leningrad completed the course under Rules last season he finished tailed off' (*Sporting Life* 11 October 1990).

run¹, runner¹   Apart from describing the action of horses in a race – and racehorses were first known as *running horses* (1608: "A race of fyve myles by a couple of Running-horses") – *run* is most commonly used in the sense 'to enter a horse for a race'. The OED's first attestation is from 1750, 'Nothing is esteemed a more laudable topick of wagering than the lives of eminent men; which, in the language of Newmarket, is called running lives.' Strictly speaking, to *run* a horse is distinct from *entering* it for a race. A trainer may well say that, although he has entered a horse for a particular race, he will only run him if the *going* is suitable.

In a more general sense horses may be said to *run to form*, or *run up to form*, meaning that they run consistently. The OED's first attestation is from 1891: 'The result of the Prince of Wales' Stakes was interesting, as it afforded a striking proof of the way

in which horses sometimes consistently run up to their form.'
This phrase has entered the general language.

That horses in a race should be called *runners* is a logical extension of their being originally called running horses. *Non-runners*
are horses which have been declared to run in a race and are then
withdrawn before the field comes under *starter's orders*. If the
horse does come under orders and then *plants* itself, refusing to
run at all, it is still called a runner.

run² In the course of a race, a horse's *run* is its finishing burst.
Depending upon the horse and the *distance¹* of the race, such a
run might be only fifty yards or two or three furlongs. A horse
which has just 'one run' is, commonly, a horse which can be
relied on to make only one effort in a race and which will not
sustain it once it has hit the front. 'She won at Yarmouth in July
and was not beaten far when seventh of eighteen... in a much
better race than this. However, she reportedly has "only one run"'
(*Racing Post* 20 September 1990). This usage is very close to the
sense of 'run' in the phrase *first run*.

run about, run around In a race, a horse *runs about*, or *runs
around*, when it fails to keep a straight course. Unlike *rolling*,
which occurs when a horse is tired, running around is usually
caused by *greenness*.

run down In *chasing*, a horse *runs down* a fence when, instead of
jumping straight over it, it jumps at an angle, taking it almost
side on. This is often caused by tiredness or a horse's unsuitability
to a left or right-handed track.

run-in As the home stretch of a race, the OED offers no racing
examples, but its earliest attestation is antedated by twenty years
in Surtees' description of the finish at Newmarket, where 'the
rude stakes and ropes... guard the run-in' (Surtees, 87).

run on When a horse *runs on* it shows its stamina by continuing
to improve through the field right up to the race's end. If a horse
runs on, this may be a sign that it should be moved up in *distance¹*
in its next race. 'Access Ski took the lead entering the final mile...
and ran on strongly to beat favourite Regal Reform' (*Racing Post*
5 September 1990).

run out In jumping and Flat racing, horses *run out* when they
leave the proper course: even going the wrong side of a *doll* can
constitute running out and render a disqualification certain.
'Northern Meadow: jumped well, led until rider took wrong
course and ran out bend approaching last' (*Racing Post 29 May
1990*).

run over Used in the passive: a horse is *run over*, or gets run
over, when it is emphatically beaten.

run up In *conformation*, a horse which lacks substance is said to *run up light*: see *light*.

runner[2] *Runners* are *workmen* employed by bookmakers. In the days before licensed betting shops *bookies' runners* were common, taking illegal bets. Now they work on the course, hunting out *prices*, *laying off* bets, and generally sizing up the state of the *market*.

running 'The action on the part of a horse, of going at (great) speed, especially in a race; racing; a race.' The first attestation is from *c*.900: 'mid swiðe ʒeswencian horse or ærninge.' Its common use now is to describe a horse's *form*: 'Cheltenham is likely to be out because the horse just doesn't give his true running there' (*Sporting Life* 13 September 1990). To *make the running* is to lead, first attested in 1837; to *make all the running* is to lead the whole way: 'making the running' has gone into the general language along with other 'running' phrases, all of them originating with the racing usage: e.g. 'take up the running', be 'in' or 'out of' the running. To be *full of running* is to be going easily towards the end of a race. Betting *in running* describes betting being carried on in the *ring* through the course of a race: see the quotation under *roar*[2]. The OED records 'running mate' as 'a horse entered in a race to set the pace for another horse from the same stable which is intended to win', from which the modern political usages developed, but the original examples indicate that this was a trotting rather than racing term.

ruof Odds of 4/1: back-slang.

rush *Do a rush* is bookmakers' slang for 'laying a dummy bet... i.e. rushing the public into betting on this horse' (Partridge, 1870). 'He already repented of his rashness. He felt, to quote the language of the Turf, that "he had been rushed" into making the wager' (Thormanby, *Tales*, 67). To *roam on the rush* was nineteenth-century slang for a horse's swerving at the end of a race, at the point when the 'rush' for the line is really on. In such a use of *rush* the earliest days of racing are recalled; for, often, the four or more miles of a race were covered at a relatively moderate pace until the final half mile or so when all of the contestants rushed for the line.

S **addle**   First attested in English in the poem *Beowulf* (?10th C.) as *sadol*, the word may be derived from an Indo-Germanic form cognate with the verb *sit*. When a trainer *saddles* a horse he runs it in a race, a usage first attested in 1928. Racing saddles are extraordinarily light: 200 grams, or just over 1lb in weight. The lightest, known as a *pound dock*, weighs 9¼ozs.

safe   To make a horse *safe* was a euphemism for *nobbling* it:

> 'Making horses safe', as they now call it, was not common in those days, though in the present fast ones it is – being, I suppose, the march of intellect... I forget the horses' names, but two, I think, in one stable were backed for large sums. Dawson knew that they were always watered from that public bucket, and Bland persuaded Dawson to poison the water. The consequence was that one horse died and another nearly did. Dawson was arrested and tried; and... sentenced to death.
> (Osbaldeston, 119)

The safety involves is the bookmakers': the horse is safe to *lay to* any amount. Partridge records *safe 'un* as slang for 'a horse that will not run, certainly will not (because not meant to) win' (1871).

St Leger   The final *classic* of the season, run at Doncaster, over 1m 6f 132yds, for three-year-old colts and fillies. Until 1813 the race distance was two miles. The race was established in 1778 and named after a popular sportsman of the time, Lt.-General St Leger of Park Hill. Of the five classics the St Leger, although the oldest, is the most vulnerable to sniping criticism: its Northern location, *distance¹*, and proximity to the Prix de l'Arc de Triomphe, all make it unattractive to owners and trainers of the top three-year-olds.

sand   A familiar term for *all-weather* surfaces, as opposed to turf: 'Postage Stamp and Longshoreman are old hands at the sand, the pair finishing clear of the field in a Southwell maiden in May' (*Racing Post* 20 September 1990).

savage   The word goes back, via Old French *sauvage*, to the Latin *silva*, 'wood, forest', and was originally used in English to describe wild animals: the first attestation, from 1300, is 'leones sauvage' (savage lions). Since the *thoroughbred* is entirely domesticated, describing it as *savage* implies a regression to a primal state. The OED's first example for the sense 'a bad-tempered horse' is from 1889. Steve Donoghue had this to say about savage horses:

There are incomparably fewer savage horses at the present than there used to be. Bloodstock breeding is studied so much more carefully, the mating of suitable lines of blood so much more scientifically planned, and then training methods are so immensely improved from the old days of chifneys, scourges, chains, etc. – horses are, with few exceptions, handled very differently nowadays, and it is all to the good. (Donoghue, 186)

save To *save on* a horse is to *hedge* one's bets: a backer may bet on one horse in a race and save on the *favourite*, by putting enough on it so that if it beats the first horse he has backed he will come out quits. Such a bet is a *saver*. The OED quotes, from 1891, 'Wells says Perfection will win . . . but I've put a saver on Caloole.' To *save oneself* is to hedge in such a fashion: Partridge quotes, from 1869, 'Men who received the news at least saved themselves upon the outsider.'

school From its original senses of teaching and educating, the verb soon developed a meaning 'to discipline, bring under control, correct', as in this line from *Macbeth*: 'My dearest Coz, I pray you schoole your selfe.' By the nineteenth century *school* had two horse senses: 'to train or exercise a horse in movements' and 'to ride straight across country'. The first of these is an obvious development of the word's earlier senses, the second more difficult to explain – perhaps it emerged from the idea that the horse (and rider) had to be educated to go straight, over obstacles, rather than taking an easier, less direct route. The modern use of the verb, to train a horse to jump hurdles and fences, has elements of both nineteenth-century senses: the OED quotes, for the second of them, from 1885, 'we schooled back to the Poorhouse Gorse, and a couple of fences of the order intricate had to be jumped.' *Schooling* can also be used to describe the training of Flat horses. It is commonly found in the offence of *schooling in public*, that is when the *stewards* judge that a horse has been run in a race solely for the purpose of educating it rather than trying to get it the best *place* in the race: 'They found him to be in breach of Jockey Club instruction H2 headed "Schooling in Public" and fined both trainer and jockey £150' (*Racing Post* 20 September 1990). As a cure for this common practice, the idea of *schooling races* is sometimes floated. They would be 'races' on which there is no betting, and for which there is no prize money, for the purpose of introducing *green* horses to the racecourse. *Loose schooling* is schooling a horse without a rider on his back: 'Ultra Violet is a real test of skill and needs driving. We have loose-schooled him since his last win' (*Sporting Life* 24 May 1990).

scope[1] *Scope*, and its adjective *scopy* (or *scopey*), is one of racing's favourite words. Its horse sense is defined by the OED as 'the ability of a horse to extend its stride or jump', and it cites, in support, a usage like this one from the *Times* in 1980: 'The final Liverpool fence of sloping poles at six feet requiring more scope than most of the contenders possessed.' But in racing *scope* is generally used in two other distinct, but connected ways. One refers to the size of a horse, in particular the symmetry of its growth in relation to its age – and, in this respect, it is worth considering that the earliest forms of the word *shape* were *scap*, *schap*, *scape*, and *sceap*, and racing people often speak of a horse *shaping* well in a race; i.e. it runs promisingly enough to show that it is developing well. The second sense is that of opportunity for development, potential for growth: a horse *with scope* is a well-proportioned one which looks as if it should grow and develop into a fine racehorse. In practice, there seems little limitation to the way racing people use the word. I have even heard of a racecourse being described as scopy. ' "She's a lovely scopey filly", he said, "but I don't want to make any plans until we see how she comes out of this" ' (*Racing Post* 19 May 1990); 'At weight-for-age he meets Inneghar on level terms, yet the three-year-old should have more scope' (*Sporting Life* 13 September 1990).

scope² A verb formed from a contraction of *endoscope*. A fibreoptic endoscope is an instrument designed for looking at the internal parts of a body. 'We take blood tests every week and his test showed he had a low red cell count, so it was suggested that we scoped him. He was found to have a bit of muck down his windpipe' (*Sporting Life* 14 September 1990).

score *At score*, preceded by a verb of action, describes a horse making 'a sudden dash at full speed': 'It's a beautiful race – run at score the whole way, and only two tailed off within the cords' (Surtees, 91). *Score*, meant 'a line drawn' (1501), from the sense of the verb, 'to cut', the line being scored along the ground. This was used in the specialised sense of the 'line at which a marksman stands when shooting a target, or on which the competitors stand before beginning a race'. Thus the racing phrase describes a race run at full speed right from the start. 'Of course I told Walton to get away; and get away he did at score' (Thormanby, *Tales*, 78).

scrappy A *scrappy mover* is a horse which does not *stretch out* properly: such a horse *goes scrappy*. Perhaps derived from *scrape* – i.e. scraping the ground rather than striding over it – but the word in its general use means 'consisting of scraps; made up of odds and ends; disjointed and unconnected', and the last of these senses probably explains the word's racing use, the horse's *action* not flowing as a *thoroughbred*'s should.

scratch¹, scratching-board   As in other sports, *scratch* is used as a verb to denote the withdrawal of a horse from a race: 'Although the horse was announced a non-runner in the Press and on television the day before, the official scratching was issued a day later' (*Sporting Life* 5 October 1990). Such horses are known as *scratches*. The origin is the phrase *scratch out*, originally the erasure of writing with a penknife (1711) and then deletion 'by crossing through with a pen'. In the sense of erasing 'the name of (a person) from a list' the word was in common use in the nineteenth century, and the OED's first example of the racing usage is from 1859: 'Tomboy was scratched for the Derby at 10 a.m. on Wednesday.' Scratching was always a source of contention, especially in the days when all bets were on, runner or not; and not until British courses put up *scratching-boards*, listing the non-runners, were backers given a fair idea of whether the horse they were betting on would run. The OED's first attestation of this is from 1892: 'Judging from the scratching-board there would be good fields.' Like many other of the best innovations in racing, the scratching-board originated in Australia.

scratch²   In the nineteenth century *scratch* had two other racing senses as well as *scratch¹*. Pierce Egan uses the word to denote the finishing line of a race:

> Mr Osbaldeston objected on the ground that Steeple Chases generally ended in the middle of a field, and not in an abrupt leap. This matter was soon adjusted by naming a small drain or gutter in the centre of the meadow, as the final 'scratch', the first horse over this gutter to be considered the winner. (Egan, 165)

Egan also writes of the losing man who 'cannot come exactly to the scratch on settling day', who will be allowed 'time to make it "all right"' (Egan, 185). This may be only a variation of 'up to scratch', but there seems to be some idea here of the *scratch* as a place (a line?) where bets were settled.

scratch-race   A race in which any horse, of any age, a winner or a *maiden*, carrying any weight, could run: here *scratch* is used in the sense 'hastily improvised'.

scratchy   *Scratches* had long been used (since 1595) to describe a horse disease in which the *pastern* appears as if scratched; hence the first use of *scratchy* was with reference to a horse with the disease. Its more common sense today is to describe a horse's *action* when it is 'ill-sustained, uneven, "ragged"'; the OED's first attestation, from 1881, relates to rowing.

screw   Racing slang for 'a horse not perfectly sound'. The OED suggests that it may come from the idea that such a horse can be 'made to obtain a place by "screwing" on the part of the jockey'. In this case the verb *screw* means 'to force', but it has specific racing senses: a horse can screw its way through a fence, a jockey can screw it over one, and *screw in* is used to describe the successful forcing of a horce into the lead at the end of a race. The OED quotes, from 1856, 'Alfred Day... screwing in Virandière half a head in front of Butler.' Today, however, *screw* is more commonly used as a short form of *corkscrew*: a horse *screws a fence* when it jumps it with its body slightly twisted.

scrub   When a jockey moves his arms and legs vigorously while riding a finish he is *scrubbing*: 'Do not try and "scrub" (move your arms and legs as when riding a finish) too fast or too violently, or you will find yourself losing balance and rhythm' (Hislop, 67). The word is not attested in this sense until the middle of the twentieth century. Its racing usage derives from the similarity of the jockey's action to the vigorous rubbing movements which 'scrub' normally describes. 'Eddery, pushing and scrubbing virtually from the start...' (*Sporting Life* 9 June 1990).

scurry   A sprint. Four furlong *scurries* were discontinued in 1913, and the word has since gone out of use in racing; but the OED quotes, from 1898, 'There are still at Doncaster too many of the five furlong scurries.' Five or six furlong races are still common, but always now called sprints. 'Scurry' is itself a short form of *hurry-scurry*, a redupicative of *hurry* on the model of 'helter-skelter'.

season¹   The racing year is divided into two overlapping *seasons*, the Flat season, from March to November, and the *National Hunt* season, from August to May. The idea of the Flat season has been somewhat compromised by the introduction of *all-weather* racing, since Flat racing now goes on throughout the year; hence the introduction of the phrase 'turf season' to signify the traditional Flat-racing season: 'Birch out for remainder of turf season' (*Racing Post* 20 September 1990).

season²   A mare which is *in season* is on heat – also known as *in use*: the phrases are common to many species. Coming into season is often offered as an *excuse* for defeat: 'She also came into season in the parade ring before she finished third to In Excess at Newmarket' (*Sporting Life* 30 May 1990).

section, sectional   In America, for timing purposes, races are divided into *sections*. *Sectional timing*, common there, and now being introduced into Britain, gives separate timings for the first quarter of a race, the second quarter, and so on, even breaking up the quarter times so that it is possible, for instance, to estimate how fast a horse is travelling in the last furlong of a mile-and-a-half race.

seller, selling   In a *selling race*, usually known as a *seller*, the horses which take part are liable to be sold after the race. Normally, the winner is auctioned, and any other horse in the race may be *claimed* for a fixed sum. If the winning stable bids successfully for its own horse, the horse is said to be 'bought in'. The first recorded seller dates from as early as 1689, when the *conditions* for a race included the stipulation that the winner must be sold to 'him that throwes most at three throwes with two dice for 40 guinnies' (Prior, 220). Although the lowest kind of race nowadays, sellers used to be of higher prestige: a nineteenth-century steeplechase, including the famous Moonraker, had the condition that 'the last horse to pay the second horse's stake, and the winner to be sold for 400 sovereigns, if demanded within three hours after the race' (Egan, 162). Horses which run in such races are known as *selling platers*, or, more simply, *platers*. Racecourses put on sellers in order to gain valuable income – a proportion of the selling price going to the course – and stables enter their horses for these races partly because they do not expect to win with them in any higher grade, and partly because they offer good opportunities for betting *coups* because of the generally *moderate* abilities of the opposition. More than most races, in sellers it pays to *follow*[2] the market. Spectators enjoy sellers if only for the auction which follows and which may sometimes be more exciting than the race.

send down   When *off-course* bookmakers *lay off* with bookmakers on the course they are said to *send down* the money. Sending down used to be done on the *blower*: see *top man*.

set   A horse is *set fast* when it gets a spasm of muscular stiffness. In the *Sporting Life* of 6 April 1990 it was reported that 'McCain attributed Sure Metal's past jumping errors to the fact that the gelding suffers from a type of set-fast and ties up in his races if he doesn't get warmed up enough before the start.' Here *setfast* seems to be a noun derived from the idea of setting fast, but in the past *setfast* has been an alternative form of *sitfast*, which means something quite different. See *sitfast*.

setback   'Setback in training' is a common racing expression, covering the thousand and one reasons why a horse does not appear on a racecourse. *Setback* is first attested in 1674. Its popularity in racing comes from its succinct aptness. Training a horse is a matter of gradual development over months and years, any impediment setting back the whole progress of the horse 'Priolo is a very good horse who has had his share of setbacks. I could run him only once at two because of a leg problem' (*Sporting Life* 28 May 1990).

setfast   See *set* and *sitfast*.

settle¹   The verb *settle* – Old English *setlan*, from *setl*, 'a place of rest, seat' – developed a variety of senses from its original meaning 'to seat'. One describes an important part of a jockey's task, to get his horse to *settle* in a race; that is, to get it to run with the field without *pulling¹* (Cp. *switch off*). The sense here is 'to place... in an attitude of repose, so as to be undisturbed for a time'. There are dangers in getting a horse to settle. Dancing Brave lost the Derby because his jockey settled him so well in the early part of the race that he took too long to wake up to his task. On the other hand, a horse which will not settle will lose many races which it should win.

settle², settler   In betting, *settle* is used to describe the working out of bets according to a bookmaker's rules – from the sense 'to close (an account) by a money payment'. The *settler* is the clerk who works out the *returns*: first attested in this sense in 1963. The quotation from Egan under *scratch²* gives an early example of *settling-day*. Mondays were settling-days, institutionalised by Richard *Tattersall*'s opening of the Subscription Rooms at Hyde Park in 1815. Large sums were involved: £300,000 was settled in the Monday after the 1816 Derby. In 1836 Berkely Craven, a member of the *Jockey Club*, who had laid heavily against the successful Derby favourite,

> retired to his house in Connaught Terrace, flung himself on his sofa, and later shot himself with a duelling pistol... Rather than face a Settling Day at the Rooms, he preferred the greater and final reckoning. (Orchard, 178)

shadow-check   See *sheepskin*.

shake up   To *shake up* a horse is to ask it for an effort, particularly when it is *idling*. Under the definition 'to rouse with a shake' (1850), the OED quotes, from 1896, 'the favourite always had his race well won... although... Loates had to shake him up.' This gets the sense exactly. Shaking up a horse is not as vigorous as *scrubbing*, nor does it involve much use of the whip, but usually describes the act of *keeping* a horse *up* to its work. 'That shaken-up victory over Time Gentlemen certainly paved the way for this success' (*Sporting Life* 20 June 1990).

shape   See *scope*.

shark   A professional backer: derived in part from the fish whose nature had led to a class of persons with 'predatory habits' getting the same name, and perhaps in part from the earlier use (17th C.) of *shark* as a form of *shirk*, describing 'a worthless and impecunious person who gains a precarious living by spying on others, by executing disreputable commissions, cheating at play, and petty swindling.' On his way to Newmarket, Jorrocks is suspected of being 'either a shark or a shark's jackal' (Surtees, 78).

sharp[1] A *sharp* horse is one which is suited to sprint races. A horse which *looks sharp* is one which seems to be fully fit and ready to race. 'Macs Imp was much sharper and never diverted off a line, as he did at the Berkshire course' (*Sporting Life* 20 June 1990).

sharp[2] A *sharp* course has short straights and tight bends, Chester being the outstanding British example now that Alexandra Park has ceased to function.

sharp[3] In betting, a *sharp* is a backer of horses who is in the know and whom the bookmakers, accordingly, watch out for. In many cases a sharp is a *face*, but the word has slightly more nefarious connotations. While a face comes by his information legitimately, as it were, a sharp may have gained his knowledge more deviously. *Sharp*, as a short form of *sharper*, is attested from 1797 – 'the sharps have queered me' – and for the sense 'an expert, connoisseur, a wise man or one professing to be so', the OED's first example is from 1865: 'The long list of "sharps" who advertise their "tips" in the sporting journals.' For a modern use of the word, see the quotation under *warm*.

sheepskin Some trainers make their horses wear a *sheepskin noseband*. Known in America as a *shadow-check*, one of its purposes is to keep a horse looking straight ahead so as not to be distracted by shadows on the course.

shirt To *bet* one's *shirt* on a horse (1892) or *put* one's *shirt* on one (1897) is to put on all of one's money: if unsuccessful, of course, the backer *loses* his *shirt*. The echo here is of the old saying, to describe extreme poverty, of 'not having a shirt to one's back'.

shop From the sense of *shop* as a place – 'any place whatsoever' – developed the slang use of the word to denote a *place* in a race. To be *shopped*, or to *get a shop*, means 'to gain first, second or third place' (Partridge, 1870).

short[1] To *ride short* is now to ride with short stirrup-leathers. It used to mean, until the eighteenth century, that one rode with a short rein. In its modern sense, the original short riders were the American jockeys who came over to ride in Britain early in the twentieth century, particularly Tod Sloan and Danny Maher:

> Before Tod came here (it was the famous Lord William Beresford who introduced him in 1897) the fashion was for our jockeys to ride long, to sit at least halfway down their horses' backs, to dawdle (almost walk sometimes) in the earlier stages of a race, and then come with as fast a swoop as they could contrive in, say, the last half furlong. Shades of Sam Chifney,

George Fordham and Fred Archer still haunted our race-courses, and, anyway, had not these legendary figures won thousands of races between them? It seemed good enough.

Mr Todhunter Sloan proceeded to alter all that. He rode with his knees higher than we had hitherto seen and got so near his horse's neck that the famous "monkey-up-a-stick" song is said to have been inspired by the sight of him in action. He always tried to anticipate the starter, sometimes so success-fully that he was halfway home before other jockeys in the race realised proceedings had begun. (Bland, 186)

short²   In America, but not commonly in Britain, *short* means 'of a racehorse, not in top form', as in the OED's example from *Time* in 1977: 'Horsemen were quick to point out that he was slightly "short" – not in peak form – for the Kentucky Derby.'

short³, shorten¹   When a horse *goes short* it goes temporarily lame. The expression probably comes from the perceptible *shortening* of its stride when this happens. In a horse which is not lame, a shortening stride is a sign of tiredness.

short³, shorten²   In betting, a horse's *price shortens* when it comes in, e.g. from 3/1 to 2/1. A *short* price is, accordingly, one whose odds are very cramped. In America, however (and paradoxically), a *short horse* is one whose odds are long: 'If, after reaching the betting-ring, he finds this same "good thing", instead of being first favorite at 6/5, is an outsider or short horse, say 8/1' (Goodwin Bros., 24).

short-coupled   Describes a horse whose body is nicely propor-tioned, not too long between fore and hind legs.

short runner   A horse which regularly fails to get the minimum sprint distance over the Flat, or the two miles minimum over the jumps.

shot   With the odds preceding, *shot* describes a horse's place in the *market* and its chance in a race: 'Thunderbolt is a 20/1 shot.' Derived from the sense of the word as 'a random guess attempting to "hit" the right answer' (18th C.), the usage emphasises the uncertainty of betting on horses. It was probably first used in connection with long odds – the OED quotes Bertie Wooster, from 1923, talking about 'a hundred-to-one shot' – but it is equally common now to describe a *favourite* as 'a 6/4 shot'. A *long shot* was originally a naval term, the OED quoting, from 1791, 'What our sea men call a long-shot fire is the most destructive of any to the rigging of ships.' Its first racing usage is attested in 1869: 'He may also... learn to systematise his turf speculations, may know when it is prudent to "back a jockey" or a long shot.' The OED defines this sense as 'a bet laid against considerable odds', but it is apparent, even here, that it is the actual horse which is so described. A long shot is more commonly a horse whose odds are long than a bet laid on such a horse.

show[1]   A horse *shows* in a race when it is among the leaders, up with the pace: *never showed*, or *made no show*, means that it was always in the rear. 'Ivory Way never showed when he was well backed at Chester last month' (*Sporting Life* 12 June 1990).

show[2]   Horses are described as *showing* form, particularly in *gallops* or *trials*: 'Old School must have shown something at home to have been so well backed', or 'Dedication has never shown on the course what he has shown on the gallops.'

show[3]   In betting, the *show* is the display of *prices* on the bookmakers' boards, from the beginning of betting until the race begins, although one can have a *show in running* as well. In effect, each change of price is another show: 'At first show Thoroughfare was 6/1 but he had come into 3/1 by the last show before the off.' By extension, *show* describes the information signalled by the course *tic-tacs*. This may be a simple semaphoring of prices, or may involve the showing of more detailed information:

> The telephone was situated high up in the stands and the operator, wearing earphones, would be attended by the 'Top Man', a very expert tic-tac. The operator would relay any instructions received on his instrument to the tic-tac verbally and the Top Man would use the 'Show' to signal to another tic-tac on the floor of the Ring. The Show used by the Blower people was more complicated than the ordinary tic-tac as it required the transmission of words whereas most of the tic-tacs working for Bookmakers could get along quite well knowing only the code for numbers. The floor man on the floor of The Ring would have a runner to pass on the messages verbally. The floor man would then 'Show' his Top man what the runner has done and the answer, confirmation or bet was passed back to the S.P. office via the man with the earphones and his office, the whole process consuming no more than a couple of seconds. Sometimes the floorman would execute the commission himself by showing to a layer's own tic-tac, thus speeding up the operation, somewhat. (Sidney, 76)

show[4]   In America, *show* describes the third place in a race: a show bet pays a return when the horse finishes in the first three. The OED's first attestation of this as a noun is from 1925, but the verb, meaning 'to finish third or in the first three in a race' occurs in 1903. Its origin may lie in *show[1]*, such a horse being among the leaders at the finish.

shut   A horse is *shut in* when it cannot get out of the body of the field to make its run (cp. *box*): 'While it is important to go the shortest way, whenever possible, it is equally important to avoid getting shut in' (Hislop, 117). *Shut out* can be used in a similar way. Two horses closing in on each other *shut* another one *out*.

shy A horse *shies* at something when it starts back or shrinks away from it. The OED quotes, from 1796, as the verb's first reference to a horse, 'Thoroughbred hacks are . . . the least liable to shy of all others.' The verb is recorded with reference to people from 1650, but possibly goes back much earlier, given the probable existence of an Old English verb *scyhan*, 'to take fright'. The adjective *shy*, meaning 'easily frightened or startled' is first attested in 1000, and has specific reference to horses; its modern senses – 'easily frightened away; difficult of approach owing to timidity, caution, or distrust' not appearing until the seventeenth century.

side[1] *Side* can be a thoroughly confusing concept for newcomers to the races when the commentator refers to the position of horses on the course in relation to the rest of the field, or with regard to which part of the track they are running on. This is the *Racing Post*'s definition of the various terms he is likely to use: 'Near side, stands side and (for races on a round course) outside are all the same; far side is the same as inside.' Now, everything should be clear.

side[2] In betting, a backer has a horse *on his side* when he has put enough on it so that if it wins he will break even, no matter what else he has backed in the race.

> The horse was a bit of a head case, as his earlier handler, Bernard van Cutsem, confirmed, but if Ryan was right he was coming on song at the *moment critique*. Before leaving for holiday I took a little 10/1 and advised readers to be sure to have him on their side. (O'Sullevan, 292)

Cp. *right side*.

side door A jockey goes *out (of) the side door* when he is **unseated** and falls off sideways.

> Stephen Carroll had a hair-raising ride on Rosemede, whose saddle slipped round as he dived left out of the stalls. He was stuck half out of the side door for five furlongs but finally got his left foot out of the iron and baled out. (*Racing Post* 19 May 1990).

sighted, unsighted When a horse is not *sighted* in a race it is never in contention, never *shows[1]*: '"I guarantee you, Peter," he insisted, "they will not be 'sighted' against the older horses".' (O'Sullevan, 248). On the other hand, if a horse is *unsighted* the reference is to *chasing*, when a horse's view is obstructed and he is not able to see the fence he is about to jump, often with calamitous results:

> At Uttoxeter Peter Scudamore had come off a horse and was in a foul mood. He had his head down and when I ran up to him I didn't know what to say so I said: 'Unsighted, Scu?' and he completely blew his top... He came out with 'Unsighted!' and a lot more besides. (*Sporting Life* 21 April 1990).

silk Racing *silks* are the jockey's jacket and cap – although the breeches were made of silk too – now generally made of a synthetic material like satin nylon. The OED's first attestation in this sense is from 1891, but it gives earlier nineteenth-century examples of 'don silk' and 'wear silk' used with reference to jockeys. The other common verbs to use with 'silk' are 'carry' and 'sport'. A German visitor to Epsom races in 1710 describes the jockeys all having 'small special caps, almost like those worn by the people of Hamburg, and short silk riding doublets. Two had bleumourant, two white and another one of red damask' (Orchard, 62). Recent years have seen the importation of close-fitting aerodynamic silks from America, on the theory that less wind-resistance leads to more speed.

silver ring The *silver ring* is the cheapest *enclosure* on the racecourse, so called because bets there were commonly made in the smaller denominations of silver coins – florins and half-crowns – rather than notes. The first attestation is from Edgar Wallace (1921): 'I found a poor little bookmaker in the silver ring – the silver ring is the enclosure where smaller bets are made in the Tattersall's reservation.' Shrewd backers go to the silver ring today to back short-priced *favourites*, since they may often get slightly better odds in a place where most of the *punters* are backing longer-priced horses.

single A bet on one horse, as opposed to a double or other *multiple* bet. Singles may constitute part of a multiple bet: a patent, for instance, comprises three singles, three doubles, and a treble.

sire The father of a foal, derived from Old French *sieur*, going back to Latin *senior*. The word could, originally, be used to describe human parents, and is first attested to describe a *stallion* in 1523: 'She shall have most commonly a sandy colte... neyther lyke syre nor damme.'

sitfast Or *setfast*: a growth on a horse's back, produced by the chafing of the saddle, tending to ulceration – a combination of the verb *sit* and the adverb *fast*; but see the quotation under *set*.

skate To *skate in*, or *skate up*, is to win easily; i.e. as if gliding away from the other horses, with little effort. Not in OED. 'Hasbah looked back to her best when skating in by eight lengths from

Arabat at Leicester' (*Sporting Life* 20 June 1990).

skin, skinner The OED's first attestation of the verb's use is from an 1864 Dictionary of Slang: 'When a non-favourite wins a race "bookmakers" are said to skin the lamb.' As a definition, this is a little loose. It needs to be an *outsider*, rather than simply a non-favourite, to be described as a *skinner*. The OED records, from 1874, the bookmakers' prayer, which has not changed in over a hundred years: 'May we have a skinner.' *Skin* had slang senses of winning all a person's money from early in the nineteenth century, and one can compare the use of *fleece* to mean something very similar. 'Nordic Brave and Diet, the only two horses out of the handicap...gave the bookmakers a virtual skinner when fighting out the finish to the £15,000 added feature at York yesterday' (*Sporting Life* 16 May 1990).

skinny *Skinny* prices are poor *odds* offered by a bookmaker on one or more horses – even the whole field when the book is heavily over-*round*. There may be some connection with 'skin the lamb' (see above), but the sense 'mean, miserly, niggardly, stingy' which the OED offers for 'skinny' in its general usage adequately covers this racing usage too.

skipjack The OED's definitions make instructive reading: '1. A pert, shallow-brained fellow; a puppy, a whipper-snapper; a conceited fop or dandy. 2. A horse-dealer's boy; a jockey.' All of these are sixteenth or seventeenth-century senses, but the *jack* element looks forward to *jack-boy* and *jockey*.

skittish Derivation unknown: *skittish*, to describe a horse which is 'apt to start or be unruly without sufficient cause', dates back to the sixteenth century. If anything, the sense has weakened a little. Whereas it used to describe somewhat savage behaviour – as in the OED's quote from 1882, 'A very skittish, and at times vicious, thoroughbred colt' – it tends now to describe more playful behaviour.

skullcap Originally *skullcap* described a soft, close-fitting cap (17th C.), but in the nineteenth century the word was used, historically, to describe close-fitting steel helmets. The latter sense looks forward to its use to describe the tight-fitting jockey's helmets which, in 1956, were made mandatory for Flat race riding, and which are now obligatory in all areas of racing, including riding *work*.

slapping The adjective had two senses in the nineteenth century which are still occasionally heard. A *slapping* horse is a big, strongly-built one – often one able to run very fast: from 1828, 'One by Comus, and the other by Jonathan, both slapping colts.' A *slapping* pace is a very rapid one: 'The remaining competitors came galloping in at intervals: some of them at a slapping pace, anxious to avoid being last' (Egan, 163). The origin of the second sense may be connected with the use of *slap* to denote a sharp blow with the whip.

slate From *slate* in the sense 'to criticise severely' (Partridge, 1848) developed the idea of *slating* a horse; that is, betting heavily against it.

sleeper A bookmakers' term for a winning bet which has not been collected or claimed: probably included in the OED's definition 'a thing in a dormant or dead state', with this example from the *Complete Hoyle* of 1897: '*Sleeper*, a bet left or placed on a dead card at Faro.'

slide A horse's *price* is *on the slide* when it *lengthens²* throughout the betting exchanges.

slip¹ To *slip the field* is to go off into a long lead – as the well named Slip Anchor did when he won the Derby. The OED defines this sense as 'to pass by, get in front of; to outdistance' (1856).

slip² A mare *slips* its foal when she miscarries. The OED's first attestation is from Pepys's Diary: 'My Lady Castlemaine is sick again; people think slipping her filly.'

slip³ *Betting slips* now come in the form of a top-copy and a carbon, the betting-shop punter keeping the carbon. But the use of *slip* in this context antedates the 1961 act which set up these shops:

> The Street Bookies did, of course, operate illegally, for almost all their business was conducted on a cash basis. The bets were written out by the punters on 'Slips' – again the accepted terminology for any scrap of paper bearing a bet – and the cash stakes were wrapped in them and handed surreptitiously to the Pitch operator. (Sidney, 77)

The OED's first attestation of *betting-slip* is from 1927: 'Betting agents or touts are often had up before the courts for passing betting-slips in the streets to would-be backers.'

slip up A horse *slips up* when it falls on the flat. This may occur in a normal Flat race, or in a jump race between the obstacles.

slug Not so much a slow horse as one of a sluggish character: '...[Bill Scott's] tremendously energetic finishes when riding a coarse slug like Mundig, out of whom he cut the Derby with whip and spur' (Badminton, 232).

snaffle A word of doubtful origin, which must come from the same form which underlies the German *schnabel*, a forked instrument used in training dogs to keep the head up. A *snaffle* is the simplest kind of bridle-bit, consisting of a single-jointed or unjointed mouthpiece – the type of bit almost universally used in racing. The OED's first attestation is from 1533. A common expression in the eighteenth and nineteenth centuries was 'to ride in, on, or with the snaffle', meaning 'to rule easily, to guide with a light hand'.

snatch   See *stringhalt*.

snatches   When a horse runs *in snatches* it keeps taking hold of the bit and dropping it through the course of a race, not maintaining an even pace: 'Garden Centre Boy: pulled hard in rear, hit sixth, ran in snatches after, lost touch three out' (*Sporting Life* 8 September 1990). The OED's first attestation is in Barnaby Googe's *Horseback Hush* (1577), 'by snatches (as it were) and not thoroughly'.

snip¹   'A white or light mark, patch, or spot on a horse, esp. on the nose or lip.' The OED's first attestation is from 1562, 'A younge baye geldinge with a whyte snypp off the nose'; and it compares the German dialect word *schnippe*, 'a horse with a mark on the nose'.

snip²   Racing slang for 'a good tip' (Partridge, 1890), from which developed the general sense of 'a bargain', which came back into racing in the sense of a *handicap snip*, a well *handicapped* horse at a reasonable *price*.

soaping   Describes the excessive sweating of a horse, which has all the appearance of a soap lather: *lathering* is also used, and 'all of a lather' may well be the source of the phrase 'hell for leather'.

sock   A white mark extending a short way up a horse's leg: first attestation 1893. See *stocking*; *white*.

solid   *Solid in the market* means that a horse has been consistently backed. It is normally used to describe not the first and second *favourites*, but one of the better backed horses in a race.

sort   With 'good', or some other term of approbation, *sort* denotes a horse which seems *genuine* and has *scope*. 'Lotus Pool, unbeaten in two starts, is an improving sort' (*Sporting Life* 19 May 1990); 'This progressive sort must have just as good a chance as her stablemate' (*Sporting Life* 12 September 1990). Frequently the word is used merely as a synonym for horse: 'Henry Cecil does well with lightly-raced sorts in handicaps' (*Sporting Life* 3 October 1990).

sound   Its original sense, still common, was 'of persons, animals: free from disease, infirmity, or injury' (1200). In racing it is used to describe freedom from lameness or from breathing problems: a horse *goes sound* when it walks freely, and is *sound in wind* when it does not *roar* or even *whistle*. In his evidence to the House of Commons Select Committee on Gaming in 1844, Richard *Tattersall* had the following to say, in response to a question about informing the public if a well-backed horse goes lame in the days just before a race:

I may venture to say no horse in England is sound; I breed a
great many myself; I have 30 brood mares, and I never bred
a colt in my life that was not lame before he was a year old;
there is no such thing in existence as a sound horse. (Orchard,
290)

sour   Formerly used to describe horses (and other animals) which
looked 'heavy, coarse, gross': the OED quotes, from 1713, 'A
strong, sower Horse of £6 Price.' Its common usage in this century, however, is to describe, at worst, a horse of a vicious or
savage temperament; at best, one which is out of love with racing
– usually the consequence of poor *schooling* or having had too
many hard races (cp. *sweet*).

Let Fly was a very sour horse, in the opinion of every jockey
who rode him; he had been through some hard tussles as a
two-year-old, which no doubt helped to spoil his temper...
He would 'stick his toes in' if pressure was applied, and swerve
right out of his ground. (Donoghue, 45)

S.P.   Short for *starting price* (see *price*). The abbreviation has been
popularised by television police series, where the *S.P.* stands for
the low-down: 'Give me the S.P.' says the hard-bitten detective
to his juniors as he arrives at the scene of a crime.

spare   Jockeys get *spare rides*, or *spares*, when they ride a horse
for which they have not been booked, usually because the booked
jockey is late, injured, or otherwise unavailable. *Spare* also
describes the second horse which a stable lad has to *do¹*, and a
horse in partial training not doing work with the main string.

speech   A tip: in the phrase *give the speech* (Partridge, 1872) –
probably a development of *speech* in the sense 'a report or rumour'.
Cp. *talk*; *whisper*.

speedy-cutting   See *plait*.

spin   Although the verb *spin* is long established – it is first attested
in 725 – the noun is not found until the middle of the nineteenth
century. The sense of the noun, 'continuous movement by way
of exercise or pastime', now common when we talk of going for
a spin in a car or on a bike, seemed to have emerged from the
training of horses. The OED's first attestation, from 1856,
describes 'shorter spins of three-quarters of a mile' which will be
adopted 'as often as the trainer sees fit'. Perhaps the derivation
is from *spin out*, 'to render lengthy or protracted' (1603), a *spin*
being a lengthy ride – in spite of the 'shorter spins' of the OED's
quote. The word is still common in training reports: 'In the
Groove did a seven-furlong spin this morning and finished with
ears pricked' (*Racing Post* 8 June 1990).

spiv   Partridge defines *spiv* as 'one who lives by his wits – within

the law, for preference; esp. by "the racing game"', and traces
its usage back to the 1890s 'by and among race-course gangs...
and had been known to a few police detectives since 1920 or so.'
He conjectures that it is a shortened form of *spiffing*, as in 'spiffing
fellow'.

splint   A bony growth which can agitate a horse's tendon. The
horse is said to *throw a splint* when it develops one: first attested
early in the sixteenth century. Its origin may lie in the idea that
the growth is a splinter in the bone or, less likely, that it gives
the leg the appearance of being in a splint. 'The West Awake
throws splint – misses Gold Cup' (*Sporting Life* 24 January 1989).

split   A jockey *gets the split* when the horses in front of him part
so that his own horse can go through the gap between them.
Towards the closing stages of a race he may have to decide whether
to wait for the split or to pull his horse out and go round the
horses in front of him. 'Sally Rouse got a tight split between the
Wragg runner and Bold Russian' (*Sporting Life* 21 June 1990).

spook   From Dutch *spook*, German *spuk*, the noun came into
American English at the beginning of the nineteenth century,
and the verb by the end of the century. The sense of the verb in
racing, when a horse becomes alarmed or unnerved by something
it sees, hears, or senses, is first attested in 1928, with reference
to cattle. *Spook* is a good word to use because of its supernatural
implications: often a horse will spook for no discernable reason.
Spooky describes generally apprehensive behaviour. 'He pointed
out that his horse spooked at something inside the final furlong'
(*Racing Post* 19 May 1990).

sport   The *sport of kings* is a favourite cliché, but in spite of Charles
II's example, it has only lately come to be synonymous with horse
racing. First it described war (17th C.), then hunting (18-19th
C.). After a day out at Newmarket, Jorrocks challenges the racing
fraternity with a counter toast – ' "the chase... I say it's the sport
of kings! the image of war without its guilt" (hisses and immense
laughter)' (Surtees, 93). Its first use to describe racing does not
seem to be until the twentieth century: from 1918, 'Weep for the
King of Sports, the Sport of Kings... On thousand tracks unrid-
den, desolate, Hay waves from winning-post to starting-gate.'
That *sport* should relate mainly to racing is borne out by the title
of the *Sporting Life*, a daily newspaper which is chiefly concerned
with horse-racing. From early in the eighteenth century until the
beginning of the twentieth, racecourses were often dignified by
the title *place of sport*.

sprawl   A horse *sprawls* when it loses its *action* completely in a
race: 'Steve Cauthen reported heavily-backed Private Tender

"sprawled" when he tried to pick him up three out' (*Sporting Life* 19 May 1990).

spread   See *plate³*

spread-eagle   A horse *spread-eagles* its field when it wins very easily: 'Shaking off Anonoalto at halfway, Never In The Red spread-eagled his field to win by six lengths' (*Sporting Life* 19 June 1990). The verb, in common use now, has its origins in ice-skating: a spread-eagle was a figure cut in the ice, in imitation of the old inn sign, 'The Spread Eagle'. From the skating sense developed that of tying up a person for punishment (1829), and the racing sense of beating emphatically. The OED's first racing attestation is from the *Daily Telegraph* in 1864: 'When poor old Flash-in-the-Pan spread-eagled his field for the Chester Cup.'

Spring double   A popular *ante-post* bet, aiming to get the winners of the Lincoln Handicap, on the Flat, and the Grand National.

springer   A *springer* – more fully, *springer in the market* – is a horse which should, on *form*, be an *outsider*, but whose *price* shortens very quickly because of the large amount of money wagered on it shortly before the *off²*. Its use may derive from the idea that the horse is a surprise sprung on the bookmakers. The OED's first attestation is from Edgar Wallace's *Flying Fifty-Five* (1922): 'The "springer" in the market, the horse that opened at ten to one and came rapidly to five to two.'

sprint, sprinter   A *sprint* is a race of five or six furlongs for horses of three years old and upwards; for two-year-olds the sprint distance is five furlongs only. A *sprinter* is a horse which specialises in such races. The word is connected with the verb *sprent*, of Scandinavian origin, meaning 'Of persons, animals, etc: to spring, spring forward...move quickly or with agility'; first attested in the fourteenth century. Early horse-races were long-distance affairs, of four miles and more, but since they were often run at a dawdle – even a walk some of the time – with horses running flat out for only the final few furlongs, the sprint was already inherent in them. See *dash*; *scurry*.

spur   One of the artificial aids. The OED defines it as 'a device for pricking the side of a horse in order to urge it forward, consisting of a small spike or spiked wheel, attached to the rider's heel.' *Spora* in Old English, the word is recorded as early as 725. If spurs are ever used in racing today they will be of the 'blunt' variety.

squeeze   A horse is *squeezed*, or *squeezed up*, when it is trapped between two or more horses coming in on him from either side. This often happens when a jockey thinks he gets the *split* and then finds the gap closing back on him: see *tighten*. *Squeeze* also

describes a jockey's action when he grips the horse firmly with
his knees: 'Although Runaway Romance quickened, the champion jockey had only to squeeze up the filly to win by a ready
length' (*Sporting Life* 4 October 1990). See also the quotation
under *washing*.

squiggle   The symbol in the *Timeform* guides which indicates that
a horse is un*genuine* is known loosely as the *squiggle*, or, sometimes, thinking of the *connections'* feelings, 'the dreaded squiggle'.
Timeform describes such a horse as being 'of somewhat unsatisfactory temperament; one who may give his running on occasions
but cannot be relied upon to do so.' In extreme cases a *double
squiggle* is attached, to a horse which is 'an arrant rogue or
thorough jade; so temperamentally unsatisfactory as to be not
worth a rating.'

stable   From Old French *estable*, ultimately from Latin *stabulum*,
literally a standing place: first attestation 1250, 'Vor hors a stable
and oxe a stalle.' A horse is trained at a *racing stable* (1810).
Punters may *follow³* a *stable in form*; i.e. back all the runners of
a trainer whose horses are performing well. Equally, a stable may
be 'out of form', ready to 'strike form', be 'under a cloud', etc.
In every case the essential idea is that when some horses of a
stable run well, then others from it will run well too, and when
some disappoint, then others from it are likely to.

A *stable jockey* is one paid a *retainer* to ride all a trainer's horses.
Stable-mates are horses which belong to the same stable (formerly
stable-companion). A *stable-pea* is 'the horse fancied by members
of its stable' (Partridge, 1920): the phrase plays on the idea of its
being the 'sweet pea' of the stable. For *stable lad* see *lad*.

stake¹   The OED says that the derivation is uncertain, but suggests
that the sporting senses of *stake* may come from the phrase 'on
the stake', referring originally 'to a custom of placing on a "stake"
or post the object . . . hazarded on the event of a game or contest.'
However, there is no evidence that such a custom ever existed.
A *stake* is 'that which is placed at hazard; especially a sum of
money . . . to be taken by the winner of a game, race, contest'
(1540). In racing, the sums which owners pay to enter their horses
in a *stakes-race* are then divided, proportionately, among the
placed horses. Such races may be modest, but include the top
events, whose titles are, properly, the Derby Stakes, the Eclipse
Stakes, etc. Today races like these usually have a sum of money
added to the stakes to increase the value of the prizes. In the past,
without such additions, stakes races were worth remarkable sums:
in 1889 the Eclipse Stakes was worth £11,165, and the Prince of
Wales's Stakes, at unfashionable Leicester, £11,000. Two horses

of that period, Isinglass and Donovan, each won over £55,000 in stakes races. *Produce Stakes* are races 'in which the runners must be the offspring of horses named and described at the time of entry' (1833).

Anyone who bets on a race has a stake in it, hence the use of the word to mean the amount of money wagered: a *minimum stake* means that the bookmaker has a lower limit to the amount of money which he will accepts as a bet.

stake²   A horse gets *staked* when it impales itself upon some such stake as a fence post or, on the racecourse, one of the rails posts or the rail itself. The use of plastic rails has led to a great reduction in such injuries. The OED's first example is from 1687: 'A bright bay Gelding...a...Scar on the far side near the Flank (where he had been stak'd).' Steve Donoghue describes his riding in a race in France where the two other runners were ridden by jockeys who hated each other so much that they knocked each other off their horses and engaged in a furious fist-fight. Donoghue passed the post the winner, 'so helpless with laughter that I almost had to be helped off my horse when I rode him into the enclosure'. The joke turned sour, however: one of the runners, 'a very nice mare, was very much injured, having got "staked" so badly that her racing career was perforce ended, though it was eventually managed to save her for the stud' (Donoghue, 61).

stale   Perhaps from Old French *estaler*, the verb *stale* means 'to urinate, said esp. of horses or cattle' (15th C.):

'I kept him away from the course as long as I could,' he said confidentially; 'he's as quiet as a sheep, but he knows what he's here for: he's staled twice since we got here.' (Sassoon, *Memoirs of a Fox-Hunting Man*)

stall   The Old English *steall* first appears in the eighth century as a gloss for the Latin *stabulum*: its sense is 'a standing-place for horses or cattle'. The chief use of *stall* on the racecourse now is in the *starting-stalls*, which have replaced the *starting-gate*, and which ensure a fair start in all but a very few Flat races – the exceptions are long-distance races for which the stalls would be an obstruction on the second circuit of the course. *Stalls handlers* load the horses into the stalls.

stallion   From Old French *estalon*, related to *stall*: an entire male horse, at least four years old, capable of reproducing the species. First attested in 1388.

stamp   The physical shape of a horse; corresponding to the OED's definition 'physical or outward form, cast' (1598), as in a statement like: 'He's a lovely stamp of horse, every inch a chaser' (*Racing Post* 31 July 1990). The word can be used to describe a horse's potential development, but here *scope* is more common; and *stamp* generally describes its achieved appearance rather than its future development.

stand¹, stands   The *stands* at a racecourse look back to the first examples of raised platforms for the viewing of a sporting event. The OED's first attestation is in connection with racing, from a notice concerning Doncaster races in 1615. In spite of its early date it has a familiar ring: 'It is agreed that the stand and the stoopes shall be pulled upp and imploied to some better purpose, and the race to be discontinued.' Such stands were quite different from today's constructions, as Jon Bee's definition demonstrates: 'a house for accommodating the spectators at horse-races.' When such constructions became grander in size and purpose, the word *grandstand* was introduced, defined in the original OED volume G, in 1900, as 'the principal stand for spectators at a race-course, etc. with the highest price of admission,' its first British example being from 1841: 'The first brick of the Grand Stand at Ascot was laid on the 5th of December, 1838', although it gives an American example from 1834. From this close racing association came the phrase a *grandstand finish*, meaning a close and exciting one.

stand²   A stallion *stands* at stud to serve mares. The OED quotes, as its first attestation, from 1766, 'Merry Tom stands at my house, and covers mares at a guinea the leap.' The usage is originally American, this quotation coming from the *Virginia Gazette*.

stand³   Bookmakers *stand* a horse when they keep taking money for it without shortening its price: possibly derived from the phrase to 'stand in' a price, as in *Pickwick*, 'It'll stand you in a pound a week.' Behind the usage, also, there is some sense of withstanding heavy pressure. If a bookmaker 'takes a view' on a horse – i.e. decides that it is going to be beaten – then he may stand it for large sums of money without *laying off*.

stand down   Stewards *stand down* a jockey when they suspend him from riding for a stipulated period: a development of the phrase's general sporting sense, 'to withdraw from a game, match or race' (1890); but the military sense, 'to come off duty' (1916) might have some influence, given the military backgrounds of many stewards. 'Michael Roberts...was stood down for two days...for excessive use of the whip' (*Racing Post* 20 June 1990). Jockeys may also be stood down for medical reasons.

stand in   In its definition of *stand in*, the OED quotes a Slang Dictionary of 1865, which defines it as 'To make one of a party in a bet or other speculation'. In racing it refers to those backers who *get on* a horse at a fair price: 'Nor was he ever known to

scratch a horse merely because the public had so far backed it as
to prevent him from "standing in", as the racing slang hath it'
(Thormanby, *Famous*, 33).

standing dish   A horse which *farms* a particular race or, more
commonly, wins regularly at a particular course. 'It was easy to
see why Tauber had become a standing dish here this season
when she landed a six furlong handicap last week' (*Racing Post*
20 September 1990). Literally, a standing dish was one 'that
appears each day or at every meal' (1876).

stand off   A *chaser stands off* when he takes a longer jump than
usual, taking off half a stride before he would normally do so.
Not in OED.

star   The white mark on some horses' foreheads, smaller than a
blaze.

star-gaze, star-gazer   A horse *star-gazes* when it holds its head too
high, a dangerous habit in *steeplechasing*, and undesirable in Flat
racing since it means that the horse is not concentrating. *Star-gazer*
is first attested in 1785.

stare, stary   A horse's coat *stares* when it stands on end: first
attested in 1573. A horse which looks *stary* is one whose coat is
patchy or threadbare.

start, starter[1]   because of the frequency of *false starts* Lord George
Bentinck introduced the *flag start* in the middle of the nineteenth
century: a flag start is still used in a limited number of long-
distance races, where the use of starting *stalls* is not practicable,
or on occasions when the stalls fail to work. In jump races a
starting tape is used, absolute equality of starting not being important in a medium where the minimum race distance is two miles.
Although much care is taken to ensure that starts are fair, they
do not count for anything in betting. If a horse is *left at the start*,
or refuses to start, it is still considered a *starter*; that is, a runner
in the race. Before 1862 horses were allowed to make a *running
start*. From that date the *Jockey Club* ruled that horses must 'walk
up' and be started at a walk. In 1898 the *starting-gate* was tried
on British racecourses, having already been used in the colonies
some years before. By 1900 all two-year-old races were ordered
to be started by a 'starting machine', the official name for the
starting-gate. In 1901 they were ordered to be in use at every
meeting, with special exceptions where its introduction would be
impracticable.

starter[2]   The official who gives all the orders necessary for securing a fair start: the OED quotes an example of this title from 1622.
When horses come *under starter's orders* the race is deemed to
have begun and a horse which, for whatever reason, does not

start, is still counted as a runner.

starting-stalls See *stall*.

starting price See *price*.

stay, stayer A horse which *stays* is one which *gets[1]* long distances: how long depends upon its age – a two-year-old which gets a mile, a three-year-old which gets a mile and three-quarters, an older horse which gets two miles may all be described as *stayers*. Such descriptions are less often used in jump racing, where staying is the name of the game, except that *hurdlers* which get distances in excess of two and a half miles may be described as staying hurdlers. When a horse *stays on*, in whatever form of racing, it is doing its best work towards the end of a race. A frequent *excuse* for a beaten horse is that 'it didn't stay'; and a true long distance horse will 'stay forever'. Since the principal senses of *stay* mean coming to a halt and standing still, it is possible that this racing usage comes as an extension of the sense 'to stand one's ground, stand firm'. 'Tender Type, who looked a picture beforehand, stayed on well to beat favourite Podrida' (*Racing Post* 19 May 1990); 'He gives every indication that he stays all day' (*Sporting Life* 21 June 1990).

steady[1] To *steady* a horse is to get it well balanced, especially before a fence: 'To a certain extent horses must … gallop over their fences; but this by no means signifies that they should not be held together and steadied when they jump' (Badminton, 310).

steady[2] *Steady in the market* means that a horse's *price* stays the same through the course of the betting, from the opening of the market to the issuing of the *S.P.* Cp. *solid*.

steal Jockeys *steal* races in two ways: either by slipping the field and not getting caught, or by coming with a late run, to *get up[1]* just on the line. 'I thought Steve had stolen it and it took Batshoof a long time to get there' (*Racing Post* 20 June 1990).

steamer Popularised by John McCririck on television's Channel 4, a *steamer* is a horse which is strongly backed on the morning of a race, so that its *price* shortens dramatically. The probable derivation comes from the idea of punters 'steaming in' to back it; although there may also be some connection with the use of the word as a slang expression for punter, on the basis that steamer = steam tug = mug.

steeplechase Alternative forms are *steeple-chase* and *steeple chase*. Races across country used to be from one church steeple to another one a few miles away – or, more accurately, to the shadow of the steeple. This steeplechasing seems to have originated in Ireland. There is record of a *match* raced in 1752, between Mr O'Callaghan and Mr Edmund Blake, from the church of Buttevant to the spire

of St Leger church. The first recorded English steeplechase was
in Leicestershire in the early 1790s, over an eight-mile course.
However, Elizabeth Eliot cites a letter from a gentleman at Newmarket, in the suite of the Duke of Monmouth, which describes
a race in which the duke 'got a very terrible fall'. He was 'bleeding
at the mouth, and dead for a time', but recovered well enough to
see his horse win him £100 later in the day. The writer, Thomas
Ross, goes on to imply, in Eliot's words, that these were 'races
in which the riders of distinguished horses were expected to break
their necks' and, therefore, 'might reasonably be supposed to
include the leaping of ditches, hedges, payles, rails or fences'
(Eliot, 13). If right, her conjectures would push our records of
the sport back to 1662. By the nineteenth century steeplechase
matches were well established. The *Sporting Magazine* describes
a match which took place in 1804, 'which among that community
is determined a steeple race – the parties undertaking to surmount
all obstructions, and to pursue in their progress as straight a line
as possible'; and in the same year 'a veritable case of steeple
hunting, as it was called' was a race run in Newcastle-on-Tyne,
from Chapel House to the Cowgate, between Captain Prescott
and Captain Tucker, each of the Fifth Light Dragoons:

> The conditions laid down that the riders were not to deviate
> from the object in view by more than fifteen yards, no matter
> how formidable might be the fences encountered. Within the
> limits of fifteen yards the leading horse was to have choice of
> the country, and the other, while not permitted to jump at the
> same place, had nevertheless to keep within the fifteen yards
> 'and choose another road for himself'. Presumably Captain
> Tucker led most of the way and had his choice of road, for he
> won by something like a quarter of a mile. (Eliot, 22)

This form of racing seems to have been a development of the *wild
goose chase*.

By the 1870s steeplechasing had been 'tamed' into regular races
on specially prepared courses, with artificial rather than natural
obstacles – no walls or ploughed fields, and brooks and ditches
reduced to the *water jump*. The sport fell into great opprobrium
in the nineteenth century, partly because of the lack of control
over it – see *illegitimate* – and partly, no doubt, because of the
dilution of what had once been a gentlemanly pursuit. In the
words of a writer of the 1870s, disparaging 'steeplechasing in its
modern form', it now consisted of

> jockey boys on cast-off race horses, riding round and round a
> course, jumping hurdles, sham brooks, and other artificial
> fences . . . Now sport gives way to shillings and sixpences, and

the circus business best suits those enterprising lessees who
have solely an eye to gate money. (Eliot, 35)
In the twentieth century the sport gradually increased in popularity. Offering a genuine test of stamina on the horse's part and
bravery on the jockey's – although the horses need to be brave
and the jockeys tough also – steeplechasing seems to many now
to be the most legitimately sporting area of horse-racing. *Steeplechasers* stay in training for many years, in contrast to Flat horses
whose careers are often finished by the end of their three-year-old
season.

steer Frequently used as a synonym for ride: to *steer* a horse
home is to ride a winner – or, one can speak of steering a horse
into second or third place. The usage is very old. The OED quotes,
from 1375, 'Ther may no man haf worthy hede, Bot he haf wit
to steir his stede'; and, from 1890, 'Tapp was the jockey... and
"steered him to victory".' The quotation marks in this last example
indicate that even before the word's increasingly narrow reference
to driving motor vehicles, its horse sense was becoming thought
of as figurative. A *steering-job* is when a horse wins – or is expected
to win – very easily: all the jockey has to do is to sit tight and
steer it round the bends. 'The two-year-old proved the proverbial
steering job, duly hacking up by seven lengths' (*Racing Post* 19
June 1990).

steward 'A person appointed to supervise the arrangements or
maintain order at a race-meeting' is how the OED defines *steward*,
although this definition better describes the job of the *clerk* of the
course. The stewards' function is primarily to ensure that the
rules of racing are observed, their word being law – although the
decisions of local stewards can be overruled by the *Jockey Club*
stewards. A *stewards' enquiry* indicates that the running of a race
is to be reviewed so that the result is not yet official – see *enquiry*.
The chief qualifications for being a steward are that one should
have been to a good school and should have no experience of
riding horses in a race. Stewards were first officially appointed
in 1770. See *stipe*.

stick¹ Used familiarly to describe the whip and the winning-post.
From the former comes the expression 'give some stick', meaning
'to encourage punters to bet freely on a certain horse, especially
the favourite' (Partridge, 20th C.). *Over the sticks* is a familiar
term for jump racing.

stick² In betting, a bookmaker *sticks* a horse when he keeps taking
money for it without *laying off* – cp. *stand*. Alternatively, one
might *stick* a horse oneself if given a *commission* to back it and
one chooses, instead, not to lay it off:

Among bookmakers who have made it from scratch, one of the leading layers in the north of England started his working life as a bobbin boy in a Lancashire mill. Appointed the factory 'runner', it didn't take him long to realize that the money he collected on behalf of his workmates from the bookmaker generally amounted to less than he had delivered. He began by sticking a few bets, and then the lot. It has worked for some, but not all. (O'Sullevan, 78)

stiff¹ In nineteenth century racing slang *stiff*, or a *stiff 'un*, was synonymous with *safe*, or safe 'un; that is, used to describe horses 'certain to lose or not to run at all'. The OED quotes, from 1871, 'Most assuredly it is the bookmakers that profit from the "safe 'uns", or "stiff 'uns", as ... horses that have no chance of winning are called.' A development of this was the use of the verb *stiffen* to mean 'prevent a horse from doing its best' (Partridge, 1900). However, the OED records an alternative use of *stiff*, of Australian origin, to mean a horse certain to win, quoting from 1890: 'After the Melbourne Derby and Cup of 1880, Grand Flaneur was considered stiff for every race for which he was entered.' The writer explains this as a metaphor, meaning 'something that cannot be diverted'.

stiff² A *stiff* course is the opposite of a *sharp* or *easy* one. The origin is in the use of the adjective to mean 'of an ascent or descent: steep so as to be difficult' (1704), from which there derived a special hunting sense, 'difficult (said of a tract of country presenting many obstacles)': from 1817, 'the ground gone over was through a stiff country.' A stiff course over the jumps is likely to be one where the obstacles are difficult – Haydock Park, for instance; on the Flat it is likely to be one where much of the racing is done on the *collar*: 'The Curragh mile is even stiffer than Newmarket in the eyes of many racing professionals' (*Sporting Life* 19 May 1990).

stifle 'The joint at the junction of the hind leg and the body ... in a horse or other quadruped' – corresponding to the human knee, but the knee of a horse is on its foreleg. The word's origin is unknown, although a connection with 'stiff' has been suggested. It is first recorded in 1330, referring to deer.

stipe Slang for Stipendiary Steward, the racecourse official who acts as the *stewards'* secretary. Partridge identifies its use as originally Australian (1942), but *stipe* as a short form of stipendiary magistrate goes back to the 1850s.

stirrup Old English *stigrap*, a compound of *stig*, 'climb', and *rap*, 'rope': first attested in the tenth century. A *stirrup* is an arched piece of metal with a flat plate to receive and hold the rider's foot.

As the word's etymology shows, the original stirrup was a looped rope; and the OED points out that in other Teutonic languages the word has been used to refer to the stirrup *leather*, the stirrup itself having another name. See *irons*.

stocking Longer than the *sock*, a white mark extending from the horse's knee or hock to the hoof. See *white*.

stoke up To *stoke up* a horse is to ask it for an effort: a frequently used idiom, probably because of the vigorous arm movements involved. Not in OED. Cp. *scrub*.

stone-cold Slang for a horse which has no more to give in a race.

stop¹, stopper To *stop* a horse is to tamper with it before a race so that it will not be able to run up to its form. Not in OED. Any such treatment is known as a *stopper*: '"In racing terms it is a stopper," Neville Dunnett of the Horse-racing Forensic Laboratory said. "It will quieten a horse very carefully but effectively."' (*The Independent* 4 October 1990).

stop² A horse is said to *stop* in a race, not when it comes to a halt – that is to *pull up* – but when it slows down: 'Honeydew ran on while others were stopping'. Not in OED.

store Since the fifteenth century *store* has been used to describe animals kept in reserve. A *store horse* is one bought young, to be kept for several years until it is ready to go chasing. 'Josh Gifford set the European record of 68,000 guineas for a jumps "store"' (*Sporting Life* 15 May 1990).

straight¹ A horse is *straight* when it is fit to race. Not in OED. 'Though Miss the Point was an easy to back 6/1 shot . . . he looked pretty straight and battled on to lead inside the distance' (*Racing Post* 20 June 1990).

straight² *Straight*, in the sense of a straight portion of a race-course, is first attested in the OED in the middle of the nineteenth century, but the usage is much older. Cheny's 1732 *Racing Calendar* offered to provide a 'list of courses of the Kingdom . . . also a Description of their Forms and Ciutations of their Streights and their Turns' (Prior, 108). Cp. also the use of 'streight course' in the quotation under *distance³*.

straight³ In betting, in America and other places where a *pari mutuel* operates, a *straight bet* is one laid to win. The use of this term antedates the setting-up of the pari-mutuel system:

> This starts you to thinking. Thirty dollars is somewhat of a swell bet to put on a horse straight at that price; better to play it all three ways. So, after a mature deliberation, you take 45 to 10 straight, 14 to 10 1-2, and 5 to 10 1-2-3. (Goodwin Bros., 31)

For *straight forecast* see *forecast*; for *straight tip* see *tip*. 'Straight from the horse's mouth' has been stable slang since 1830, according to Partridge, and by 1900 had become a common colloquialism.

strap To *strap* a horse is to groom it. The OED quotes, from 1875, 'When the groom took off his clothes to strap him . . . my hopes of winning . . . vanished altogether.' See, also, the quotation under *wisp*.

stretch¹ When horses stride out properly they *stretch*, or *stretch out*. When they are *on the stretch* they are having to work hard to keep their place: 'It is always better to walk or trot too slowly than too quickly, because there is nothing worse for a racehorse than being on the stretch when he is trotting' (Hislop, 46).

stretch² The *stretch*, as a synonym for the *straight²*, is now more common in America. Its first attestation is in an 1895 Dictionary of Slang, where it is defined as 'the straight or nearly straight sides of a course as distinguished from the curves or bends.' Its derivation may lie in the idea of the course being stretched out, as it were, but there may also be an influence from the verb *stretch¹*, since this is the part of the course where horses stretch out most fully. A racecourse normally has two such straights: the *back stretch* and, as a phrase which has broadened into the general language, the *home stretch*.

stride Horses – and jockeys – *see a stride* when they approach a fence and are able to take off at exactly the right distance from it to put in a fast jump.

strike¹ The verb is used to indicate a change in a horse's pace. The OED quotes, from Sir Walter Scott, 'No sooner had the horses struck a canter . . .' An older sense of *strike* refers to a horse's putting down of its fore-foot short: first attested in 1683, and the OED quotes from 1850, as an explanation of 'strike short', 'to put down his fore-feet perhaps a yard short of his usual stroke or stride.'

strike² In betting, a bet is *struck*: a development of striking a bargain, itself a development of striking hands, when the two parties shake hands in agreement. The handshake is still an appropriate idea for horse-race betting because, no matter how large or small, betting debts are not recoverable in law – and yet much betting still depends upon credit rather than ready money.

strike into A horse *strikes into* another when it clips its heel with its own fore-leg:

> The condition of New Mexico, badly struck into after winning at Beverley on Tuesday, was yesterday reported to be 'not very good' as vets continued to fight to save him. The six-year-old was found to have completely severed his off-hind flexor tendon

when third placed Shifting Breeze ran into him as he was pulling up. (*Sporting Life* 4 August 1990).

string   A trainer's horses are known as his *string*: 'This was only his second winner this year from his nine-horse string' (*Sporting Life* 12 September 1990). The first attestation with reference to racehorses is in 1809, the sense being derived from the use of the word to describe 'a number of animals driven in single file tied one to the other', the OED quoting, from 1686, 'they generally plough with their oxen in pairs, but with their horses in a string, to prevent poaching the land.' Jon Bee writes: 'Dealers fasten the halter of one horse to the halter and tail of another, and so on to the amount of sixteen, twenty, or more, and either is a *string*.' For *put strings on* see *rope*.

stringhalt   Or *springhalt*: a condition which affects the hind legs of a horse, causing a spasmodic muscle condition. The OED's first attestation is from 1523, giving a fair enough description: 'The stryng-halte is an yl disease, and makyth hym to twyche up his legge sodeynly.' It derives the word as apparently from 'string' and 'halt' in the sense of 'limping, lame'. The condition was also known as *snatch*.

strip[1]   *Strip* is used to describe the appearance of a horse when blankets, etc. are taken off it just before a race. 'Peter Hudson's lightly-raced three-year-old will strip fitter after her comeback ninth to Dream Talk at York eighteen days ago' (*Sporting Life* 3 July 1990). The sense 'of an athlete, a pugilist, etc: To take off one's ordinary wearing apparel in preparation for a contest' is first attested in 1688; and the OED quotes, from 1833, 'Whether it be the prize-fighter who strips in the ring, or the race-horse at the starting-post.'

strip[2]   To *strip* a horse's ears is to pull them 'gently through the hand from base to apex', to quote from the OED's one recorded usage (1908). *Strip* here comes from a verb cognate with *stripe*, originally used to describe the milking of a cow, especially the extraction of milk remaining in the udder after the normal milking. A similar gentle hand movement is involved in *ear-stripping*, a practice which horses greatly enjoy, and which helps comfort a tired horse.

stripe   The use of *stripe* as a verb or noun to describe a beating with a whip goes back to the fifteenth century. It is still used to describe a jockey's vigorous whipping of a horse: appositely, because the stripe marks of a whip are easy to see, especially on a thin-skinned horse, and jockeys sometimes try to smoothe them away before returning to the unsaddling enclosure and the stewards' scrutiny. See the quotation under *washing*.

stuck into   Backers *get stuck into* a horse when they bet heavily on it: the phrase originates in military slang (Partridge, 1916).

stud   From Old English *stod*, first attested in 1000, its original meaning, 'an establishment in which stallions and mares are kept for breeding' is still the current one. The *General Stud Book* first appeared in 1803, 'containing pedigrees of race horses etc. etc. from the restoration to the present time.' The first record of any kind of *stud book* is in 1605, when the 'gentleman of the Horse' is ordered to 'keepe a note in a booke when everie mare is coverede, and with what horse.'

stuffy   The original, and now obsolete sense of *stuffy*, a simple adjectival form of *stuff*, was 'full of stuff and substance', and the OED example from 1667 shows that the word had positive connotations when describing a horse, which should be 'short from the head to the croup, and stuffy'. Now, however, the word describes a horse which is in need of a race to get fit, as if its lungs are not clear. However, an echo of the original sense survives when a horse in the paddock is said to look stuffy, as if it is too solid in appearance to run athletically.

stumer   The word came into the language, perhaps from Yiddish, to mean a horse which had no chance and which bookmakers were therefore happy to take bets on. From this it broadened its sense to mean anything worthless – the racing sense only exists now as part of this general one; but cp. Wodehouse in *The Inimitable Jeeves* (1923): 'The agony of having put his little all on a stumer that hadn't finished in the first six.'

stump   To *stump up* a horse is to wear it out, 'exhaust by excessive strain'. The OED, whose first attestation is from 1875, traces it to *stump* in the sense 'to render penniless', although there may well also be a sense of the horse's legs having gone, and hence a recall of the verb's earliest meaning, 'to walk stumblingly'. 'He doesn't need a lot of work . . . he won't be going there stumped up or sore' (*Racing Post* 6 June 1990).

style, stylish   A jockey's *style* is his manner of riding. *Stylish* is usually a strong term of praise – 'he rode a most stylish race on Father Deer to win' (*Sporting Life* 12 September 1990) – but it can be used negatively when a rider is thought to be too flashy. The best definition of style is John Hislop's: 'Style only means riding in the way that is easiest for the horse to carry you, and in which you can help him most' (Hislop, 107).

supplement   In the past, if a horse showed unexpected improvement from two to three, and it had not been *entered* for a *pattern* or *classic* race, it was not possible to do anything about the omission: Vaguely Noble, in the 1960s, was one example of an outstanding three-year-old colt of his year who did not run, because not entered, in the Derby. Now, in some races (but still not the Derby), a supplementary fee can be paid to enter late such a horse, hence the verb *to supplement*. The supplementation fee is prohibitively high, compared with the normal entry fee, but supplementing is becoming popular, the signs being that owners are less prepared than they were to pay entry fees for all of their potential classic colts and fillies, preferring to supplement the one or two which turn out to be really good:

> The advisers have simply pointed out to their bosses that it would be cheaper to supplement late with the few horses they already know to be good rather than to enter *en bloc* before half of them have even had a proper gallop. (*Racing Post* 14 April 1990)

surcingle   From Old French *surcengle* (the Latin *cingulum* means 'a girdle'): a piece of webbing which passes over the racing saddle to keep it in place, secured by a strap or buckle. The OED's first attestation is from 1390.

sweat   Horses *sweat up* before a race, either because of the heat of the day, or, most often, because they get nervous (or both). In some cases this is not a good sign, but in others it is virtually a prerequisite for the horse to run a good race. Snow Knight looked to have sweated away his race in the *parade* before the Derby in 1974. *Sweating* a horse was a practice carried on by trainers well into the nineteenth century, often exercising them in blankets or coats specially made for the purpose. A *sweat* was, accordingly, a training run for a racehorse: a notice in *The London Gazette* in 1705 advertises a race for hunters that have not 'been kept in sweats above 12 weeks before the day of Running'.

sweepstake   Originally a race in which all of the stake moneys, including *forfeits*, are taken by the winner, as in this title from 1785: *Authentic, Historical Racing Calendar of all the Plates, Sweepstakes, Matches, etc. run for at York 1709-85*. Jon Bee defines *sweepstake* as 'the subscription of three or more, which only one of the parties can *sweep off*, or carry away, by winning the race.' He adds that neither the Oaks nor the Derby is a sweepstake, 'the second horse, in both cases, having £100.' The use of *sweep* to mean winning all the stake was well established: the OED quotes, from 1635, 'Death's a devouring gamester, and sweeps up all.'

sweet, sweeten   Horses can go *sour* with too much racing, or after a hard race, and need to be sweetened up: an easy race is, therefore, a *sweetener*. Another way of sweetening a horse is to send him to a new *stable*. Horses may be said to *run sweet* for a particular jockey. 'There's a chance that hurdling might keep Rainbow

Bridge sweet, but he had plenty of chances on the Flat' (*Sporting Life* 14 September 1990); 'Brunico, formerly smart on the Flat and over hurdles, has been considerably sweetened up by a spell of hunting' (*Racing Post* 6 October 1990).

swerve   Another word for *hang*:
> Horses swerve or hang from different causes: a weakness in a leg or foot, which he naturally feels more acutely when he is tired; a bad, or hard, or one-sided mouth; defective eyesight; exhaustion; the whip, or lack of courage; but generally for a reason of some sort – never without one. (Brock, 143)

swing, swinging   A horse *swings off* the pace when it bowls along just behind the leaders: perhaps from *swing* in the sense 'to drive or cause to move in a curve' (often used in hunting), or 'to go along with undulating movement, or in a vigorous manner'. From this comes a *swinging* pace; i.e. an easy pace, with the horse moving comfortably: 'We did a nice swinging half-speed behind Shavian for five furlongs' (*Sporting Life* 5 June 1990).

swish   An imitative word, not attested until the second half of the eighteenth century. A *swishing* tail is usually a sign of discomfort or that the horse is not *genuine*. 'Tudor D'Or: led, jumped well, clear third, headed two out, soon ridden and swished tail...' (*Sporting Life* 19 September 1990). Cp. *thrash*.

switch   To *switch* a horse in a race is to pull it out from behind one or more horses, out of the *line[1]* it was racing on, to give it a clear run. A difficult and sometimes dangerous manoeuvre, it may fail because the horse has to make up too much ground, and the jockey would have done better waiting for the *split* to come. Equally, it may cause *interference* with horses behind and lead to disqualification. The sense derives from the meaning 'to turn (a railway train, car, etc.) on to another line by means of a switch' (1875). 'Ashdren ...always in touch, effort over two furlongs out, switched and kept on well towards finish' (*Racing Post* 7 September 1990).

switch off   The mark of a good jockey is his ability to *switch off* a highly strung racehorse in the middle of a race, conserving its energy for the final burst. 'In the fastest Queen Anne on record, Dettori switched off Markofdistinction in the rear' (*Sporting Life* 20 June 1990). The OED's first example of such a figurative use of the phrase is from 1929: 'Without great discourtesy one couldn't switch off Binkie.'

system   A method of backing horses according to a predetermined formula, ranging from the complex, involving much research and calculation, to the simple, such as backing 'the outsider of three': 'only your experienced turfite comprehends the enormity of the idiocy of backing horses by systems' (*Pitcher in P*, 81).

T **ack** An abbreviated form of *tackle*, 'the equipment of a horse, harness', from Middle Low German *takel*, meaning 'equipment generally'. But *tack*, from French *tache*, was itself a word which in earlier times meant 'a contrivance for fastening two parts together' or 'a hook for hanging anything on'. Since most riding tack involves fastening and hanging, the latter word may well have influenced the adoption of the shortened form. Its use as a verb is also found: 'We go on to show how to tack-up a horse in racing equipment' (*Sporting Life* 16 May 1990).

tail off A horse is *tailed off* when it falls far behind the rest of the field: first attested in 1852. The phrase has now completely replaced *distanced* and double distanced. 'Tadbir: blundered 1st, tried to refuse 2nd, tailed off when refused 3rd' (*Racing Post* 29 May 1990). A horse can be described as tailing itself off when it refuses to keep up with the field.

take, take out When bookmakers shout *take* before a horse's *price*, e.g. 'Take 6/4', this means that they are betting *odds on*; so that, in this case, the price is 4/6. Punters *take* a price when they back a horse at particular odds: 'Take 5/1 if you can get it; if not, don't take worse than 9/2.' Backers are, therefore, *takers*: first attested in 1810, 'Two to one were offered... but there were no takers.' The best definition of *take*, as opposed to *lay* is the one offered by Charles Sidney: 'A taker of odds is one whose liability on a particular transaction is smaller than his expected winnings' (Sidney, 7). So, if a backer takes odds of 2/1 offered by a bookmaker, his liability is one unit, his expected winnings two units (he is *returned* three units, the two he has won and the one he staked). If, however, the bookmaker offers odds of 1/2 on a horse, the backer's liability is two units, his expected winnings one (again, he is returned three: the one which he wins and the two he has staked). In this latter case the bookmaker is the taker and the backer is the layer, hence his call 'Take 2/1', meaning 1/2.

Bookmakers use *take out of* to indicate the amount which backers have put on a horse – the backers will take a certain sum out of the horse – and also to indicate how much they stand to lose if a particular horse wins – it will take a certain amount out of their book. In this anecdote *take* is used in two specific bookmaking senses. First, with *out of*, to show how much money had been put on the favourite, and then, with *money* and with *odds*, to emphasise that the favourite was odds on. The context is that the bookmaker hopes, but does not know for sure, that the favourite in a three-horse race has been doped:

The Bookmaker, a fearless bettor anyhow, decided to take a chance that the solution was of effective strength and 'painted' 4/6 on his board. He was inundated with layers and took some twenty-odd thousand pounds out of the favourite, and as he took money he had it on the second favourite which was about a 9/4 chance. All during the betting period our intrepid young layer kept taking odds while his tic-tacs and outside men were shovelling on the second best, and at the off the market had not altered from the opening offers. This fact was somewhat unusual as the large turnover was equivalent to some hundred times the value of the entire field – the reason for the steady market will appear in a moment.

The race was run, the dozy favourite fell at the first jump and the second-best made a little more show until succumbing to an obstacle a few yards farther down the course, leaving the outsider to plod on and win. It later transpired that another Bookmaker... 'had' [i.e. had doped] the second favourite and it was from this layer that all the money for the favourite had come. (Sidney, 26)

Take out, in the sense of the amount which the bookmaker stands to lose on each horse in the race – 'In the first race Safawan was plunged on at 2/1 and 7/4 to take out well over £150,000' (*Sporting Life* 20 July 1990) – is also used as a noun. One simple way of assessing the degree to which a book is over-, or under-**round**, is to calculate the *£100 take-out*; that is, to add up the amount it would cost to win back £100 on each horse in the race. A simple example – if unlikely in practice – is to imagine a five-horse race in which each horse is offered at odds of 3/1. The £100 take-out for each horse is £25: if a backer stakes £25 on each horse, the return will be £100, whichever one wins (= 3x£25 plus the £25 stake which is returned). With five runners the book is 25% over-round (5x25 = 125). If there were only three runners in the race, each at 3/1, the book would be 25% under-round (3x25 = 75). With four runners at 3/1 the book would be exactly round. I say that this is a simple method, but only relatively so. In the real world, try now to calculate, using the £100 take-out, the percentage over-round of a nine runner race, with horses showing at odds of 7/2, 4/1, 5/1, 6/1, 7/1, 8/1, 10/1, 12/1, 20/1, 20/1.

talent The *talent* was a common nineteenth-century term for the betting public, or at least those members of it supposed to be 'in the know'. The OED quotes, from 1883, 'Xarifa was the most in demand, and the talent again proved correct in their choice. Mr Valentine's filly winning a capital race by a neck.'

talker   A horse which *roars*: stable slang (Partridge, 1870).

talking horse   A horse, often an unraced one, which is the subject of great rumours about its ability. The implication is that the horse may never live up to its home reputation: 'True Dividend is something of a talking horse. Not for the first time he was backed at Chester three weeks ago but failed to make any impression in the handicap won by Hackforth' (*Sporting Life* 30 May 1990).

tan   Crushed bark, especially from the oak: the Latin *tannum*, meaning oak-tree, is probably of Celtic origin. An infusion from the crushed bark was used to convert hides into leather, hence the range of senses which *tan* has, from bronze in colour to the tannery where hides are processed. In racing the word is used literally, to describe *gallops* made of crushed bark. The OED quotes, from 1887, 'After the usual canter [she] galloped him a mile and a quarter on the tan.' The Newmarket tan gallop was laid down in 1830, developed against the wishes of the *Jockey Club* by an American circus proprietor, Jack White. The OED quotes, from 1849, 'Circus – with its tan and tinsel.'

tap   A shorter form of the phrases *tap for speed* or *tap for foot*. A horse is *tapped* when it is left behind as another one accelerates. The origin of the usage may lie in the idea that all of the horse's speed has been drawn out of him, but the general implication of its use is that the horse in question is simply not fast enough to keep up with the other. Perhaps the usage comes from *tap* meaning 'ask for' (Partridge, 20th C.), as in tapping someone for a fiver: in this case the horse is found wanting. The OED does not record the phrase. 'Ballet Classique continues to be tapped for foot and this looks to be a hot race' (*Sporting Life* 14 September 1990).

Tattersalls, Tatts   Richard Tattersall (1724-95) has given his name to three racing senses. First, the principal horse auction at Newmarket, still run by Tattersalls and known as Tattersalls Bloodstock Sales. These sales began in the Tattersall premises at Hyde Park Corner: the Subscription Room there became the location for the formation of a betting market, hence the use of *Tattersalls* to describe the most expensive public *enclosure* on a racecourse, where the *ring* is located. This is commonly abbreviated to *Tatts*. From this location comes the name *Tattersalls Rules* to describe the rules which govern transactions between bookmakers and their clients. In all three senses it is more common to spell the name without an apostrophe, but *Tattersall's* and *Tatt's* are also used.

tenderly A jockey rides *tenderly* when he uses only *hands and heels* and not the whip: usually a sign that he is on an inexperienced and well-thought-of horse which the stable wants to keep *sweet*. The word is often used euphemistically, implying that the jockey did not try too hard: 'The stewards inquired into the running and riding of Dashing Prince, who finished fourth...and was apparently tenderly ridden...in the closing stages' (*Sporting Life* 5 July 1990).

terms A horse which looks well is *on terms* with itself – short for *good terms*. It is *on terms* with the field when it keeps up with it – short for *equal terms*. To *get away on terms* is not to be left at the start. *Never on terms* means that the horse was always behind: 'Say Shanaaz: never able to get on terms, tailed off from 6th' (*Racing Post* 29 May 1990).

there Bookmakers' slang for an exactly *round* book, in which £100 in total would have to be staked on all the runners to win back £100, whichever one won (see *take*).

thereabouts Close to winning: usually in predictions, e.g. 'From her good draw and with her liking for the going, Disdain should be thereabouts.'

thief An *ungenuine* horse. One which does not run up to its form in a race. 'A really good horseman on any sort of horse...and able to get the last ounce out of a lazy, sluggish horse, or a "thief"' (Bland, 79).

thimblerig Like the five-card trick, the *thimblerig* was a popular nineteenth-century entertainment aimed at duping mugs out of their money. The OED's first attestation is from 1825: 'An unfair game known among the frequenters of races and fairs by the name of "the thimble rig".' The game itself was based on guessing under which thimble a pea was hidden; but the *thimblemen*, as they were known, were a general scourge of racecourses. In 1830 the Doncaster stewards, with the aid of the police, and with the military in reserve, attacked and arrested some 150 thimblemen, many after a pursuit over open country.

think, thinker A horse which *thinks* – often known as a *thinker* – is one which takes too much care of itself in a race and often will not, therefore, try hard enough. 'Glenstal Abbey, one of the leading contenders for the tag of jumping's biggest thinker, was in a winning mood for the first time in his career' (*Racing Post* 19 May 1990).

thin-skinned Describes a horse which marks easily when it is hit with the whip. 'The stewards...interviewed Dwyer as Galway Gal was found to be marked, but no action was taken as the mare is thin-skinned' (*Racing Post* 6 October 1990).

thoroughbred From *thorough*, meaning 'completely', *thorough-bred* is first recorded in the sense 'thoroughly educated or accomplished', the OED's first attestation being 'A thorough-bred soldier weighs all present Circumstances, and all possible Contingents'; but by the end of the eighteenth century it had come to be used to describe a horse whose pedigree is fully recorded in the *General Stud Book*, going back over several generations. From this usage its modern senses derive: thus, a 'thoroughbred soldier' today would be one who came from a family with an ancestry of soldiers. In this respect it is worth noting that the distinction between *through* and *thorough* only gradually emerges in English (cp. 'thoroughfare'), and that the point of a thoroughbred horse is that its pedigree can be traced right through a line back to one of the three great Arabian sires: the Darley Arabian, the Godolphin Arabian, and the Byerley Turk. Vincent Orchard quotes the Earl of Bristol as the first user of the word, offering to send horses from his stud to the Elector of Hanover, because 'thro-bred English horses are allow'd to surpass most of the same species' – the date was 1713 (Orchard, 68). While in practice the purpose of horse-racing might seem to be to provide opportunities for betting – or even to give people pleasure – in theory, the thoroughbred is its prime and sole reason. Improving the breed of the thoroughbred horse is the stated purpose of racing. The statement came in the *Report of the Duke of Norfolk's Committee on the Pattern of Racing* in 1965:

> The thoroughbred is a British creation, and is part of our national heritage, which is worth preserving... the foreigner looks to the thoroughbred as a typically British creation... It is the duty of the Turf authorities to try to preserve the supremacy of the British thoroughbred as far as possible... and if they fail in this duty racing is liable to be debased to the level of roulette, and does not deserve to survive.

thrash A horse *thrashes* its tail when agitated or unhappy: sometimes a sign that it is not *genuine*. The word has a long history, forms of it being found in many cognate languages, but this sense, 'of air, branches, or anything free at one end: to flap, whip, lash', is not attested until the second half of the nineteenth century.

throw[1] The OED records, as a specific sense of *throw*, the meaning 'of a horse... to cause the rider to fall off' (1531); but in a race this is more likely to be described as *unseating*, although *thrown* is used when a jockey is unseated before or after a race. In effect, the distinction is between a deliberate act on the horse's part and an accidental one.

throw[2] Describes the producing of domestic animals. The OED's first attestation, from 1845, relates to horses: 'You cannot possibly tell what sort of a horse your mare may throw.'

throw in, throw out   A horse is *thrown in* when it is given what appears to be a very lenient weight in a *handicap*. It is *thrown out* when the *stewards* disqualify it after a race which it has won or been placed in. For both usages, cp. *chuck*. In earlier centuries *throw out* was used to describe a horse's being *distanced*[2] in a race; i.e. left so far behind that the horse was disqualified from riding in further heats. The OED quotes from Scott's *Quentin Durward* (1823): 'I had been unluckily thrown out, and was riding fast, to be in my place.'

thumb   In *tic-tac* signalling, thumbs up indicates that a price is being taken; so, *with the thumb* indicates that a price on offer is being taken by backers and is, accordingly, likely to shorten.

tic-tac   Originally spelt *tick tack*, derived from *ticker* in the sense of 'a telegraphic recording instrument' (1883), *tic tac* is the 'telegraphing' system, using hand signs, employed at the racecourse to keep bookmakers in touch with movements in the market all over the course. First attested in 1899, this quotation from 1905 explains its development:

> A prisoner puzzled the Kingston Bench by describing himself as a 'racecourse telegraphist'. . . A detective explained that the man practised what is known as 'tick tack telegraphy' – signalling by means of the arms to outside bookmakers.

Contrast this quotation, from the *Guardian* in 1972, to see how widely the usage caught on: 'The policeman tic-taced to the judge what the punishment should be.' Many of the *prices* are known on the course by their tic tac signs; e.g. 'on the shoulders' is 9/4, 'earhole' 6/4, 'tips' 11/10, 'up the arm' 11/8, 'top of the head' 2/1, 'shoulder' 7/4, 'wrist' 5/4; and see *thumb*.

tidily   A horse wins *tidily* when it wins easily enough not to have appeared in danger of defeat in the closing stages, but not so easily that it draws right away from the field. Compare *cleverly*, which implies a slightly closer finish.

tighten   Horses *tighten up* in a race when they drift closer together. A horse gets tightened up when it is squeezed out, either by one horse coming across and pushing it towards others, or towards the rail, or by two horses drifting towards each other when it is going for the *split* in between them.

> There were several cases of interference in the closing stages as Masnun and Bertie Wooster, making their runs on either side of the leading pack, drifted in towards each other causing a general tightening up. (*Sporting Life* 6 September 1990).

In an *objection* a jockey may accuse another of 'tightening me up'.

tilt To have a *tilt*, or, more fully, a *tilt at the ring*, is to bet with
large sums of money on the course. The image is of jousting, the
word describing originally an armed combat between two men;
the sense here is the transferred one of 'a thrust of a weapon, as
at a tilt'. In this case the weapon is enough money to worry the
bookmakers:

> There were famous names betting in Tattersalls Rings all over
> the country and punters were accommodated for almost any
> amount. Percy Thompson led the Ring in the South of Eng-
> land, while such names as Hoppy Beresford, Bill Chandler
> and, of course, Parker made the Ring worthy of a tilt. (Sidney,
> 79)

tip, tipster In the sense of 'a piece of useful and private information', *tip* is derived either from 'the notion of tipping or lightly
touching the arm or elbow of a person by way of a private hint',
or from the phrase 'to tip the wink'. *Tipster* is first attested in
1862. It means not just someone who gives a tip, but one who
does it professionally. For the verb the OED's first attestation is
from the unlikely source of the Georgian poet Ernest Dowson,
writing in 1889 about the November Handicap at Manchester:
'Ye gods . . . I have been tipped (i) Lady Roseberry (ii) Goldseeker
(iii) Phil – by you.' The *straight tip* became a common slang expression in the nineteenth century: 'Both Crowe and the Captain's
man . . . were made much of by a company laudably desirous of
obtaining what is known in sporting circles as the straight tip'
(Thormanby, *Tales*, 68). The OED quotes, from 1873, 'The
"straight tip" is the tip which comes direct from the owner or
trainer of a horse. Of late years a "straight tip" means a direct
hint on any subject.'

tissue Originally used to describe 'a sheet of paper showing the
"form" of the horses competing in a race' – hence James Joyce's
description of a character in *Dubliners* as one whose profession
was unknown, but 'his name was vaguely associated with racing
tissues'. *Tissue* was used because of the flimsiness of the paper.
Now it describes the sheet which bookmakers have on the morning of a race predicting the likely starting prices:

> Some courses . . . provide a 'Tissue' which is a betting forecast
> for each race of the day drawn up by some acknowledged
> 'judge' to assist those layers who have no sources. In the end,
> however, the criterion for price is demand. (Sidney, 113)

toe A horse with *toe* – 'some toe' or 'a bit of toe' – is one with
speed: virtually a synonym of *foot*. The OED identifies this usage
as Australian and New Zealand slang, first attested in 1963. *Toey*,
meaning 'restive, anxious, touchy', comes from the same area, the

OED's first attestation, from 1930, being 'Wise Force was "toey" before the race, and behaved in an alarming fashion on his way to and at the post.'

tonguestrap A horse whose tongue comes 'over the bit' is more difficult to control, hence the use of the *tonguestrap* in racing. It is a band which must, by regulation, be at least one inch wide, fastened under the horse's jaw.

tool¹ 'He's a real tool!' said Jamie Osborne, after having ridden a winner at Newbury (*Sporting Life* 2 November 1989), harking back to a slang use of *tool* which emerged in the nineteenth century, first to describe travelling smoothly in a horse-drawn vehicle (1812) and then, in the phrase *tool along*, to mean any kind of smooth travelling (1839). A *tool* is, therefore, a horse which gives a jockey a smooth, easy, fast ride.

tool² On the racecourse the pieces of equipment which make up a bookmaker's *joint* are called the *tools*: mainly, the *board*, on which prices are marked, the *flash*, the *hod*, and the *mush*. 'Lulu, despite several unfruitful pleas for a spare set of tools, took off for the Silver Ring where he found an away bookmaker willing to lend his tools for the giveaway sum of £100' (*Sporting Life* 3 October 1990).

tooth A horse is *aged* by its teeth: hence the phrase 'long in the tooth' (Partridge, 1910). Horses which are so old that they have lost the distinguishing marks in their teeth are described as *old in the tooth* or *up in the tooth*.

top¹ *Top of the ground*, or *on top*, describes *going* on the firm side of good. Not in OED. 'Morley Street, a rangy and, at present, rather unfurnished gelding, has won well on top-of-the-ground as well as on heavy; he has yet to race on very firm' (*Timeform Chasers and Hurdlers 1988-89*, 511).

top² In betting, a bet laid *on top* is one which is made by a bookmaker's accomplice to encourage others to bet on a horse. It is entered by the clerk 'on top', not in the body of the book.

top man An expert *tic tac* who takes instructions from the *blower* man and relays them to a tic tac in the *ring*. 'Top' here refers to his expertise as well as his location up in the grandstand – see the quotation under *twist*.

topped Refers to a horse's appearance. A *heavy topped* horse is a burly one who may, therefore, be prone to weakness in the legs. 'He was a big massive chestnut, with a white blaze, and being so heavy-topped he had developed a weakness in his knees after running as a two-year-old' (Donoghue, 202).

topweight The horse which carries the highest weight in a race, usually in a *handicap*. 'Alex Greaves...finished third on topweight Super One' (*Sporting Life* 3 October 1990).

Tote Short for *Totalisator*, the government-owned betting organisation, in competition with the bookmakers, in which all stakes in a race go into a *pool*, a proportion of which is paid out to winning bets. The word's first attestation is in Australia in 1879, but *totalisateur* was in scientific use in France in the 1860s. The Tote was only introduced on British racecourses after the Racecourse Betting Act of 1928, and first operated in July 1929, at Newmarket and Carlisle. However, *pari-mutuel* machines – effectively the same thing, except that each machine made a separate return – were introduced at York in 1871, when the basic stake was 2s 6d (12½p). *Tote odds* are those paid out on Tote bets, as opposed to *S.P.* *Tote monopoly* describes a system of racing in which there is no private bookmaking, only pool betting being allowed: effectively the way racecourse betting is run in most countries except for Britain. The disadvantages of such a monopoly are many, including, notably, the loss to backers of the opportunity to take a *price* on a horse – on the Tote they are stuck with whatever dividend is declared – and the loss of the hurly-burly of the *ring* which makes British racecourses so much more fun than their sombre, tote-monopolised, continental and American equivalents. The one great advantage of a Tote monopoly is that all profits from betting would go back into racing, leading to richer and better supported racecourses and higher prize money.

touch[1]   A betting *coup*. Backers *go for a touch* on a horse, or *land a touch* when it wins – in either case it is the good *price* which makes it a *touch* rather than the simple fact of its being successful.

> If there was a cunning plan for Mellottie to win the Newbury Ladies Handicap and land a bit of a touch in the process, it fell down on two counts. First he was never a better price than 5/2...and second...he did not win. (*Racing Post* 19 May 1990).

The OED records a sense of 'touch' meaning, originally, 'an act of theft, especially of pocket-picking', and developing into 'a sum of money gained at once, especially by theft' around the turn of the twentieth century.

touch[2]   In accounts of the betting market before a race, a horse's extreme price – normally the longest, but sometimes the shortest – is described by the verb *touch*. 'Killjoy opened at 10/1, touched 12/1 in some places, and came in to 8/1 by the off.'

tout   Developing from a verb meaning 'to peep, peer, look out' (15th C.), the noun *tout* meant originally 'a thieves' scout or watchman' (early 18th C.) and came to mean 'one who surreptitiously

watches the trials of racehorses, so as to gain information for
betting purposes' (1865; but *touter* is attested in this sense in
1812). In expressions like 'ticket tout' the word has kept its negative associations, but in racing the profession of the tout, in its
nineteenth-century sense, has turned respectable, many newspapers now employing people whose job it is to find out horses' form
on the *gallops*. Accordingly, the name has changed – 'watcher',
'our man at such-and-such a training centre', or even 'reporter'
tend to be the preferred forms – and *tout* is generally confined
now to the shadier kinds of tipster. Some idea of the opprobrium
in which touts were held a hundred years ago can be seen in this
definition:

> Touts are thieves who steal stable secrets, either by spying on
> horses in their gallops and trials, or by bribing servants to
> betray their masters, and to reveal any important information
> acquired in the opportunities of observation which the nature
> of the work necessarily affords. (Badminton, 262)

Much of the early history of racing is taken up with efforts of
stables, *laying out* horses for big races, to disguise their form from
the touts by such means as galloping them with extra weight. In
his evidence before the House of Commons Select Committe on
Gaming, in 1844, Richard *Tattersall* had the following exchange
on touts with MPs:

> Supposing a horse a favourite, and that just before the race
> he fell lame, or fell so sick that he became a certain loser,
> would that information, according to the general custom, be
> made known to the public as well as to the owner? – *The public
> know it before the owner generally, and the horse would go back
> instantly in the betting. There is not a horse ever comes out and
> gallops at Newmarket but if there is anything the matter with it
> the touts soon make it known. It is known as soon in London as
> the owner knows it, or before the owner knows it.*
>
> Do you consider a horse unsound if he has ever been
> unsound in his life? – *There is no horse that you can warrant for
> three days.*
>
> What is the business of the touts? – *Men that watch horses.*
> Then it is through the touts that this information is given
> to the public as to the lameness of a horse? – *Yes.*
> Would it not be open to the touts to spread false as well as
> true information? – *So they do.*
> Therefore what reliance can the public place upon any such
> information? – *They cannot place reliance upon it any more than
> upon what you read in a newspaper.*
> Then the truth would not be known to the public as to the

condition of the horse, as it is to the owner of the horse? – *Yes, it is; because the tout is a very quick man upon those occasions. The trainer very seldom sees the faults of his horses as another person does; the trainer is the last person generally to do that; they are so fond of their own animals that they do not see it* . . . (Orchard, 290)
A nineteenth-century term for tout was *rail-bird*, so named because of 'his vantage-point on gate or hurdle' (Partridge). A polite term for touts today is *workwatcher*: 'Fellow workwatchers expressed surprise to find that Steve Cauthen partnered Redden Burn, but the . . . colt pleased in his work' (*Sporting Life* 6 September 1990).

trace   Middle English *trays*, from Old French *traix*, plural of *trait*, 'action of drawing, rope or leather strap by which a draught beast is harnessed': the traces are the 'ropes, chains, or . . . leather straps by which the collar of a draught animal is connected with the splinter-bar or swingletree.' From this comes the phrase *trace clipping*, when only the belly and the upper part of the horse's four legs have their winter coat removed.

traffic   *Traffic problems* are difficulties which a horse meets when trying to thread its way through the field in the closing stages of a race. 'He overcame traffic problems to reach Tirol's quarters inside the final furlong' (*Sporting Life* 19 May 1990).

train, trainer   Ultimately from the Latin *trahere*, 'to draw, drag'; the use of *train* to describe disciplining first occurs in gardening (to train plants) in the fifteenth century. It is used to describe the disciplining and instruction of a horse in 1609: 'Richard Eastwood, for his paynes, and his coache, to trayne the horses theirin, xxxs (i.e. 30 shillings).' *Trainer* only appears in this sense in 1812, at about the time when owners were beginning to employ, on a large scale, people whose job was to prepare horses for races. Nimrod, writing in 1833, refers to a 'training-groom' whose job is to look after the health of, feed, and exercise a racehorse.

train on, train off   A horse *trains on* when it maintains its *form* into a new season: 'Qui Danzig . . . had the most sympathetic race of the quartet, and was a neck further back in fourth. He appears to have trained on' (*Sporting Life* 19 May 1990). A horse *trains off* when it has had too much racing and no longer runs up to its form: 'Her dam Areola, a very fast filly as a youngster . . . trained off early in her second season' (*Racing Post* 29 May 1990).

trappy   In *chasing*, *trappy* fences are those which are deceptive and likely to 'trap' unwary jumpers into a mistake. The OED's first attestation of the word is in this sense in 1882 – see under *open*. Races, particularly *handicaps*, where many horses stand a chance of winning are also described as trappy, the pitfalls here being the punters'. 'Yesterday's Portland result suggests high numbers will have the advantage in the trappy-looking Kyoto Handicap' (*Sporting Life* 13 September 1990).

travel[1]   Describes the way a horse moves in a race: 'Steve Cauthen told them he had tried to make the early pace but the colt was never travelling on the ground' (*Sporting Life* 20 June 1990). The OED records this sense, describing animal movement, from 1877, noting that it was used with special reference to deer.

travel[2]   Partridge records the phrase *travel in the market*, meaning 'the way or extent in or to which a horses is betted on or against', from 1870. 'Anshan, who travelled badly in the market, ran the worst race of his career' (*Sporting Life* 20 June 1990).

treble   See *multiple bet*. The *Daily Treble* used to be a popular *Tote* bet, involving the nomination of the winners of the second, fourth, and sixth races on the *card*.

trial   The word is used in two distinct but connected senses: (i) galloping a horse at home, on its own or against others, to see how ready it is for a race – see under *tout*; (ii) to describe certain races which may be either official or unofficial *trials* for big races: early in the season three-year-olds may run in Derby trials at courses like Lingfield or Chester. Trials in the first sense were very common in the nineteenth century, but as trainers became more wary of 'leaving races behind' on the *gallops*[2], the second sense came to be more common. Still, the use of the word to describe certain races was not uncommon in earlier periods. It clearly developed from the appreciation that particular races had become, in practice, stepping-stones to better things, and they grew to be known as e.g. Cesarewitch or Cambridgeshire trials. Cheny's *Calendar* of 1727 describes a race held at Kipling-Coates in Yorkshire on the third Thursday in March as, 'although but sixteen Guineas, yet, as the time of Running for it is the Infancy of the Season, 'tis looked upon as a proper Taste-Tryal, or Proof for Horses, how they have come through the Winter' (Prior, 113).

tricast   See *forecast*.

trier   See *judge*.

trip   From French *treper*, 'to strike the ground with the foot in sign of joy or impatience'(!), *trip* in the sense of a short journey, was originally a sailors' term (17th C.), but soom came to refer to travel on land. In racing, the *trip* is, first, the *distance*[1] of a race – the OED's first attestation of this sense is as late as 1959 – and a horse which does not *stay* the distance is said not to *get the trip*. Of course, getting the trip is often only a relative judgment, to be qualified by the context of a race: a horse may get beaten in a mile and a half *pattern* race, the *excuse* being that 'he didn't get the trip', but he might then win a mile and a half *handicap*, getting the trip against inferior opposition. The more general sense of *trip* is to signify a long distance, say anything over a mile and a half on the Flat. A horse which only shows its best form in such races is one which *needs a trip*. 'The extended mile and a quarter at York was too far for her. Seven furlongs is her best trip' (*Sporting Life* 6 July 1990).

triple crown   The original *triple crown* was the papal tiara. Its use in racing is to describe the three *classics*: for colts, the Two Thousand Guineas, the Derby, and the St Leger; for fillies, the Thousand Guineas, the Oaks, and the St Leger. If a horse wins all three, he or she wins the triple crown – not an actual prize, but a title of distinction. The OED's first attestation of this racing sense is in 1897. The American equivalent is the Kentucky Derby, the Preakness Stakes, and the Belmont Stakes.

trixie   See *multiple bet*.

trot   From the French *trotter*: first attested in English in 1300. The *trot* is the slow pace of a horse, between walking and running. The beat is two and two, near front and off hind then off front and near hind hitting the ground together. To *trot up* is to win easily.

try   All horses in a race are supposed to *try*; that is, try to win, or, failing this, try to get the best placing they can. *Non-triers* are of two kinds: horses which refuse to do their best, and, more sinisterly – and more commonly in racing usage – horses which are not being *asked* to do their best.

tubed   A *tubed* horse is one which has had a tracheotomy, with a tube inserted in his windpipe to help him breathe properly. The word is first attested in 1925, but *tuber*, describing such a horse, occurs a little earlier. 'Now tubed and prone to break blood vessels, Glencroft is currently rated 77, compared to 110 when he was at his peak' (*Sporting Life* 5 June 1990).

tug   A horse which *pulls¹ takes a tug*. A jockey *takes a tug* when he pulls on the reins, usually to keep the horse from making too much *use¹* of itself early in a race.

tumbler   Partridge notes this as slang for 'a worthless horse' (1904), suggesting that it is so called 'because it tumbles about'.

turf   Old English *turf* can be traced back to Sanskrit *dartha*, 'a tuft of grass'. *The Turf* – without or without a capital – is 'the grassy track or course over which horse-racing takes place; hence, the institution, action, or practice of horse-racing; the racing world.' The first attested use of the word in a racing context already gives it its broadest sense: from the *Gentleman's Magazine* of 1755, 'If you are a true sportsman, and have the honour of the turf at heart.' The word has always kept its posh associations, and so has been used to euphemise the everyday practices of racing: *turf accountant* is a bookmaker (1915) – hence the story of the young lady who went into one bookie's office in search of a new lawn; *turfite* is a frequenter of racecourses (1836); *turf guides* are *form* books (1868); *turf horses* are racehorses (1802); *turf parlance* is racing slang (1884); and *turf writers* are racing journalists (1865). Surtees offers an evocative compound as the climax to a series of imprecations over a fixed race: 'honour – rascals – rogues – thieves – robbery – swindle – turf-ruined' (Surtees, 87). The word's most engaging use comes in the toast which Jorrocks and company are offered after a day at the races: '"The Turf", and may we be long above it' (Surtees, 92).

turn[1] At the start of a race not started in *stalls*, the *starter* may ask the field to *take a turn*, i.e. turn away from the tape and come back round to the start again.

turn[2] *On the turn* describes a course where the *straights* are short and the bends long, so that the horse is running round a bend, *leading* with the same leg, for nearly the whole race.

turn around See *form*.

turn of foot See *foot*.

turn out[1] To rest a horse between one season and another. The idea here is of turning the horse out into a field, from the sense 'to drive or put out (beasts) to pasture or to the open', first attested in 1560. 'The summer months, when a horse is turned out and resting himself, are just as important as those months when he is in strict training' (Brock, 171).

turn out[2] To present a horse properly groomed and equipped for a race; a development of the phrase's sense 'to equip, "rig out", "get up"'. This is one of the stable *lad*'s jobs and many races now offer a prize for the 'best turned out' horse. This racing sense is not given by the OED.

turn over For one horse to *turn over* another is to beat him unexpectedly – commonly used in the passive, the *favourite* being turned over when it gets beaten. The *hotter* the favourite, the more likely the phrase is to be used.

> In what appeared the increasingly unlikely event of Be Friendly being 'turned-over' in the six runner Vernons Sprint Cup, Lester Piggott had arranged for his old rival to take over on the apparent 'good thing', Harbour Flower, for which he'd been booked in the last. (O'Sullevan, 271)

turn-up An unexpected result. Derived from 'the turning up of a particular card or die in games of chance'; its first racing attestation is in 1873, when it was defined as 'an unexpected slice of luck'. Among sporting men bookmakers are said to have a turn up when an unbacked horse wins – hence the common expression 'a turn up for the books'.

twist card   Because *tic tac* is a form of signal telegraphy, understood by anyone who knows the signals, the *twist card* was developed, particularly for use by *top* men, to disguise latest *shows*[3] and hedging *commissions* from all but subscribers. The card is, in effect, a coded race *card* in which the horses are given different numbers.

two horse   See *one horse*.

type   Used like *sort*: 'He has always looked a second season type and should go close' (*Sporting Life* 14 June 1990).

U ndone   See *come undone*.
uneasy   In the betting exchanges, an *uneasy favourite* is
one which is being opposed in the market, with its odds
going out; e.g. from 5/4 to 7/4.

undergraduate   Late nineteenth-century slang for a horse 'in training for steeplechasing or hunting' (Partridge); probably on an analogy with *schooling*.

under-round   See *overbroke*; *round*.

united   A horse's *action* is *united* when the leading fore leg and leading hind leg appear to be on the same side. The OED defines this sense of the verb 'unite' as 'to cause (a horse) to move with the hind and fore-quarters in union or agreement', its first example being from 1753.

unseat   Originally *unseat* meant to dislodge someone from a horse, as in a joust; but in racing the reference is to some kind of shock in the horse's movement – a sudden stop or buck – which causes the jockey to fall off. In *chasing*, where the word is most commonly used – abbreviated as *u.r.*, unseated rider – it is often interpreted as an insult because of the implication that the jockey fell off although the horse itself did not fall. Many a strenuous debate has passed between jockeys and race readers to insist that an 'unseated rider' ought to have been recorded as 'fell'.

unsighted   See *sighted*.

unstuck   See *come unstuck*.

up[1]   In the saddle, riding: as in the order 'jockeys up', or the popular cry 'Archer's up'. The OED's first attestation is from 1812, and it quotes, from 1857, 'A match for £50, 10st 7lb each. Owners up.'

up[2]   Used about horses, in the same sense as *out*, as in 'First time up Pot of Gold ran a poor race.'

up[3]   When jockeys are required to attend an *enquiry*, they are said to be *up* before the stewards.

upsides   The original meaning of the word, in the phrase 'upsides with', was 'even, equal, or quits with... by means of retaliation or successful rivalry'. The more gentle sense, 'on a level with; alongside of', appears late in the nineteenth century, and is the general racing sense. Horses are *upsides* when they are level with each other. 'The whole face of the race changed at the last hurdle in the back straight, where Luke Harvey asked strongly-fancied

On His Own to go upsides with a long one' (*Sporting Life* 31 August 1990).

use¹ In a race, to *make use of* a horse – or, sometimes, just to *use* it – is to keep it up with the leaders throughout a race: 'A very great many races are lost each season because riders do not make enough use of their horses. They are told to wait, and wait they do accordingly, though it may be that the horse is a fair stayer' (Badminton, 326).

use² May be used reflexively in the sense of *use¹* – 'he made too much use of himself in the race' – but more often the reflexive has another sense, going back to a common sixteenth-century meaning of the verb, 'to conduct or comport oneself'. In racing, the way a horse *uses itself* is the way it *acts* on the prevailing *going*. Peter O'Sullevan here describes the jockey Rae Johnstone's apprehension about his mount Asmena in the 1950 Oaks:

> The filly had a rheumatic tendency and was so apprehensive on the, to her, unfamiliar firm ground, that as they walked across the downs to the 1½ miles start Rae told Charlie Elliott (on third favourite Plume II) he'd have to pull her up after a quarter of a mile if she didn't use herself better. (O'Sullevan, 80)

Asmena won the Oaks.

V **alet** The attendant in the jockeys' room who looks after boots, saddles, silks, etc. The OED records a "rare" military sense, first attested in the sixteenth century, of 'a footman acting as attendant or servant to a horseman.'

value In betting, *value* is one of the more complex ideals – something sought by both backer and bookmaker. The principal OED definition of the word is 'that amount of some commodity, medium of exchange, etc which is considered to be an equivalent for something else; a fair or adequate equivalent or return.' Such a definition applies more to a bookmaker's conception of value than a backer's. The latter will, relatively simply, regard *getting* 2/1 about a 6/4 shot, or 12/1 about an 8/1 horse, as value. If a *skinny* price is offered about a *favourite*, a discerning backer will not bet on it because, although it may well win, there is no value in the price offered: 'If the markets were a little different and the favourites stood longer I would advise an each-way double on Salsabil and Macchiavellian, for I would then believe they represented value' (*Racing Post*, 3 May 1990); Salsabil won the Thousand Guineas at 6/4, Macchiavellian was second in the Two Thousand Guineas at 6/4. For the bookmaker, value is not simply equated with profit, but, more subtly, with 'the profit-making potential of the transactions entered into in the course of the betting'. Charles Sidney, whose words these are, describes value as 'the basic concept on which the Practice of Bookmaking rests' and he devotes eighteen pages of his book to its definition (see Sidney, 112-30). His advice, finally, is that value lies in consistency. The bookmaker who follows well-tried rules of practice in the framing of a book and the laying of prices will, in the long run, always achieve value, while one who alters his practice inconsistently, in search of short-term profit, will fail.

van In the early days of racing horses were walked to races – even if the journey was a hundred miles or more. Then, in 1816,

At the First October Meeting the Newmarket St Leger was won by Mr Terrett's bay colt Royal Sovereign, who started at 30/1 . . . This is the earliest instance of a horse being vanned to a race meeting . . . Mr Terrett was a large grazier in Worcestershire, and wishing to save his horse the long journey on foot, put him in the bullock float, and so travelled to Newmarket. (Prior, 185)

231

The OED's first attestation of *van* as a verb refers to the vanning of horses (in 1840).

velvet To be *on velvet* is to be certain to win: not nearly certain or morally certain, but absolutely. To take a simple example, if, in the early betting exchanges on a two-horse race, a backer *gets* 6/4 about one horse, and, later, he is able to back the other for the same amount at 5/4, then which ever wins he does too. The expression originally had the general meaning of being 'in a position of ease or advantage', but in the nineteenth century it was narrowed down to betting and gaming.

visit In the betting exchanges, a horse *visits* a certain *price* when it goes out in the betting and then comes back in: the price visited is the furthest price it reaches. 'Imperfect Circle ended sound after visiting 3/1 in places from 9/4, back to 5/2' (*Sporting Life* 4 October 1990).

visor Half-way between *blinkers* and a *hood*: a head covering for a horse which keeps the ears uncovered but which offers more of a mask than a simple set of blinkers. Not in OED.

W ait Keeping a horse off the *pace* until the late stages of a race is called riding a *waiting race*. The verb, in the nineteenth century, was to *wait off* – first attested in 1856: 'He partially waited off, while Sancho forced the running' – now it is simply to *wait*, as in: 'Cautious Pete: waited with, joined leaders seven out' (*Sporting Life* 13 September 1990). Traditionally, the first great exponent of waiting was Sam Chifney (1753-1807), but the practice undoubtedly goes back to the earliest days of racing. A German visitor to Epsom races in 1710 made the following observations about the winner's tactics:

> The manner in which these fellows outdistance each other is astonishing, so that often a man who led by twenty paces at the start will come in last. A horse must, nevertheless, win twice running or it is not valid. A blue-grey horse, which looked the least likely of all the five, won both times. But this was largely owing to the man who rode it. For he was wise enough to spare his horse at the beginning, let the others pass him and tire themselves out; he only took care not to be left too far behind, and in the second time round, especially when they were nearing the post, he gave the horse its head and passed the others. (Orchard, 63)

In each period the jockey who uses this tactic most successfully is known as the *head waiter*. The craftiest kind of race is one in which the jockey *waits in front*:

> The art of 'waiting in front' is a great one to learn . . . The leader sets the pace, and if he, while leading, is going well within himself, so much the greater reserve of speed will he have when it comes to racing. (Badminton, 326)

walk¹ To *walk the course* is often done by jockeys and trainers before racing begins, with the purpose of finding the best ground to race on.

walk² To *walk it* is slang for a very easy win (Partridge 20th C.), usually in the prophetic sense, '*x* will walk it', sometimes countered by wags with the observation that the rest of the field will be running.

walk³ To go for a *walk* in the market describes a horse's *price* drifting in the betting because of lack of support for it. 'The original market leader Kingsley went for a walk from 6/4 on to 13/8' (*Sporting Life* 1 June 1990).

walk⁴   The OED records a nineteenth-century use of *walk* to indicate a jockey's natural weight: 'He was about 5ft 5ins in height,
walked about 9st 5lbs in the winter months, and could ride, if
required for a great race, 7st 12lbs to the last.'

walk-over   Or *walkover*. Literally, a race in which, for whatever
reason, only one horse goes to post and has, therefore, only to
walk over part of the course to win the prize moneys. For obvious
reasons, there is no betting on a walk-over. The phrase 'walking
over the course' is attested in 1779; and Jon Bee, in his definition,
combines the two ideas implicit in the single word, its literal sense
and the figurative one of a horse's total superiority over others:
'To "walk over" another, is...to set him at naught, as a racer
that is so vastly superior to other cattle that none dare start, and
he walks over the course.' Even in a jump race, the horse is
required only to walk over part of the course, not to jump any
obstacles. The figurative use of the word, to signify a very easy
victory, has extended to many other contexts: the OED quotes a
political example from the 1830s.

Theoretically, it ought to be impossible to lose a walk-over,
but in racing anything is possible. In a *point-to-point* race in 1990
the one declared runner was disqualified because the horse bolted
while being unloaded from the horse-box, and could not be caught
in time to weigh out and weigh in again. To add insult to injury,
the rider was fined £25 for declaring the wrong colours.

walk up   Horses are instructed to *walk up* at the start of a race in
which *stalls* are not used: see *start*.

wall-eyed   *Wall* comes from the Middle English *wawil*, from Old
Norse *vagl*, perhaps meaning 'a film over the eye'. From its begin-
nings the word described both humans and horses. It means 'having one or both eyes of an excessively light colour, so that the iris
is hardly distinguishable from the white.' Gervase Markham,
writing in 1607, describes 'The Horse that is whale-eyde, or white
eyed' as being 'for the most part shrewd, craftie, full of toyes,
and dim sighted'. Thoroughbreds are only rarely wall-eyed.

wand   Often used to refer to the whip: *wand*, in the sense 'a rod,
stick or switch used for chastisement', is first attested in 1297.

wander   A horse *wanders* when it comes off a true *line¹*, especially
towards the end of a race: 'Howjal: prominent, chased leader
from 6th, wandered before last, switched right' (*Racing Post* 29
May 1990).

warm   Bookmakers' slang for a backer who often *finds* winners,
and whose bets, therefore, need careful treatment. The sense may
be derived from the idea that such a backer is nearly 'hot', in the
sense 'exceedingly skilful' (Partridge 20th C.); or from the use of

warm in games to indicate 'being near the object sought; being on the verge of finding or guessing' (1860).

If and when the guessing became too accurate, the layer no longer treated them as ordinary clients but re-classified them as 'warm' if not 'sharps'. There were two remedies for this eventuality, either the layer requested that they take their business elsewhere or he might use the betting as a source of information and as a guide to his other business. Value could be obtained in this way by laying, more heavily, those horses that the 'warm clients' did not back. (Sidney, 126)

warn off The complete expression is *warn off the course*. It describes the extreme penalty inflicted by the *Jockey Club* upon those who infringe the rules of racing. Originally, the operative phrase was *warned off Newmarket Heath*. The Jockey Club owns the heath, warns transgressors off it, and thereby effectively forbids them from riding or running a horse at any official race meeting. The first racing attestation of *warn off* dates from 1856, as an extension of its sense 'to notify (a person) to keep at a distance' (1815). The first public warning-off notice appears much earlier, in 1711, although the expression itself is not used, in connection with Chester races:

In order to save Mr Quirk, Mr Castle, or any of the Ascott Confederacy the trouble and expense of training, they are desired to take notice that none of their horses will be allowed to run for any of the above plates, neither will they be suffered to run for any of the plates at Conway, Nantwich, or Holywell; nor will Thomas Dunn be permitted to ride. (Prior, 150)

In the Jockey Club Rules of Racing, the decision to 'warn off Newmarket Heath' excluded the offending party from all racecourses. In 1969 the phrase was deleted from the Rules, but is still in common use. Warning off can be the punishment for trainers, owners, jockeys, newspaper men, stable staff, and, indeed, any member of the public. Horses, too, can be warned off: the first to be so was a horse called Vigilance in 1910, on account of his *savage* behaviour.

washing *Out with the washing* is racecourse slang for a horse which is completely out of contention, either during a race or at the end. In the former case all may not be without hope:

It was difficult to tell from the stands how much ground Sayani had covered (150 yards was the post race estimate) when he stumbled on to his nose and I lost him momentarily, as he would have lost a less accomplished horseman than Rae [Johnstone]. Reidentified, he appeared 'out with the washing.' I was focusing on another even bigger French gamble...

Philadelphe II, when the binoculars revealed Sayani almost rejoining the pack. With two furlongs to run he could even make the first six – if he sprouted wings. He did. When Rae 'picked him up', taking a firmer hold and squeezing him but *not* administering a gratuitous striping, the Lieux family's 'young ox' devoured the hill as if it were the equine equivalent of caviare.

The judge posted the verdict: Sayani by a head from Claro. (O'Sullevan, 55)

waste   Describes jockeys' efforts to lose weight: an extension of the word's use to describe a person's or animal's loss of strength and substance ('wasting away'). The OED's definition is 'to reduce one's weight by training', but in a jockey's case it is more often starvation and the sauna which keep the weight down. Pierce Egan, writing in 1832, tells of a jockey, Fitzpatrick, who 'caught cold in wasting, and died in the prime of life.' The great Fred Archer, over 5ft 9ins tall, regularly *wasted* from his natural 10 stone to 8st 9lbs: he shot himself at the age of twenty-nine, 'a martyr to wasting' (Brock, 223). The articles for the Newmarket Town Plate, framed in 1666, include the following stipulation regarding weight: 'Weight twelve Stone, one Pound and a half for Waste' (Prior, 113).

water   The *clerk* of the course's dilemma is whether or not to *water* the course. If the *going* is too firm, then few runners will be attracted and attendances will be down. As soon as he chooses to water, however, it may well rain, and what would have been good going will turn heavy, so that runners will be withdrawn, trainers will complain, and attendances will be down.

water jump   A fence with a shallow ditch of standing water after it: the most spectacular obstacle on most *steeplechasing* courses and, therefore, usually sited in front of the grandstand. In practice, it is the easiest of the obstacles to clear, and it is rare to see a horse fall at it. 'A foot in the water' is often a sign that a horse is not going well and will soon drop out of contention. Its title marks it as a survival of early steeplechases, where streams and ditches were part of the course. Squire Osbaldeston, writing about the six steeplechase *matches* which he won, describes one of his horses, Clasher, as 'an extraordinary fencer, a capital water-jumper, and very fast' (Osbaldeston, 57). For a description of a fearsome early water jump, see the quotation under *collect[1]*. Water jumps used to be a mandatory element in steeplechase courses but are no longer so.

weaken   The fate of most horses in a race is to *weaken* in the closing stages; i.e. to lose contact with the leaders. A horse *weakens* in the market when its *price* gets longer.

Weatherbys In 1773 James Weatherby published his first *Racing Calendar*, in which he described himself as 'Keeper of the Match-book at Newmarket'. The firm which he founded, *Weatherbys* – the apostrophe is commonly omitted – performs the major administrative duties in racing, acting as general stakeholders, distributors of prize moneys, collectors of entry fees and forfeits, payers of jockeys' fees, printers of the *General Stud Book*, and, most prominently, acting as the central organisers of each race meeting: every horse entered for a race has to be entered through Weatherbys.

weaver A horse which does not run straight, but weaves from side to side in a race: perhaps connected to the boxing sense, for boxers who weaved from side to side have been known as *weavers* since the early nineteenth century.

weigh Jockeys *weigh out* before a race and *weigh in* after it. The *weigh-in* is, in practice, the point at which the race result becomes official, hence the announcement *weighed in*, after which book-makers will pay out. In Shirley's play *Hyde Park* (1632), before the race is run, the page describes his lord as having 'left Virgo... to go to Libra, To see the horsemen weighed' (Act 4:3). That weighing in was taken very seriously in the early days of racing is borne out by Conrad von Uffenbach's account of racing at Epsom in 1710, although one might suspect a little ribbing of the German tourist here:

> As soon as the fellows have dismounted and got their breath a little, they are again weighed, and if one of them has lost even his whip, which must weigh half a pound, he cannot win. We were told some time ago that there was a man who, feeling unwell, had to vomit, did so in his hat, and brought it back with him, so that he should not be any lighter. (Orchard, 64)

The *Racing Calendar* for 1805 includes the rule 'That every person who shall ride at Newmarket for Plate, Sweepstakes, or Match shall be obliged to weigh when he comes in.' *Weigh in* is first attested in 1867; *weigh out* in 1877.

weighing room The *weighing room* is where the *clerk* of the scales operates, and because it is out of bounds to anyone not directly connected with the racing it has become the location for rumour and speculation – 'weighing room gossip'. In the eighteenth and nineteenth centuries jockies were weighed at the *weighing post*.

weight First attested to denote the burden a horse carries in a race in the *London Gazette* in 1692: 'None but Gentlemen to ride: the weight 12 stone.' *Weight* was then used in the *conditions* of races: e.g. in the 1734 *List of Horse-Matches*, 'The highest Horse to carry 12 stone and all under his Size to be allow'd Weight for Inches.' The common *allowance* now is *weight for age*, where horses are given weight concessions when running against older horses. In the eighteenth century these races were known as *Whim* – or, *Whimsical – Plates*, typical conditions being that seven-year-olds and upward carried 10 stone, six-year-olds 9st 7lbs, five-year-olds 8st 11lbs, and four-year-olds 8 stone. Jon Bee defines *dead weight* as 'that addition which a light-weight jockey wears about him, to bring him to a certain ponderosity.'

weight cloth   A cloth under the saddle which contains lead weights to bring the weight which the horse carries up to the required amount.

weight for age   See *weight*.

welsh   Or *welch*. A term which originated in racing circles, meaning to cheat out of a bet (first attestation in 1857). A *welsher* is a bookmaker who refuses to pay out or who absconds. The OED says that the word is of obscure origin but, as Partridge suggests, the idea that 'Taffy was a Welsh man, Taffy was a thief' is likely to have reinforced the usage. Since the 1930s the word has widened in sense to mean any failure to keep a promise. Other slang terms for welshing are *shice* – c.1860, from Yiddish *scheisse*, 'shit' – and *knock* – a *knocking-joint* was slang (c.1932) for 'the stand of a bookmaker that intends, if unlucky, to welsh' (Partridge).

whim plate   See *weight*.

whip   In your right hande you must have a long rodde finely rush-growne, so that the small ende thereof bee hardly so great as a round packe-thread, insomuch that when you move or shake it, the noyse thereof may be lowde and sharpe.

So Gervase Markham in his *English Horseman* in 1607; but the word *whip*, which he seems carefully to avoid here, had long been used. Its first attestation, in 1325, is in connection with horses, and the first printed English Bible (1535) includes the verse 'Unto the horse belongeth a whippe, to the Asse a brydle, and a rodde to the fooles backe.' Today, use of the whip is one of the most contentious issues in racing. Some countries ban its use; and in Britain the *Jockey Club* issues *guidelines* which, if transgressed, lead to the fining and suspension of jockeys. The jockeys, for their part, complain that they are equally likely to be punished for not *trying* if they do not use the whip. See *reminder*; *stripe*; *wand*.

whipper-in   A hunting term, describing the huntsman's assistant who keeps the hounds from straying by driving them back into the main body of the pack with a whip. In racing, the *whipper-in* is the last horse in the race, *hunting up* the field.

whisper A *tip*, as in 'The whisper is for Earhole.' The idea is that good tips are given in secret, to be known to only a few. 'Jallad was a persistent whisper when making his debut in the Convivial Stakes at York' (*Sporting Life* 7 September 1990); see also the quotation under *outsider*. The *whisper at the post* was 'an owner's final instructions to his jockey' (Partridge, 1870): at the post, so that the jockey could not pass them to any of his accomplices and thereby dilute the odds which the owner would hope to get, and the instructions were probably the simplest – win, or don't win.

whistler See *roar¹*.

white All white horses are *grey*. For white legs, see *sock* and *stocking*. An old verse measures a horse's reliability by such markings:
Four white legs, keep him not a day;
Three white legs, send him far away;
Two white legs, give him to a friend;
One white leg, keep him to the end.

wild goose chase An early form of *steeplechasing*. The expression was current in the seventeenth century; John Fletcher's play *The Wilde Goose Chase* was performed in 1621. The rules of such a race probably varied from place to place, but one apparently typical version stipulated that after 240 yards of the race all the riders had to follow and keep behind the leader. He could take any course he liked and the others had to follow with an agreed distance between them (i.e. two or three lengths). Triers (judges), who rode alongside, whipped those who transgressed. The chase, in its equal spacings, resembled the flight formation of wild geese.

win, winner Horses are commonly said to *win* a certain distance, dropping the preposition 'by': 'Gold Muffin won a length' or 'won half the track'. As for *winner*, such is the enduring optimism which informs all levels of racing, that the word is most often used to describe horses which will – or, more accurately, may – win a race.

wind-sucker Describes a horse which has 'the vice of noisily drawing in air': first attested in 1825. From the noun the verb *wind-suck* has also been formed: 'Newmarket October Sales... Lot 12 (Elegant Air filly), has been seen to windsuck. Lot 125 (Rousillon colt),·is NOT a windsucker' (*Sporting Life* 13 October 1990).

wind up To *wind up* a horse is to get it fit for a race, a development of the phrase's use, since the seventeenth century, to mean 'set in readiness for action'. The OED quotes, from 1871, 'There's one that's we call wound up: going to run next week in a big handicap.' Trainers talk of giving a horse its *winding-up* gallop – its last piece of serious *work* before a race. Several 'winding up' senses fit the racing usage: e.g. to wind up a string instrument making it fit to play (1605), or, to wind up a clock (1601). From a workwatcher's notes in the *Sporting Life* (6 September 1990): 'Geoff Wragg's Nayland wound up for a handicap at the same venue with Welney.'

winning-chair   A nineteenth-century alternative for the winning post. 'It was too much for the young one – he tired the sooner, and the Flying Dutchman passed the winning-chair first by a short length' (Thormanby, *Famous*, 91). The chair is the *judge*'s chair.

winning post   See *post*.

wisp   From the noun meaning 'a handful, bunch, or small bundle (of hay, straw, grass, etc.)', the verb *wisp* means to rub down a horse. The OED's first attestation, from 1598, is 'A fair bryde is soon buskt and a short horse soon wispt.' 'At evening stables they'd be tied up with three-rack chains, one fastened from the hayrack to the head collar and one to each side while they were wisped and strapped' (O'Sullevan, 204). Traditionally, a *wisp* is a pad made of coiled straw, rope, or hay.

withdraw   If a horse is taken out of a race for which it has been *declared* to run, it is described as *withdrawn*. It can be withdrawn at the start, but if it has come under *starter's orders* it is regarded as a runner and all bets on it are lost. In the early days of racing the word was contracted to *draw*, and applied to the horses themselves and to the stakes. The OED quotes, from 1698, '[The match] betwixt the Yorkshire mare and Mr Frampton's horse the Turk for £500 is drawn by consent.'

withers   The bony peak where the horse's back joins its neck. A horse's height is measured from the top of its withers. The word was originally *widersome*, first attested in 1541 in an act of Henry VIII:

> Every horse... to be... in heyght xiiii handfulles... measured from the nether parte of the here of the houghe unto the upper part of the Wydersomes, That is to saye, the upper parte of the Shulders.

work   The exercise which a horse does at home in preparation for its races. Different forms of exercises are known as *slow work*, *fast work*, etc. To be *held up in his work* means that the horse's preparation has been interrupted. To *ride work* is part of a stable jockey's job, exercising the horses each morning. The idea of work is extended to the race itself when a horse has to be *kept up to its work* – see *keep*. The OED has a general sense, 'exercise or practice in a sport or game; also, exertion or movement proper to a particular sport, game, or exercise', dating from 1856; but it offers no specific racing sense. 'I thought he might be a bit short of work and lacking in experience to win first time out' (*Sporting Life* 30 May 1990); 'She was back in strong work during Ebor week' (*Sporting Life* 6 October 1990).

workman   A bookmaker's assistant who does the menial rather than the brain work:

> A workman went to the races knowing that after the last race he would have his day's wages in his pocket... The major attraction, however, for a workman was of a slightly different nature... there always existed the possibility that an opportunity might exist whereby [he] could advance his position to unbelievable heights in a few hours – there were chances. Thus many workmen were prepared to work 'on results'. If the Guvnor had a good day then the wages were good, sometimes enough to buy a share in the business. A bad day – no wages at all. (Sidney, 69)

workmanlike   A word which originally described a good piece of work, and then was extended to describe the smart appearance of people or animals. The OED quotes, from 1878, 'two very workmanlike little horses'. In the twentieth century the word came to be applied to the way a horse performs in a race. A *workmanlike* victory puts the emphasis upon the effort rather than smartness, meaning that the horse did not win brilliantly but did its job well enough. 'Miss Alleged won the Group Three Prix de Royaumont, beating Vue Cavaliere a workmanlike length' (*Sporting Life* 28 May 1990).

workwatcher   See *tout*.

wrap   Taking a *wrap* is an Americanism for taking a *pull¹*, so called because the jockey wraps the reins tightly around his hands. 'McCaughlin, not wishing the favourite to get pumped out, took a double wrap on him' (Goodwin Bros., 69).

wrong¹   Partridge conjectures that the general slang senses of *wrong 'un* – 'a welsher or a whore, a base coin or spurious note' – were derived from the use of the phrase in the 1890s to denote 'a pulled horse'. Another racing usage, also from the 1890s, described a horse that had run at a *flapping* meeting.

wrong²   A horse *goes wrong* when it suffers a major *setback* in training. A horse is *wrong* when it is not able to show its *form* for any of a multitude of reasons: 'She was clearly wrong when getting a hiding from Chimes of Freedom at the Curragh and was later found to have injured a shoulder' (*Sporting Life* 20 June 1990).

Yankee   See *multiple bet*.

yearling   A horse in its second year: see *age*. The first recorded example of a *yearling* racing was in 1791, when the yearling filly Cash beat the three-year-old Eliza, getting three stone. In 1859 the racing of yearlings was prohibited.

Bibliography

Badminton (1889) *Racing and Steeplechasing* in 'The Badminton Library of Sports and Pastimes', London: Longmans Green. 'Racing' is by the Earl of Suffolk and W.G. Craven; 'Steeplechasing' by Arthur Coventry and Alfred E.T. Watson.

Bee, Jon (John Badcock) (1823) *Slang*, London. Entries are alphabetical.

Bland, Ernest, ed. (1950) *Flat-Racing Since 1900*, London: Andrew Dakers.

Brock, D.W.E. (1949) *The Racing Man's Week-end Book*, London: Seeley Service.

Donoghue, Stephen (1923) *Just My Story*, London: Hutchinson.

Egan, Pierce (1832) *Book of Sports and Mirror of Life*, London.

Eliot, Elizabeth (1957) *Portrait of a Sport: a History of Steeplechasing*, London: Longmans.

Goldschmidt, Lieutenant-Colonel S.G. (1947) *Bridle Wise: a Key to Better Hunters and Better Ponies*, London: Country Life.

Goodwin Bros. (1895) *How to Make or Lose Money on a Small Capital*, New York. The book's subtitle is 'Showing the Weakness of Human Nature and its Susceptibility to the Speculative Magnet'.

Hislop, John (1958) *From Start to Finish: First Steps to Flat-Race Riding*, London: Hutchinson.

McGuigan, John (1946) *A Trainer's Memories*, London: Heath Cranston.

Orchard, Vincent (1954) *Tattersalls: Two Hundred Years of Sporting History*, London: Hutchinson.

Osbaldeston (*c.*1857) *Squire Osbaldeston: His Autobiography*, edited by E.D. Cuming, London: John Lane, 1926.

O'Sullevan, Peter (1989) *Calling the Horses: a Racing Autobiography*, London: Stanley Paul.

Partridge, Eric (1948) *A Dictionary of Slang and Unconventional English*, 8th edn, London: Routledge & Kegan Paul.

Pink 'Un (1903) *A Pink 'Un and a Pelican* by Arthur Binstead, London: Sands & Co.

Pitcher in P. (1903) *Pitcher in Paradise* by Arthur Binstead, London: Sands & Co.

Prior, C.M. (1926) *The History of the Racing Calendar and Stud-Book*, London: The Sporting Life.

Sidney, Charles (1976) *The Art of Legging*, London: Maxline International.

Surtees, R.S. (1831-4) *Jorrocks' Jaunts and Jollities*, I have used the Everyman edition, London: J.M. Dent, 1928.

'Thormanby' (1882) *Famous Racing Men* and *Tales of the Turf*, London: James Hogg.